FRASER HILL

THE CEO'S GREATEST ASSET

THE ART AND SCIENCE OF LANDING LEADERS

First published by Pecker Publishing 2022

Copyright © 2022 by Fraser Hill

First edition

ISBN: 978-1-7345445-3-4

To mom and dad, who taught me that hard work, humility, and kindness are the real currency of success, and to Karina for proving them right every day.

Contents

Preface

For over 20 years, I have worked with some of the biggest companies in the world, as well as many start-ups, recruiting externally as a headhunter and working in-house in executive search. In the second half of my career, my focus has been on C-level executives and their global and regional direct reports. I have lived and worked in recruitment in London, Hong Kong, Poland, Canada, and the US, and consistently, across all the regions, not one organization has managed to master the art of building high-performing teams on a consistent basis.

Throughout my career, I have often questioned the interview and selection process of experienced hires. I never managed to find the time to really get into the detail because it's a very complex problem to unravel and understand, let alone improve upon. Then COVID-19 came along, and I finally had the time to give this serious consideration. I always thought, "How is it that despite having terrible interview processes, Fortune 500 companies and others are still able to hire great people?" They no doubt use the fact they're still hiring great people as justification for their interview processes because "They clearly work. Look at who we hire?"

Do they work, though? Is it that the questions are effective? Or is it perhaps that, instead of the popularized notion of the "best person for the job," there are actually several people sufficiently competent enough to do the job, and the interview process only serves to select one of the competent chosen few? Even then, is it that these questions drive the decision-making process, or do they merely serve to act as a decoy to the underlying confirmation bias that exists in the human interactions that take place as part of the interview process?

It's a big problem that hasn't been addressed in any great detail. This is clearly evident in the fact that we continue to use behavioral competency questions and other terrible questions as a way to qualify candidates in or out when in actual fact, these questions are simply not fit for purpose. I have come to the conclusion that, for experienced hires, what we have at play instead of a perfect interview process, is strong confirmation bias driving decisions, with competency interview questions masquerading as the influencing factors in the decision-making process.

How can a bunch of disparate answers to questions, each seeking one example from a whole career of experience, paint any kind of informed opinion about a candidate? Moreover, how do you even begin to compare the answers from one candidate's examples to another? Furthermore, how do you then compare a candidate's answers to one interviewer's questions to the answers given to their colleague's questions when they're not even asking the same questions? These archaic assessment methods, still used in all Fortune 500 companies, are a breeding ground for biases to flourish and dominate the hiring process, holding us back from our goals to have more diverse and inclusive organizations. Things have to change.

This book is the result of an eight-year study and 1727 interviews with experienced hire executives, followed by a review of 100 of the most important pieces of scientific literature from the last 100 years of psychology. The end result is a completely new interview framework for experienced hires that does away with competency questions and finally justifies the notion that people are the CEO's greatest asset.

Introduction

A CEO's role, broadly speaking, is to formulate and execute a strategy to create shareholder, employee, and customer value. Those shareholders may be private owners, the public stock market, a government, or their employees. To execute a great strategy, the CEO needs to have high-performing teams in place, or at the very least, teams consisting of people that are sufficiently competent to deliver on the company objectives. Most of what you will learn in this book falls under the remit of the CEO's direct team and their direct reports. However, unless the CEO also understands how unfit for purpose the current approaches to leadership hiring are, as outlined in this book, then change is less likely to happen. It has to be a top-down initiative that permeates every layer of the company. In doing so, all hiring managers are clear on what to do and are also held accountable for doing so.

Ask almost any CEO what their most valuable asset is and what sets them apart, and they will invariably say, in one way or another, their people. It seems apparent that they would say this, yet the actions of many companies tend to imply that there's enormous room for improvement. Fortune 500s, global public listed companies, start-ups, and long-established private companies are all guilty. All of them. Companies cannot always compete with the best when it comes to new customer acquisition and revenue size. Still, when it comes to being a place where people want to work, all companies appear to be asleep at the wheel or, at the very least, having unsolicited naps as they travel. As a result, the competition for talent is a level playing field where all companies can compete. If you win the competition for the best talent, and you can keep them, then you have an excellent foundation for success.

Interviewing for experienced hires in most companies is chaos. People don't think it's chaos because there is, by some definition, a structure to it. That structure, however, is mostly competency interview-based, with the hiring manager and HR executives conducting interviews and then inviting multiple people to interview the candidates and share their opinion on each one. These opinions are often based on answers to superficial questions that do nothing more than affirming the biases they walked into the interview room with. They certainly can't compare answers because they're not even asking the same questions, despite the candidate having only one career and life story.

In the entertainment world, Oprah Winfrey is regarded as a good interviewer. She has enormous credibility, for one, which means people respect her and are more likely to engage in the level of rapport required to make someone comfortable enough to answer some tough questions. She's not afraid to get beyond the veneer of shallow answers given to interviewers who may be less experienced than she is. How interview processes are currently conducted in companies, both large and small, is the equivalent of Oprah pointing to camera number two and saying:

"Hey John, you do a great job as our cameraman, but I'd really like to get your opinion on Clint Eastwood here. Can you just come down and ask him a few questions and let me know what you think?"

Perhaps the cameraman isn't senior enough to be taking on this task. Maybe she calls in her television producer, who is the most senior person there. Oprah puts her finger to her earpiece:

"Clare, listen, I know you're doing a million things right now, but we've got Clint Eastwood here. Can you come down and interview him for a few minutes? I just want to get your take on him."

"Sorry, what's that? What should I ask him?"

"Oh, whatever you like. I just want to see what you think."

The way candidates are currently interviewed is like getting a group of part-trained psychologists together and getting them to diagnose a patient through consensus. Only once they'd asked each other what they thought would they come to a consensus on what the diagnosis is. Given that they're not fully trained psychologists, they would, in part, just be making it up as they went along. That's obviously not what happens. One trained psychologist follows a well-established process to conduct a full interview and investigation. Then their report can be reviewed by other doctors, safe in the knowledge that one of their fully qualified peers would have reached the same conclusion, given the very specific process they must follow.

It would be an insult to the years of training and expense that psychologists go through to suggest that interviewing candidates for a job is analogous to a psychologist interviewing patients. However, it is equally insulting to candidates whose next important career move is being assessed by a hiring manager that has no formal interview training in any meaningful methodology designed to get deep, rich content from a candidate's life story. Unfortunately, in candidate selection, there is no scientific formula that ensures outcomes will be predictable. If there were, they would lead to scientifically sound evaluations of candidates, whereby every candidate in an interview process is always asked the same questions, with measurable, comparable results. That just can't happen. Furthermore, when you add the element of bias on top of this, the scientific robustness of an interview process is further eroded to the point where it is entirely unscientific. That in itself is not a problem, but it is something to recognize and be aware of as we seek to find the next best alternative to a scientifically measurable process.

Reading Guide

This book isn't designed to be read cover to cover with some ice cream while watching an episode on Netflix. It may, at times, remind you of a textbook. That's because humans are unbelievably complex. When choosing people to lead companies, we can't just be reading a LinkedIn article about the "Top Ten Interview Questions" and hoping we pick the right person.

For too many years, companies have not taken interviewing seriously enough. This book takes the subject very seriously, and its aim is not to just give you some cool questions to ask. The aim is to help people become more objective about the science and the facts that lead us to reach better-informed conclusions about who to hire. With this, you can build your own interview questions frameworks, safe in the knowledge that they're based on a rigorous understanding of the science and the art of landing leaders.

If your goal is just to discover the new questions, you can just read Chapter 9, which should take you about a half tub of ice cream, depending on the tub size and how long you've had it out of the freezer. If you wish to become an expert at interviewing, where you're confidently able to design effective interview processes, then it will be unhealthy to eat ice cream every time you read this.

Chapters 1 to 5 are a rigorous deep dive into the psychological literature from the past 100 years as it relates to leadership, intelligence, personality, intuition and biases, and interviewing. These chapters are much heavier in parts compared to Chapters 6 to 10, which outline the practical application of the book's new ideas and concepts. These first five chapters lay the theoretical foundations upon which chapters 6 to 10 are built. You could, in theory, read this book from chapters 6 to 10 and then return to these first five chapters.

If all you are looking for is a quick read and a practical solution to the problems identified in Chapter 7, "Why All Companies Are Bad At Interviewing," then you can, in theory, read chapters 7 to 9 first. Chapter 8 outlines the new leadership trait framework devised from the study that links back to the science outlined in the first five chapters. Chapter 9 outlines the new interviewing methodology and questions that can replace outdated behavioral interview questions and personality tests.

To get the most from the book and to establish your own objective views, reading all of it from beginning to end is highly recommended. Have fun, and if you can't have fun, have knowledge.

I

THE SCIENCE

PSYCHOLOGY ISN'T ROCKET SCIENCE

This section is incredibly important to help you objectively assess the rest of what you read in this book, especially when it comes to an understanding of the studies that have been done and how loosely "facts" are defined in the world of behavioral science. Normally when you read books that quote facts from studies, those facts are absorbed without questions as, after all, the studies back up the claims. If instead of writing this section, I simply wrote that you should question what you read about in behavioral studies, you would, at best, question what you read, but you may not know what questions to ask. Therefore, the aim of this chapter is twofold. Firstly, it is to help you understand how these studies are conducted, so you can be more objective in any assumptions you make in the future when you hear about such studies being mentioned. Secondly, it is to walk you through some of the processes and references I used to develop the Bremnus Leadership Success Model, which is the basis for the proposed interview framework. With this knowledge, you will be able to make your own mind up about the validity of certain studies, models, and frameworks, and in doing so, better formulate your own objective opinions that are not entirely reliant on what you read about online.

There are certain rules in behavioral science that do not apply to the traditional scientific world, and you cannot form any kind of objective view on this without some foundational understanding of what these rules are and, more importantly, what these rules are not. The laws of physics and mathematics are governed by a set of exact, calculated principles. "Roughly" or "approximately" doesn't cut it when you're building a rocket. In the world of psychology, however, "roughly," "approximately," or even "sometimes" can be enough proof to get a paper published and then have it quoted in various credible outlets as "facts." I don't believe, however, that the intention of social scientists is to always have the results of their studies quoted as facts. Something is conveniently lost in translation between the scientist's very specific description of the results being merely probability and what we then see in the headlines as being facts. It is probably a more fair assumption to state that the media can get more clicks when probability is presented as facts, which in turn strongly influences the reader's interpretations of what facts are.

That's not to say there are no attempts to measure outcomes in any kind of scientific way. The attempts to measure behaviors and personality traits in any quantitative way are referred to as psychometrics. People typically think of psychometrics as tests like Myers-Briggs, for example. Psychometric standards weren't even invented when Myers-Briggs came out. Incidentally, most credible scholars in the field of psychology don't believe Myers-Briggs even stands up to the statistical scrutiny that qualifies it as a psychometric test. You only need to read all sixteen Myers-Briggs "types" to see they're a bit like horoscopes – all telling you something you want to hear, yet none telling you anything you don't want to hear.

True psychometrics is a field that focuses on the measurement of psychological traits such as intelligence and extraversion. All psychological traits are constructs. We cannot necessarily see them, but we can observe behaviors that show us they exist. Constructs in psychology help us to group observable and complex sets of behaviors, emotions, and thoughts into meaningful concise language.

Unlike temperature, distance, and weight, psychological constructs cannot be measured with a thermometer, ruler, or weighing scale. Even establishing whether a construct exists is a scientific process in itself. For example, we don't measure the personality trait conscientiousness directly. It is an unobservable construct. What is observable are the behaviors and actions that we have come to associate with conscientiousness, and when enough of these actions are observed concurrently on a consistent basis, it is then fair to assume that what we are witnessing is the trait conscientiousness. For example, it would be fair to conclude that someone who diligently got up at 4 a.m. to work out for two hours, before getting to the office at 7 a.m., one hour before everyone else, and working extremely hard all day and into the evening, every day is displaying behaviors of a conscientious person.

This differs greatly from measuring, for example, the temperature of water with a thermometer and concluding not only that it is hot, but it is exactly 100°C, and, therefore, by definition, boiling. There is no thermometer equivalent in psychometrics, so we have to rely on statistical analysis and probabilities, the measures of which are scientific and robust, but with the results being statistical probability in place of defined fact. This difference is very important. In rocket science, calculations cannot be nearly correct. They have to be exact every time. With probability, and specifically psychometric measurement, even a 9% correlation may be considered to be worth mentioning as evidence. This is what we're dealing with; probability rather than fact. Now we're comfortable with that, or at least aware of the difference, how do we even measure unmeasurable constructs?

RELIABILITY AND VALIDITY

In psychometrics, for research to be in any way credible, it has to be able to pass tests of reliability and validity. What constitutes reliable and valid is not based on any abstract opinions that are open to interpretation. It is based on statistical formulas, well defined since the mid-twentieth century, with the latest rules being published by the American Psychological Association (AERA, APA, NCME, 2014).

In terms of reliability, we can break it down into three areas.

Reliability over time (test-retest reliability)

For example, if you take a test twice over a period of time, the results should be at the very least nearly the same if the underlying proposed construct is valid. Myers Briggs, for example, fails this test horribly.

Reliability across items (internal consistency)

For example, with the construct of intelligence, one facet of that may be one's ability to recognize patterns, and another facet may be mathematical problem-solving. Generally speaking, someone scoring well on one of these is highly likely to score well on other items of the same underlying construct, intelligence. We know this to be true as it's part of the foundational research into IQ. We are able to check if this is indeed true using factor analysis, which we'll come onto later.

Reliability across different researchers (inter-rater reliability)

When constructs and behaviors are observed and rated by others, the extent to which one rater's score correlates with another is referred to as inter-rater reliability. This suggests that, for example, if five people were observing a candidate's responses to interviews, and all reviewers see the same footage, if their observations are the same or similar, this can help to validate the underlying construct. Currently, with competency interviews, there is no such thing as inter-rater reliability as two different interviewers aren't even asking the same questions. Therefore, it is currently a very unscientific process, to say the least.

Just because a test is reliable, that doesn't in itself make it valid. For example, If I measure a distance with a ruler that has stretched by 20%, it will reliably compare two different people's heights, but the height measurements themselves will be wrong and therefore invalid. According to the American Psychological Association, validity is the "process of constructing and evaluating arguments for and against the identified interpretation of test scores and their relevance to the proposed use" (AERA, APA, NCME, 2014). This definition has evolved over time. Now it is generally believed that it is not one of these individually that confirms validity but rather a combination of collective evidence. These guidelines are largely based on the work done by an American psychologist, Samuel Messick (1989), who elaborated on work conducted by Lee Cronbach and Paul Meehl (1955), also American psychologists.

There are five broad qualifying definitions. These are important as they are also relevant to our work on the Bremnus leadership model, outlined in Chapter 8. Classical validity theories spoke of different types of validity like content, construct, and criterion. Since then, a theory first posed in 1989 by Samuel Messick suggests that validity is one single concept, and proving validity requires the construction of a cohesive argument based largely on five evidence sources, namely:

1. Evidence based on test content

Validity evidence based on test content concerns "the relationship between the content of a test and the construct it is intended to measure" (AERA, APA, and NCME, 2014).

In other words, does the test accurately measure what it's intended to measure? For example, the purpose of the Implicit Association Test (IAT) was to measure our unconscious biases. The IAT failed this validity test. More on this later in the chapter on intuition and biases.

2. Evidence based on response processes

This tests "the fit between the construct and the detailed nature of the performance or response actually engaged in by test takers" (AERA, APA, and NCME, 2014).

If someone was doing a complicated calculus question, for example, the answer itself wouldn't suffice. Knowledge of how that answer is reached is the nature of this measure, and it would be represented, in the calculus example, with the long-form calculations written down by the person answering the question.

3. Evidence based on internal structure

This is "the degree to which the relationships among test item and test components conform to the construct on which the proposed test score interpretations are based" (AERA, APA, and NCME, 2014).

Typically here, a statistical measure called factor analysis is used to see if the relationship between the construct, like creativity, has a similar corollary relationship with each of its constituent facets. For example, if creativity was strongly correlated with vision and ideas but had absolutely no correlation with one's ability to create a strategy, we would know that evidence of that person's strategic experience would not be a contributing factor in assessing the candidate's creativity.

4. Evidence based on relations with other variables

This is how one variable correlates with another already known and validated variable. The theory is that if there is a strong correlation with an already proven and established construct or facet, it is further evidence of validity. Establishing validity here will often involve statistical equations like the correlation coefficient, outlined below in "Measuring Validity."

5. Evidence based on the consequences of testing

This is the "soundness of proposed interpretations [of test scores] for their intended uses" (AERA, APA, and NCME, 2014). This describes the extent to which the consequences of the use of the score are congruent with the proposed uses of the assessment.

MEASURING VALIDITY

It may feel like we're about to go way off-piste into a statistics lesson that's taking us far away from candidate assessment. However, it requires understanding this magical number, represented by the letter "r," to comprehend just how much of a "pinch of salt" psychometricians get to use when making claims with studies.

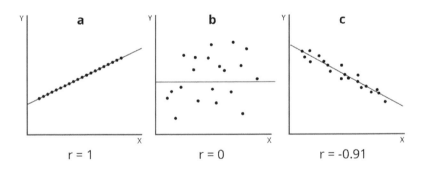

Figure 1: Illustration of Pearson's Correlation Coefficient

In statistics, there is a number called Pearson's correlation coefficient (r) (Clark & Cooke, 1978). This number represents the strength of the covariance of two variables and is always between -1 and +1. Zero means there is absolutely no correlation whatsoever. The closer to 1 represents a stronger correlation; conversely, the closer to -1 represents a stronger inverse correlation. For example, if you mapped miles traveled in a car against gas left in the tank, assuming you were traveling in a straight line with no incline at a consistent speed, you would note a perfect negative correlation. As miles traveled went up, gas in the tank would go down.

If you are looking to prove that reading ability and verbal ability are correlated, you would take, say, two hundred people, give each person a reading test and a verbal test, and then plot the scores of each on a scatter diagram like those in Figure 1. In the example in Figure 1, X will represent the reading score, and Y will represent a verbal test score. You can see from the three example charts in Figure 1 that if "a" represented the results of the reading and verbal test, it would mean that one could accurately predict the score of a candidate's reading test simply by viewing the results of the other test. If "b" represented the answers, we could say that there is zero relationship between each of the scores and that they are not correlated in any way whatsoever. If "c" was the result, which would be very odd, it would mean there was a strong inverse correlation between reading and verbal test scores. It would suggest that the higher one scores on a reading test, the lower one would score on a verbal test. Clearly, this is a made-up statistic. If you're familiar with social media, you'll know all about made-up statistics.

We could fairly assume that this number can just be directly translated into a percentage. So, in diagram "c," for example, we believe we could say that this represented 91% of the population. However, that assumption is incorrect. Rather confusingly, r cannot equate to a percentage. So if r = 0.9, we cannot say that 90% of one variable correlates with the other variable. To get the correct percentage, we have to consider something called the coefficient of determination, which is r squared. I promise we're nearly finished. That is to say, when this correlation is 0.9, the coefficient of determination is 0.81 (r squared). We can then express that as a percentage, which in this case is 81%. If r was 0.5, the percentage would be 25% (0.5 squared represented as a percentage), and if it is 1, the percentage is 100% (1 squared represented as a percentage). So as you can see, that validity number (r) has to be very high to represent a majority population.

So who cares, and why does this matter? When we see these studies being published on LinkedIn quoting "evidence," we have to get better at interpreting what the evidence actually means. A generally accepted breakdown of correlation interpretation is represented in Table 1. For negative correlations, just add a "–" and replace "positive" with "negative."

Size of Correlation	Interpretation
0.90 to 1.00	Very high positive correlation
0.70 to 0.90	High positive correlation
0.50 to 0.70	Moderate positive correlation
0.30 to 0.50	Low positive correlation
0.00 to 0.30	Negligable correlation

Table 1: Interpretation of Correlation (r) Numbers (Hinkle & Wiersma, 2003)

This is important to remember and why the above explanation was necessary. As you can see, for the correlation to be negligible, it has to be less than 0.3. Over 0.3, and it supposedly has statistical value. But remember the coefficient of determination equation, r squared. 0.3 squared is 0.09, or 9%. In rocket science, if your equations are right 9% of the time, you're not going to send a rocket to space as 91% of the time as you will have nothing more than a very expensive firework. Even if we take a less cynical look at these numbers and consider that 0.7 is a high positive correlation, then this equates to 49% of a population (0.7 squared and turned into a percentage). Sure, that's a lot of a population, and there's clearly a correlation, but we can't treat the "facts" of social science in the same way we treat the facts of rocket science. In other words, if mathematics was an equivalent behavioral construct, two plus two could equal four most of the time, or as little as 9% of the time for it to be considered an indicator of the underlying construct. Not exactly rocket science.

Besides, the above only dealt with constructs and comparing two separate constructs and how they correlate. What happens when we're trying to evaluate multiple traits? That's where factor analysis comes in. In 1904 an English psychologist, Charles Spearman, published his now-famous paper in the American Journal of Psychology, "General intelligence, objectively determined and measured" (Spearman, 1904). He proposed what is believed to be the first tenable psychometric definition of intelligence (Jensen, 1994). We will look at intelligence and his work later, but he was the first to use factor analysis to observe that different forms of intelligence are correlated and, as such, result in one underlying factor of intelligence, referred to as "g." Factor analysis attempts to reduce a large set of correlated variables to a much smaller set of dimensions. This method is useful in understanding the common nature of the variables that jointly define a given factor. It was also factor analysis that led scientists to the Big Five personality traits, which we'll come on to look at soon.

My conclusion from all of this is that statistics in behavioral science, as it relates to performance in the workplace and ultimately candidate selection, is about as useful as building a rocket without any understanding of mathematics or physics. It can work, but guessing your way to the answers is like calculating your way to interpret behaviors. That said, it cannot just be dismissed as a thinly veiled attempt to make psychology empirically scientific. There is great utility in some of the studies that have been done, and where the correlation really is significant, the numbers cannot be ignored.

I also believe we should continue to question what behavioral science is telling us because using statistics and, as a result, concluding the degree to which something is probable is not stating the degree to which something is a fact. If probability is to be used as the basis for our factual beliefs, would you conclude that a 49% chance of winning in the casino is strong enough to sell your home and all of your possessions to take that bet? I'm guessing not, for most of you, yet if a study is done and a correlation of 0.7 is found (49%), then it will be quoted as a fact by various media outlets that take an interest in organizational psychology.

As psychologists continue to fight over the definition of constructs and whether they even exist, they will do so using empirically sound statistical methods, reverse engineered into the most complex of human behaviors. This appears to be the only thing we can do given our limited box of tools borrowed from the traditional scientific world. That's not to say it's necessarily the best way to unravel the complexities of human behavior, though. I think that is yet to be achieved, which I believe is incredibly exciting for the future of behavioral science. In the meantime, we should continue to observe the highly correlated results with great interest. However, I believe we should also remain skeptical, so our conclusions do not rely entirely on the numbers, as the probability of these numbers being correct is often, at best, no more conclusive than the toss of a coin.

INTELLIGENCE - IQ & EQ

Across multiple studies, general mental ability (GMA), first conceptualized over 100 years ago (Spearman 1904), has consistently proven to be the key predictor of job performance (F.Schmidt, J.Hunter. 1998). GMA is defined as "A highly general information-processing capacity that facilitates reasoning, problem-solving, decision making, and other higher-order thinking skills" (Gottfredson, 1997). Charles Spearman (1904) observed that individuals who do well on one type of mental task also tend to do well on many others. He based this on his research into kids in school and observed which of the children did well in more than one subject. Spearman's hypothesis of a single general mental ability was challenged by Thurstone (1935), who popularized the notion that people had several independent primary mental abilities rather than a single general mental ability. For example, some people are better at solving problems verbally, while others are good at solving problems that involve visualization. Some people who are good at both of these things may only be average at tasks that rely heavily on memory (Thurstone, 1935).

Modern psychology views cognitive ability as having several dimensions, all of which seem to be correlated with one another. Many interpret this correlation as reflecting an underlying general cognitive ability, GMA, or "g," that is measured by the full-scale scores on the major cognitive ability tests. GMA tests are actually a battery of different tests that may include verbal concepts, vocabulary, arithmetic, and spatial awareness. Given the correlation between GMA test results and IQ, for example, IQ tests are often sufficient to determine one's "g," although not strictly being a test of "g" in and of itself. Following Spearman's research work, in 1905, a French psychologist, Alfred Binet, developed the first IQ test as a way of identifying a student's academic potential. That test was adapted for use in English by Lewis Terman and, in 1916, became the Stanford-Binet IQ test – still one of the most commonly administered cognitive ability tests (Becker, 2003).

Intelligence is defined as: "A very general capability that, among other things, involves the ability to reason, plan, solve problems, think abstractly, comprehend complex ideas, learn quickly and learn from experience. It is not merely book learning, a narrow academic skill, or test-taking smarts. Rather, it reflects a broader and deeper capability for comprehending our surroundings—'catching on', 'making sense' of things, or 'figuring out' what to do. Intelligence, so defined, can be measured, and intelligence tests measure it well" (L. Gottfredson, 1997).

Taking the concept of intelligence one step further, in 1943, psychologist Raymond Cattell, a student of Spearman, popularized the concepts of fluid intelligence (g(F)) and crystallized intelligence (g(C)) (Cattell, 1987). Fluid intelligence is roughly defined as using logic and abstract reasoning to solve problems. Crystallized intelligence is facts-based knowledge accumulated over time, so reading comprehension, general knowledge, and language development, in other words. For example, someone may be amazing at solving problems in an IQ test (fluid intelligence) but not very good when it comes to exam time, where crystallized intelligence is more associated with memory recall. Despite testing being distinctively different, the overlap of working memory, that is, the ability to process and remember information, and fluid intelligence, has been described as being almost indistinguishable (Kyllonen and Christal 1990). Therefore, given that there's no absolute test for GMA itself, IQ tests, the results of which are correlated with other GMA tests, have largely been adopted as the indicator for GMA.

The fact that high GMA is highly correlated to job performance shouldn't come as a surprise to anyone. High GMA allows individuals to learn faster, which will lead to the acquisition of new skills, leaving them in a favorable position to climb the organizational hierarchy more rapidly. High GMA also implies a greater ability to solve complex problems, although not all problems. For example, it doesn't account for the nature of human interactions, an important part of solving problems in the workplace. We will come to that later in another section, but in essence, this is something that can more readily be measured, to the extent to which it's possible, with personality tests.

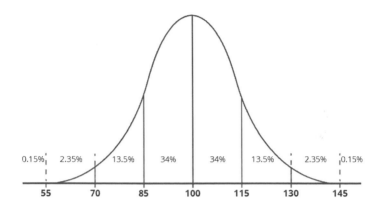

Figure 2: Average IQ And Normal Distribution

Figure 2 represents the normal distribution of IQ across a general population. The mean IQ score, or the average, is 100. What this chart tells is that 50% of the population fall to the left of the middle, and 50% fall to the right. Those with an IQ of between 85 and 115 represent 68% of the population.

The shape of this curve isn't unique to measuring IQ. You will observe a nearly identical bell-shaped curve when considering measurements like newborn baby weights, blood pressure among broad sample groups, height, and shoe size, for example. None of those measurements have anything to do with intelligence, but they are all seemingly random occurrences in populations that just happen to fit neatly into a bell curve. If a random pattern correlation with baby weights doesn't cement the validity of IQ as a measure of intelligence, how about SAT scores? Below you will see a table of SAT scores for all US university applicants in 2010.

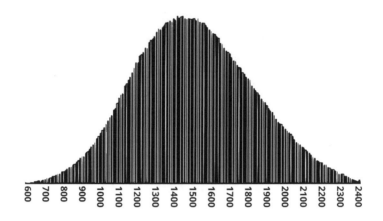

Figure 3: 2010 SAT scores for 1,547,990 US students (Man, 2011)

The sample size for this chart in Figure 3 is 1,547,990 students. It would be quite a challenge for those who deny IQ as a valid measure to explain the correlation between this enormous sample size of SAT scores and the bell shape of the IQ results.

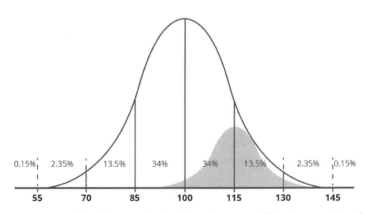

Figure 4: Average IQ of University Students Compared To Average Population

In a study done in 1997 with a dataset of around 8000 American students, the mean IQ for a US university student was 114 (Murray, 2009). If you mapped those students onto the standard IQ bell curve, the average IQ for students would look something like the grey area in Figure 4, with a minimum of somewhere around 95. From this, we can make a rough estimation that those with an IQ of 95 and above may qualify to attend university, although not all universities and not for all courses. For Ivy League schools in the US, that mean number will be higher.

People don't need a university degree unless it's for something specific that requires certain licensing, like the medical field, law, or finance, for example. That's not to say they don't need to be smart, but as we've already seen, if we are to take IQ as an approximate indicator of one's ability to learn, then around 50% of the population is apparently smart enough to go to university, but clearly not all smart people do. All a university degree does for general professional jobs is show an employer that the entry-level candidate has demonstrated a sufficient capacity to learn to get to a competent level in the job they're applying for. It certainly doesn't imply they will be a great leader or a manager. Those without degrees shouldn't be discounted from a hiring process for professional jobs that don't require special post-graduate licenses. Candidates should simply have to demonstrate their experience or the equivalent sufficient capacity to learn as that of their peers who had the opportunity to go to university.

Ivy league school graduates have the upper hand in many job applications partly due to how difficult it is to get into an Ivy League school in the first place. It's not enough to be incredibly smart and get a high SAT score, but they also have to show evidence of excelling in other areas of their lives, which often involves contributing to or even leading teams. With that, companies can be confident that if they've graduated from an Ivy League school, they have demonstrable evidence of both learning and working in teams. That's it, but then at the graduate level, that's all there can be; It's not like they have lots of experience behind them. Does that mean Ivy League graduates will make the best leaders? No.

A paper published in the Journal of Applied Psychology said that leadership effectiveness as it relates to IQ plateaus at around 120, after which there is no difference in leadership effectiveness. The article goes on to say that at very high levels of IQ, there's an inverse relationship between leadership effectiveness and IQ.

"Individuals who are too intelligent vis-à-vis the group they lead may limit how effective they could be. The leaders may be limited because they: (a) present more sophisticated solutions to problems [which] may be much more difficult to understand................use complex forms of verbal communication [and] expressive sophistication [that] may also undermine influence...............; and (c) come across as too cerebral making them less prototypical of the group" (Antonakis et al., 2017).

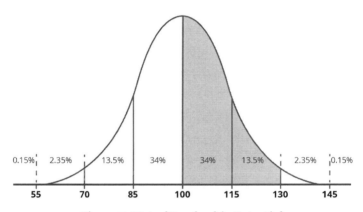

Figure 5: IQ And Leadership Potential

I believe most companies think they're good at hiring graduates because the candidate's threshold for learning potential is so high that, of course, they're mostly going to do well. When hiring at the management and leadership level, where the candidates have maybe worked in a few different companies, the only thing separating them now is their experience. All of them have sufficient ability to learn for most jobs, and so the candidate pool is, by definition, much larger than we believe it may be.

In theory, if all people with an IQ of roughly 95 and upwards have the learning ability to graduate university, whether they do or not, and optimal potential to lead, then 47.5% of the population could do most professional non-licensed jobs. This is illustrated in Figure 5. The actual number may be more, but let's consider this population as an example. I believe this is why companies with terrible interview processes can still hire good people. It's not their interview process that's good; it's the candidates who are mostly good. Sufficiently smart, motivated people figure things out. People step up in challenging times. People stretch when they're asked to do things they may have believed are beyond them.

IQ is not a definitive measure of how well someone will do. All it really indicates is someone's ability to learn and solve abstract problems. It doesn't tell us how someone will interact with others. It is not the full story of how effective a manager will be. It isn't the degree someone gets that defines how far they will climb in the workplace. It is how people conduct themselves, how they build trust, how they demonstrate integrity, how they communicate, commit, deliver, and how they push themselves that counts. All of this is in the story of their lives and careers; the challenges they overcame, the risks they took, the promotions they won, and the friendships they made. Unless we have a way to understand all of this that is consistent and in some way measurable or at least comparable, our guesswork interviews may hit many home runs, but that won't be because the interview was robust and conclusive; it's because people who can learn and who are motivated, will figure it out.

EMOTIONAL INTELLIGENCE

Emotional intelligence (EI) was first introduced as a concept by Salovey and Mayer (1990), who described it as the ability "to accurately perceive emotions, to access and generate emotions to assist thoughts, to understand emotions and emotional knowledge, and to reflectively regulate emotions to promote emotional and intellectual growth" (Salovey and Mayer, 1990). The concept of EI emerged from a long history of research into social intelligence, dating back to 1920 (Thorndike, 1920).

However, it wasn't until 1995 when EI became popularized by Daniel Goleman and his book, "Emotional Intelligence," which became an international bestseller. In it, he describes the Emotional Competency Model of EI, which has four domains: self-awareness, social awareness; self-management; and relationship management. He suggests that EI traits are responsible for high-performing employees after IQ has been considered or discounted (Goleman, 2005). This clearly has implications for evaluating candidates beyond just their cognitive ability and experiences. Goleman stated, "Intellectual abilities like verbal fluency, spatial logic, and abstract reasoning are based primarily in specific areas of the neocortex, as compared to the EI components that are noted as behavioral manifestations of underlying neurological circuitry that primarily links the limbic areas for emotion, centering on the amygdala and its extended networks throughout the brain, to areas in the prefrontal cortex, the brain's executive center" (Goleman, 2001). This suggests that IQ and EQ may not always come as a package, so basing any assessment on how smart someone is is not enough, despite it being well documented that GMA is the best predictor of success in the workplace. This theory may go some way to describe how some incredibly intelligent individuals who are gifted in certain academic domains may enter the workplace with a 1st class degree but not necessarily flourish because of less advanced EQ.

Self Awareness	Self Management	Social Awareness	Relationship Management
Emotional Self Awareness	Achievement Orientation	Organizational Awareness	Conflict Management
	Emotional Self Control	Empathy	Inspirational Leadership
	Positive Outlook		Influence
	Adaptability		Teamwork
			Coach and Mentor

Table 2: Emotional and Social Competency Inventory (R. Boyatzis. 2018)

In 2007, along with The Hay Group, Richard Boyatzis developed the Emotional and Social Competency Inventory (ESCI), which identifies 12 competencies and is used as a basis to assess EI in employees, as shown in Table 2. It is the most used behavioral measure of EI in practice and for which the most published studies have occurred (R. Boyatzis. 2018).

"Theoretically determined, EI consists of: (1) the self-awareness cluster concerns knowing one's internal states, preferences, resources, and intuitions, consisting of emotional self-awareness (i.e., recognizing one's emotions and their effects); and (2) the self-management cluster refers to managing one's internal states, impulses, and resources consisting of emotional self-control (i.e., keeping disruptive emotions and impulses in check), adaptability (i.e., flexibility in handling change), achievement orientation (i.e., striving to improve or meeting a standard of excellence), and positive outlook (i.e., seeing the positive aspects of things and the future). Social intelligence consists of: (1) the social awareness cluster refers to how people handle relationships and awareness of others' feelings, needs, and concerns, consisting of empathy (i.e., sensing others' feelings and perspectives, and taking an active interest in their concerns), and organizational awareness (i.e., reading a group's emotional currents and power relationships); and (2) the relationship management cluster concerns the skill or adeptness at inducing desirable responses in others, consisting of coach and mentor (i.e., sensing others' development needs and bolstering their abilities), inspirational leadership (i.e., inspiring and guiding individuals and groups), influence (i.e., wielding effective tactics for persuasion), conflict management (i.e., negotiating and resolving disagreements), and teamwork (i.e., working with others toward shared goals)" (R. Boyatzis. 2018).

People doing the assessment are asked to rate themselves against several statements about each of the twelve competencies. An example of a statement may be, "Tries to resolve conflict rather than letting it fester." The ranking is on a Likert scale going from 1 to 5 (ranging from "never" to "consistently" with increments in-between). This apparently works well for in-company development as in addition to the person being assessed; typically, three other parties are asked to rate them for the same set of statements. The result is meant to be a balanced view from different parties about where they are on the scale.

The nature of the measurement scale and some of the questions asked are, in my opinion, not useful. I could cite many examples, but let's take one of the comments used to assess how the person "anticipates how others will respond when trying to convince them." Let's think about this for a moment. You have the person being assessed, their boss, one of their team, and one of their peers, all using the same scale to assess the individual relating to this statement. The score uses a five-point scale from "never" to "consistently." This is meant to assess someone's relationship management and influencing skills. This is an incomplete statement, leaving it open to interpretation and therefore open to misinterpretation. It's not stating that the person correctly or wrongly anticipates when trying to convince others. It just states that they anticipate. Only the person being assessed will know whether they accurately anticipate the outcome correctly. They can only know this once the outcome is understood, and they refer back to what they anticipated the outcome to be. Anyone else can only assume whether or not the individual accurately anticipated any outcome and acted accordingly.

It is unclear if the statement aims to assess the extent to which the individual considers the potential outcomes of an upcoming conversation where they are trying to exert influence. Is the statement assessing the extent to which the person correctly anticipates the outcome, or just the fact that the individual anticipates anything at all? What does "correctly anticipate" mean? That they rightfully assessed what someone would be thinking and maneuvered their approach accordingly? There are just too many unanswered questions, or in other words, it's too open to misinterpretation, and that's just in understanding the question or statement.

If I'm the person being assessed, I'm likely to score a four or a five here, believing I am someone who anticipates outcomes and influences well. If I'm the peer, the manager, or the team member, I'm likely to score a three or a four because I may not understand the question, but it sounds like something the person would do based on my knowledge of them. Or maybe I score them a three or four because I've been in a position to know the outcome in a given situation but don't want to downgrade him or her for something they can't possibly be able to anticipate. If I don't like the person because I've disagreed with them in the past, I'm more likely to downgrade them because of my pre-formed opinions. The list of potentially distorting factors for this one question alone renders it unscientific and open to abuse.

EQ-I SCALES	The EI Competencies and Skills Assessed by Each Scale
INTRAPERSONAL	**Self-awareness and self-expression:**
Self-Regards	To accurately perceive, understand, and accept oneself.
Emotional Self-Awareness	To be aware of and understand one's emotions.
Assertiveness	To effectively and constructively express one's emotions and oneself.
Independence	To be self-reliant and free of emotional dependency on others.
Self-Actualization	To strive to achieve personal goals and actualize one's potential.
INTERPERSONAL	**Social awareness and interpersonal relationship:**
Empathy	To be aware of and understand how others feel.
Social Responsibility	To identify with one's social group and cooperate with others
Interpersonal Relationship	To establish mutually satisfying relationships and relate well with others.
STRESS MANAGEMENT	**Emotional Management and regulation:**
Stress Tolerance	To effectively and constructively manage emotions.
Impulse Control	To effectively and constructively control emotions.
ADAPTABILITY	**Change management:**
Reality-Testing	To objectively validate one's feelings and thinking with external reality.
Flexibility	To adapt and adjust one's feelings and thinking to new situations.
Problem-Solving	To effectively solve problems of a personal and interpersonal nature.
GENERAL MOOD	**Self-motivation:**
Optimism	To be positive and look at the brighter side of life.
Happiness	To feel content with oneself, others, and life in general.

Table 3: The EQ-I Scales and What They Assess (R. Bar-On. 2007)

Other attempts have been made to develop tools to measure EI. Reuven Bar-

On developed The Bar-On Emotional Quotient Inventory (EQ-I), shown in Table 3, which sought to measure EI, or as Bar-On refers to it, EQ, a deliberate reference to IQ; a phrase he coined in his doctoral studies in 1988 (R.Bar-On, 2007). The EQ-i is a self-report measure of emotionally and socially intelligent behavior that provides an estimate of emotional-social intelligence (ESI). The individual's responses render a total EQ score and scores on the following five composite scales that comprise 15 sub-scale scores: Intrapersonal (comprising Self Regard, Emotional Self-Awareness, Assertiveness, Independence, and Self Actualization); Interpersonal (comprising Empathy, Social Responsibility, and Interpersonal Relationship); Stress Management (comprising Stress Tolerance and Impulse Control); Adaptability (comprising Reality-Testing, Flexibility, and Problem Solving); and General Mood (comprising Optimism and Happiness) (R. Bar-On. 2007).

Based on six separate studies, Bar-On suggests that nearly 30% of the variance of occupational performance is based on ESI, as described by the Bar-On model. The findings indicate that high performers in the workplace have significantly higher ESI than low performers. The findings described here suggest that the most powerful ESI contributors to occupational performance are: (a) the ability to be aware of and accept oneself; (b) the ability to be aware of others' feelings, concerns, and needs; (c) the ability to manage emotions; (d) the ability to be realistic and put things in correct perspective; and (e) the ability to have a positive disposition. (R. Bar-On. 2007).

Academics that acknowledge EI is even a construct, and many strongly disagree that it is, seem to agree that high EI people have the ability or tendency to act in socially effective ways (Humphrey, Pollack, Hawver, & Story, 2011). It has been suggested that people with higher interpersonal skills are better at adapting their behavior and responses to certain social cues (Roulin et al., 2016). Thus it is fair to suggest that people with strong EI, knowledge of what is expected in social situations, and the ability to act accordingly, will lead to adapted responses in anticipation of certain outcomes. In fact, it has been suggested that people with strong EI are better positioned to do well in interviews as they are better able to perceive what answers may be desirable and adapt their answers and behavior accordingly

(Levashina et al., 2014).

DO WE EVEN NEED TO MEASURE EI?

Some researchers have questioned whether EI is a new construct that differs from other individual differences. For instance, as reported in a paper titled "Emotional Intelligence: Not Much More Than g and Personality," Schulte et al. (2004) found that cognitive intelligence, the Big Five traits of personality, and gender accounted for 41% of the variance in EI scores. A meta-analytic study by Lord, De Vader, & Aliger (1986) indicated that cognitive ability (g) correlated .52 with leader emergence. Furthermore, as previously discussed, the Big Five traits demonstrated a correlation of .48 with leadership (Judge et al., 2002), which brings to light questions about what new information EI can really reveal about people.

A literature review conducted by Farnia and Nakfukho (2016) identified a lack of consistent empirical evidence regarding the role of EI in leadership development and performance. Waterhouse (2006) argued that EI "has not been differentiated from personality plus IQ." Mayer et al. (2008) drew similarities between EI and the Big Five traits, highlighting the overlap with conscientiousness and extraversion. Furthermore, studies on the effect of EI on leader performance are founded on the notion that certain categories of personality characteristics are required for a leader to exert influence (Judge et al., 2009).

In my review of much of the literature on EI, I've witnessed very strong arguments on both sides. There are three arguments I've observed that are all strongly debated. 1. EI is an essential trait in successful leaders and anyone looking to interact with others. 2. Academics argue that more work must be done to measure EI and its implications successfully. 3. Nothing new can be gained from understanding EI as it's all understood already in the context of IQ and the Big Five personality traits. I also observed that academics can go a long way down the rabbit hole with research and scientific discourse. For example, they argue about the merits or demerits of meta-analysis where, for example, one argument is that many poorly constructed small studies don't mean the collective meta-study leads to smarter conclusions. They argue about sample sizes, the resulting validity, and other distractions that lead us further from useful conclusions to these studies. We must adopt a sense of reality and practicality when observing such studies that are often at odds with other robust and scientifically sound propositions.

For me, the concept of EI/EQ as a new construct has successfully been challenged and dethroned from a purely scientific perspective. However, I still find the concept's utility and its subset of traits useful in conceptualizing the human interaction side of what makes a successful leader. Yes, elements of EQ are already demonstrably measured when considering the Big Five personality traits. Yes, there are clear overlaps between IQ, the Big Five, and EQ, which means EQ is nothing novel or new. It is undeniable from a scientific standpoint that attempting to establish meaningful measures of EQ does not add to the scientific discourse beyond that which has been measured already by more robust IQ and Big Five assessments. However, I believe EQ still has great utility in better defining some of the softer skills that help people to articulate, beyond just being smart, how to get ahead in the workplace. For example, speaking about awareness of others' emotions and how to adapt your style accordingly to influence people has more tangible utility for the non-scientific community than simply talking academic-speak, referring to agreeableness and conscientiousness, as is the case with the Big Five personality traits. In this regard, EI, for me, is the people's language approach to the underlying and academically sound IQ and Big Five personality trait constructs.

This is why, when I write about the rabbit hole that academics go down, if we are to rely entirely on scientific studies, through stubbornly debating how scientific results are, we can miss the value of the language we've discovered in partly defining EQ. If we can reach a consensus about what EQ is, which non-academic individuals may be happier to agree upon, then we can move forward and utilize the power of the language of emotional intelligence as a way to focus on and improve how we treat one another.

PERSONALITY AND LEADERSHIP

Figure 6: The Big Five Personality Traits (Costa & McCrae, 1992)

From all of the research done in the past century on behavior and performance in the workplace, none has proven to be more valid and justified than the Big Five personality traits. That is except for GMA, or, roughly speaking, intelligence, which we've already covered. The Big Five personality traits can broadly be used to describe all of us across a spectrum of each of the five traits. It is this model that ended up forming part of the basis of the Bremnus Leadership research as it so well defines, or at least accounts for, a lot of our individual behaviors.

By way of a brief introduction to each of the five traits, Judge et al. (2002) provide a good summary: "Openness to Experience is the disposition to be imaginative, nonconforming, unconventional, and autonomous. Conscientiousness is comprised of two related facets: achievement and dependability. Agreeableness is the tendency to be trusting, compliant, caring, and gentle. Extraversion represents the tendency to be sociable, assertive, active, and to experience positive affects, such as energy and zeal. Neuroticism represents the tendency to exhibit poor emotional adjustment and experience negative effects, such as anxiety, insecurity, and hostility."

In 2007 a description of each of the Big Five was proposed by Deyoung et al., which breaks down each of the traits into two facets, which gives a more accurate description of how to interpret each of them.

Extraversion

Enthusiasm (spontaneous joy and engagement) and Assertiveness (social dominance, often verbal in nature).

Neuroticism

Withdrawal (the tendency to avoid in the face of uncertainty) and Volatility (the tendency to become irritable and upset when things go wrong).

Agreeableness

Compassion (the tendency to empathically experience the emotion of others) and Politeness (the proclivity to abide by interpersonal norms).

Conscientiousness

Industriousness (the ability to engage in sustained, goal-directed effort) and Orderliness (the tendency to schedule, organize and systematize).

Openness

Openness (creativity and aesthetic sensitivity) and Intellect (interest in abstract concepts and ideas).

(Deyoung et al., 2007)

The issue that critics take with the Big Five is that the data collection methods are largely based on self-scoring, so the results can be tainted (Viswesvaran & Ones, 1999). The issue has been that people are asked to rank their responses on a scale of 1-5 for several statements categorized under the five traits. This simply gives the respondent the ability to inflate their response. Another issue is the fact that not all jobs require the same degree of all personality traits, so their ability to predict job success is not universally sustainable. In 2008, a study in the Journal of Research in Personality (Hirsh & Peterson, 2008) sought to minimize human distortion by implementing new measures. Instead of getting people to rank themselves based on a five-point scale, they developed a new methodology utilizing three different approaches to minimize the extent to which an individual could "cheat the system." They essentially gave people choices between two different words and asked them to choose which word better represented them, and this was done several times relating to each of the personality traits. That wasn't the whole basis of the experiment, but needless to say, it only went to prove that bias is limited but not altogether eradicated when using this method. Besides, this method of choosing between one or another word has been criticized for being too restrictive (Bartram, 1996). It seems impossible to win in this game of behavioral science, but in the case of the Big Five, the outcomes are as close as we're going to get to being a credible scientific taxonomy of personality traits.

THE BIG FIVE JOURNEY

What follows is a description of how the Big Five came to be. Only in knowing the subtleties of the methods used outlined below can you fully understand the Bremnus leadership success model. Furthermore, it will help you to conceptualize how factor analysis is used and also put into perspective the time in history when psychologists went from just guessing to applying statistical methods. The journey from 18,000 words in a dictionary to the Big Five personality traits perfectly describes this transition. Credit for establishing The Big Five personality traits or the Five-Factor Model (FFM) is often attributed to Costa & Mcrae (1992), but in fact, much of the groundwork happened long before they came on the scene. Their work was merely a refinement of work conducted previously, which started with an American psychologist, Gordon Allport, back in the early 20th century, who is credited with the "lexical hypothesis" (Allport, 1937). In simple terms, Allport and his colleague, Henry Oldbert, read a dictionary and decided that 18,000 words sound like they may or could be used to describe personality. In their words, the lexical hypothesis proposes that most of the socially relevant and salient personality characteristics have become encoded in the natural language (e.g., Allport, 1937). They then got that list down to 4500 words before

Raymond Cattell, a British psychologist practicing at Harvard alongside Allport in 1943, took on the daunting task of getting this list down to a more meaningful and practical number. He, first of all, got the list down to 135 using semantic clustering, essentially observing words that seemed to group together, but without using empirical methods. He then used factor analysis to get this list down to 35 variables. From there, he conducted further factor analysis, which ultimately left him with 12 factors, which later settled on 16 factors, or the famous Cattel's 16 Personality Factors (16PF) outlined in Table 4. (Cattell, Eber, & Tatsuoka, 1970).

Reasoning	Perfectionism	Dominance	Liveliness
Openness to change	Vigilance	Warmth	Tension
Abstractedness	Sensitivity	Social Boldness	Emotional Stability
Rule Consciousness	Self Reliance	Privateness	Apprehension

Table 4: Cattel's 16 Personality Factors (16PF)

A number of psychologists worked with Catell's initial 35 variables and concluded a five-factor structure that broadly resembled the eventual Big Five personality traits (Tupes & Cristal, 1961, Norman, 1963). The name was not meant to suggest that these are the big five traits, but rather that these dimensions represent personality at the broadest level of extraction, and therefore each dimension is representative of many more characteristics. Perhaps the reason the Big Five is mostly attributed to Lewis Goldberg is that Raymond Cattell had faced criticism over his methods used to go from 4500 to 35 traits and then down to 16. It was more of a mix of practical guesswork and empirical methods, so naturally, it was open to criticism. However, when applying factor analysis to Cattell's 16 Personality Factors, as shown in Figure 7, we can see how the same Big Five traits can be arrived at when starting out with Cattel's 16PF.

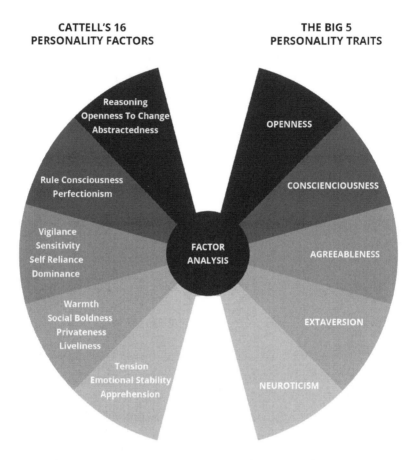

Figure 7: Factor Analysis From Cattell's 16PF to The Big Five

As a result of the criticism of Cattell's methods, Lewis Goldberg essentially started the process from scratch, expanding on work done by Warren Norman (1967) to construct an inventory of 1600 trait adjectives. This followed the same process as Allport and Oldbert thirty years previously, starting out with his own list taken from a newer version of the dictionary and then comparing self-score results with Norman's work, once again resulting in the Big Five personality traits (Goldberg, 1990).

Goldberg's work was expanded upon by McCrae and Costa, who, among others, confirmed the model's validity, and the rest of the story about the Big

Five personality traits is history. McCrae & Costa, first of all, developed the NEO Personality Inventory (NEO-PI) in 1985 (NEO representing Neuroticism, Extraversion, and Openness), and then in 1992, they published a revised version (NEO-PI-R) (R for revised), which included all five traits. In a paper by Costa and McCrae, they sought to revise the NEO-PI-R model, which appeared to be in response to critique they noted in the paper:

"If one desires a broad overview of personality dimensions, we regard the five-factor model as most promising, but if one's theoretical or pragmatic requirements are for a more differentiated, detailed perspective, perhaps other measurement models should be considered" (Costa and McCrae, 1995).

Their goal here was to broaden out the Big Five to be more explicit by describing six facets that further clarify each of the Big Five. In their own words, the Big Five "sketch the outlines of the client's personality; facet scales fill in the details" (Costa & McCrae, 1995). It appears from the article that this was done so, at a practical level, psychologists could better understand and assess their clients, which in turn would lead to more specific interventions.

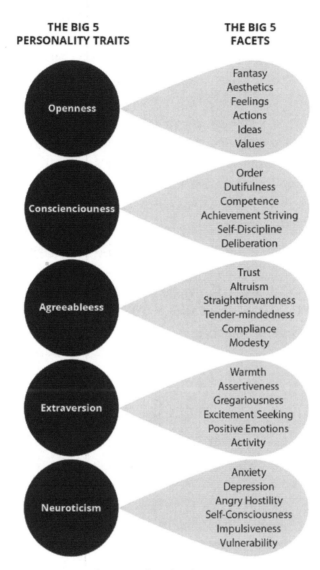

Figure 8: The Big Five Facets

The facets were selected to meet a series of criteria: "They should represent maximally distinct aspects of the domain, be roughly equivalent in breadth, and be conceptually rooted in the existing psychological literature" (Costa & McCrae, 1995). The paper then went on to describe how these facets overlapped and to what degree, with the trait theories provided by other notable scholars. The end result was a list of facets that were highly correlated with the intended Big Five traits but were independently different enough to uniquely describe a facet of the overarching trait.

HOW THE BIG FIVE RELATES TO PERFORMANCE AT WORK

The literature on leadership and the Big Five is quite extensive, albeit, in my opinion, not conclusive at all. I think the reason it's not conclusive is that the Big Five itself is a very distilled and simplified account of what personality and the related behaviors are. However, from the many studies that have been done trying to pin the Big Five tail on the leadership trait donkey, the following findings have emerged.

OPENNESS

Openness tends to indicate people who are curious, imaginative, and creative problem solvers (Carson, Peterson, & Higgins, 2005). People who score highly on this dimension have a greater tendency towards cognitive exploration and also manifest higher levels of cognitive flexibility and divergent thinking (DeYoung, Peterson, & Higgins, 2005). This is a critical trait for leaders and for me, the defining Big Five trait that separates visionary leaders from managers. Managers don't necessarily need to be high in openness. They don't need to have the ideas or be great problem solvers. They have to complete tasks and make sure teams of people are doing what is asked of them, all within the confines of a specific set of rules. That is more to do with conscientiousness rather than openness.

Openness is highly linked to creativity. Creativity includes ideas and problem solving and is highly correlated with intelligence. That's not to say that intelligent people are all creative, but one can make the argument that intelligent people know how to solve problems, at least certain types of problems. It is certainly true that creative people tend to be intelligent, but again, not on all dimensions of intelligence all of the time. Think about a spectrum between outrageously inventive entrepreneurs at one end and extremely good operations managers at another end. The psychologist Professor Jordan Peterson once said that liberals start companies and conservatives run them. Creative people tend to be more liberal, although not always, and managers tend to be more conservative. Their temperament is just different. This is one of the reasons why innovation stifles in large companies. Creative people with ideas start companies, and then they have to hire orderly, conscientious people to run them so that things get done, and tasks are completed. As the company grows, hierarchies are necessary to maintain order in the company, and so more conscientious manager types are hired, and before you know it, there's no innovation happening.

I find it interesting that large companies, like in the banking sector, for example, have these "innovation labs." They started popping up around ten years ago when the fintech space was starting to emerge. To me, they would more suitably be called "procrastination labs" as they're a reaction to the external threat of innovative companies who are nimble enough to innovate. The bank's response is, "Wait, how come these companies are carving out market share when we own this market? Why aren't we innovating? I know, let's set up innovation labs and start relationships with these startups and see what we can learn from them." All they're going to learn is that their own structure doesn't allow for incredible ideas to percolate up through the top-down management brick walls where experience is valued way more than ideas. These innovation labs are a good step forward for these banks, but, in my opinion, the root of the problem is the company structure and culture.

Identifying those who are clearly high in openness and utilizing their creativity to explore new ideas, regardless of what level they're at, will allow innovation to flourish even in the largest of companies. Instead of companies spending hundreds of millions of dollars on consulting firms to create the right management structure with the right number of layers, they should be paying equal attention to innovation, and that comes from ideas, and ideas come from thin air from people who are creatively minded.

Creativity is not like management experience. You don't have to be in a company for years before you qualify to be creative. Also, people think of creativity as art and music but rarely think of it as problem solving and ideas. Creativity is in people, but only in those that creativity resides. Not everyone is creative. Aesthetics and ideas, the two cornerstones of the Big Five trait, openness, often come hand in hand, and so companies would be doing themselves a great service to identify who these people are, give them a white coat and see what happens. They don't even need a white coat. They just need a voice.

If you're reading this as someone who's "stuck" in a company and your brain is on fire all the time with ideas, or you're super interested in ideas and maybe also art or design, for example, the chances are you're going to continue feeling stuck until you find an outlet for all of these things that occupy your brain. That outlet could be a hobby, creating music or art, or whatever interests you, but you may also just be destined to be an entrepreneur. That, by the way, is a blessing and a curse all at the same time. The curse part is that you'll never feel happy or fulfilled in a job where you can't contribute or action your ideas. You'll bounce from job to job, just feeling unfulfilled and only feeling any degree of excitement when you first start, and everything is new again. Lawyers and accountants, for example, don't tend to score very high on trait openness, but they score extremely high on conscientiousness. Think about their role for a moment. It makes sense. Their whole world is a set of governed strict rules, and unless you're Bernie Madoff's accountant, where you could successfully argue your accounting was very creative, the chances are you won't find many creative types working in that field.

In my view, the exception to this is individuals who were clearly creative at school but then followed their parent's wishes into university to become a well-respected accountant or a lawyer, for example. Those individuals will know who they are as they will be unfulfilled, unlike the highly dutiful conscientious individuals who just love working with rules and structure. Sound familiar? Neither is right nor wrong. These are just different personalities, and this appears to be poorly understood by the corporate world. If it was better understood, we'd all be much more cognizant of these issues.

The curse continues when you finally quit your job to become an entrepreneur, and you think you're all set. Unfortunately, the ideas don't stop coming just because you take action and go after one of the ideas you have. You will be forevermore distracted with new ideas, hence the reason why you need to hire a bunch of highly conscientious manager types to run your company. I had a personal journey of discovery with this, which is part of the reason I wrote this book. I grew up in rural Scotland. I lived in a small town of 13,000 people. At school, I was generally good at all subjects. I wasn't an A-star student, but I had good grades across the board. Where I really excelled was in art. At first, I wanted to be an architect, and my final year school art project was a complete re-design and a model build of my uncle's motorway cafe that I worked at on the weekends during my high school years. Then when it came time for university, everyone told me there's no money in architecture until you're 120 years old, which I now know is neither true nor relevant, so I took a business degree instead.

I then got into recruitment straight out of university, and I struggled with the repetitive nature of it, but it paid well, and in dealing with people, no two days were the same. I would go to art galleries on the weekends while working in London and stand very close to the paintings of famous impressionist artists and just stare at the strokes. I never shared that with people and almost felt embarrassed as I come from a rural part of Scotland where "people aren't into that kind of thing." I was mesmerized by it, though. I had a similar experience with music, all kinds of music. I would just get lost in it. Never for a moment did I think that this was clearly trying to tell me something about what I should be doing with my life. I don't mean I should have been pursuing a career in art, but it would have been obvious, had I known about it, that I was evidently high in the Big Five trait, openness.

Here I was, working in recruitment and executive search and managing to hold on by making the career very exciting. I moved to Hong Kong and worked there when I was 25. I moved to Poland and ran a recruiting firm in six eastern European countries when I was 27. I moved to Canada at 29 and started my first recruiting company, and I then moved to Thailand for a year to create an online recruitment e-learning product when I was 31. Soon after, I ended up back in the real world, working for J.P. Morgan doing leadership executive search, before setting up Bremnus in 2012 in London, followed by the US. That, to some, would just be too crazy, but to me, looking back, knowing what I know now, it was all because I was suffocating with the boredom of just placing candidates over and over again. So many loved the thrill of "making placements," but I really didn't. When it got to the point where I was interviewing and placing very senior candidates with packages in excess of one million dollars, I should have been delighted, but I just wasn't fulfilled, and I genuinely didn't know why. What I did enjoy were the conversations I had with a wide variety of people, many of whom became personal friends over the years. I also had a keen interest in business in general, so it was always fascinating to learn about each individual's journey and how the companies they worked for operated. It was an insider's view you simply don't get in any other profession. I learned about people's personal lives, their salaries, their insecurities, their drivers, and generally things they may not admit in any other situation or dialogue. I got to read the news and see an announcement about some C-level executive moving to a Fortune 500 company, and knowing I made that hire that was actioned months prior to the news being in the public domain. All of that certainly kept it fresh and exciting for me.

I started to research and write, just not satisfied with where my industry was but also not satisfied with where I was in it. For many, being a headhunter is a badge of honor, and rightly so. We help people change their lives by brokering new opportunities for them. However, given the repetitive nature of what we do and me having a creative and inquisitive scratch-to-itch, I became obsessed with trying to understand why it didn't appear that any of us truly knew what we were doing when it came to candidate selection. We really don't. Not even Fortune 500 companies. This statement will be explored and proven throughout this book. My goal in writing this book was to figure that out and also to try and establish a better way. The more I researched, the more I knew I had to write this book. However, in the process of writing and researching the last hundred years of behavioral science, something completely unexpected happened. I learned why I am the way I am. I learned why I'd been bored for most of my career. I learned why I felt different from those who were happy and content with repetitive task-based jobs, no matter how much you dress them up to be something different. I learned about trait openness and how it's linked to creativity, and how creativity isn't just art; it's also ideas, and as it turned out, I was off the scale on trait openness.

So there it was; the light bulb went on, and that expression that I hated and resented for my whole career, for the first time, was understood – "When you love what you do, you'll never work a day in your life." Up until this point, I worked every single day, like it was a physical back-breaking job, despite doing it from the comfort of many desks all over the world. After much of the research, I started to write this book on November 1st, 2019. I "haven't worked" since, but I have written this book, and it didn't stop there.

As a result of this research, I started to draw again, and then I started to learn Adobe Illustrator, the software used for everything from graphic design to online painting. I then learned Adobe XD, which is an online tool for building working prototypes of software products and websites, and with that, I designed all 400+ pages of my HR software company, Extraview, the online software that brings this whole book to life. In writing the book and designing the software for Extraview, it was done in two stages. I wrote the book, and I thought it was finished. I then started designing the software, and through that process, I realized there were certain parts missing from the book. Only in going through the iterative process of designing the software could I then see what was missing from the book. Something magical happened when I was able to combine my learning of Adobe Illustrator, XD, and my writing. Often I'd think in images that appeared in my mind, but I couldn't articulate them in words. However, through being able to map them out in Illustrator, then seeing a visual representation on there, and then changing bits iteratively, I was able to take some of the ideas to places you couldn't get to if you were just a writer working with a graphic designer.

That is my personal story of the revelation of the Big Five, and I should have known this a long time ago; I work in the industry where this type of research should be best understood, but it isn't understood. If those of us working in talent acquisition, both in-house and externally, don't know this research like the back of our hands, what hope do the rest of us have? That was when I knew I had to fully research this topic from top to bottom and apply myself to write this book. That story may have resonated with you personally. I'm not one to share personal stories, but it was such a profound moment in my life after years of career unhappiness that it would be wrong at this moment not to share it. You may be "that person" who is bored to death in their job and working with a brain full of constantly evolving ideas. If it has resonated and you haven't taken action to "be more true to yourself," I highly recommend it.

If it doesn't resonate with you personally, it may be the case that someone inherently creative could be working on your shop floor right now for minimum wage, daydreaming about aesthetic things, and may have incredible ideas on how to make your company more efficient. Companies seem to be more focused on people management and people's dutiful fulfillment of obligations, and they don't understand creativity or, in this case, openness.

If you are in a leadership position in a company, and you take away nothing else from this book, please digest this: You and your leadership team cannot possibly have all of the ideas. Your experience does not necessarily make your ideas more relevant than one of your team working five layers down. Ideas are not "experience." Truly novel ideas are abstractions that only come from creative people. Not everyone is creative. You may have a great leadership team of great managers, but you will have to look deeper and wider for the creative types; they could transform your company. Find them and nurture them before they end up leaving and taking their ideas with them. These types that leave are often the entrepreneurs, and it never had to be that way.

CONSCIENTIOUSNESS

The extent to which someone is conscientious, which implies they are hardworking, organized, efficient, and self-disciplined, has emerged as a strong predictor of success in the workplace (Barrick & Mount, 1991). One study even showed that self-discipline, linked to conscientiousness, was twice as effective as IQ at predicting academic performance (Duckworth & Seligman, 2005). It goes without saying that if you work hard, you'll get ahead most of the time. Conscientiousness doesn't override IQ, though. For example, someone with an IQ of lower than 90, who would, by definition, find learning hard in general, will not be able to just work really hard and become a doctor unless their IQ score was wrongly marked. Furthermore, conscientiousness without the right balance of other traits does not by itself predict strong leadership skills. In other words, for someone to have strong leadership skills, they cannot just be hard working. We will come on to look at what else they will need to be in addition to conscientious in the summary that will follow.

NEUROTICISM

After conscientiousness, rating low for the trait neuroticism, or in other words, rating high for emotional stability, has been shown to be a big predictor of success in the workplace (Salgado, 1997). Low neuroticism has also proven to be a good predictor of job satisfaction and organizational commitment (Thoresen et al., 2003). This makes sense when you consider how much pressure leaders can be under, especially when they're running enormous companies. Many of us will also know those people in our social life or work environment that just criticize everything, are always having the "worst day ever," and can't understand why things "always happen to them." Those people, if you haven't guessed, will rate high for trait neuroticism. That's not a good score, by the way. Leaders, by contrast, tend to be very calm under pressure and in a crisis, which makes logical sense.

EXTRAVERSION

A study by Gough (1990) found that naturally emerging leaders in groups were described with adjectives like "active, assertive, energetic, and not silent or withdrawn" (Gough, 1990). These are the characteristics of extraverts. Indeed, Gough (1990) found that both of the major facets of extraversion—dominance and sociability—were related to self and peer ratings of leadership (Judge et al., 2002). It's important to note that this does not mean that those that are not extraverts cannot make good leaders. It often comes down to how we interpret the word "extravert." Many of us imagine loud attention seekers when we hear this word, and that just isn't what this is.

On a scale going from introvert to extrovert, individuals can be anywhere on that scale, and their behaviors will not always represent where they naturally fall on that scale. Consider some of the most successful leaders of our time who are considered to be introverted, like Bill Gates, for example. Although he is an introvert, he's still getting on stage in front of thousands of people. Also, people closer to the introvert side of the scale tend to be less impulsive and, therefore, naturally, take more time to think, which is critical in leadership when considering some of the enormous decisions they have to make.

So, for me, the notion that leaders must be extravert is just not true. Perhaps it's more fitting to suggest that leaders have to, at times, do things that extraverts would be more known to enjoy, like speaking in front of people, for example. With that, it may be fairer to say that leaders have to be able to demonstrate moderately extraverted behavior when required, but if they are otherwise introverts, it doesn't impede their ability to succeed in any way.

AGREEABLENESS

According to the studies, agreeableness appears to carry the most amount of ambiguity when it comes to leadership effectiveness, which is really saying something. It would be too simple to state that effective leaders tend to be less agreeable because they have to make decisions and know they can't please everyone. Extremely agreeable people are pleasers and want everyone to be happy, and it's fair to say that this would not make for a good leader. However, at the other end of the spectrum are those who are entirely disagreeable, which also doesn't make for a very inclusive way of managing people. So, where do we stand on agreeableness?

There are arguments for both sides but little empirical conviction. This is one of those times when common sense may prevail. Suppose we consider a scale of one to ten. Ten is completely agreeable, where if someone suggests you should jump off a bridge, you will start Googling "nearest bridge to me." Scoring one would represent someone so disagreeable that they would argue there's no such thing as bridges. Where should a leader be on this scale? I would say they'd have to oscillate between a four and a five, with perhaps a one-point allowance on each end, depending on the situation. They have to lead with conviction and be confident, but they can't be so disagreeable that nobody wants to work for them or that they're close-minded to others' ideas.

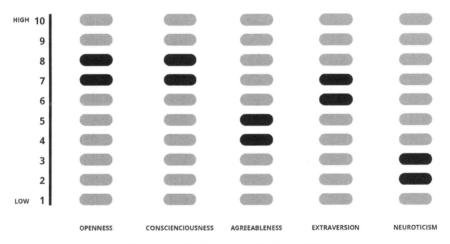

Figure 9: The Bremnus Big Five DNA

So what makes the optimal leader? Figure 9 shows the Bremnus Big Five DNA. This is our take, based on the studies we've done, on what the optimal balance of the Big Five traits is for leadership. We've taken each of the five traits and applied a scale of one to ten and suggested a sweet spot for each one consisting of two positions for each. From this chart, we can see that a good leader is typically high in openness, high in conscientiousness, moderate in agreeableness, moderate to high extraversion, and low in neuroticism.

They're typically a seven or eight in openness as openness relates to ideas and problem solving, and this is where great leaders come into their own. They don't have a textbook or someone telling them what to do. They will no doubt have trusted lieutenants advising them what to do, but the buck stops with them, and they have to make the most difficult decisions in the company. They're typically a seven or an eight in conscientiousness as they have to get things done but not in such a rigid fashion that they fail to adapt. They will most certainly want their CFO to be a nine or a ten. They will ideally be on the lower side of moderate in agreeableness, but not so low that they don't know how to listen or be open to other ideas. Extraversion will be moderate to high, at least when called for, in order to develop the right sorts of relationships with people and also to be able to lead and inspire in general. Neuroticism should definitely be low but perhaps not a one. They cannot be emotionally detached from the world but should absolutely be calm under pressure and generally be positive.

This list is not prescriptive. For example, you have great introverted leaders who are not high on extraversion at all. You have very conscientious leaders who may not be extremely high in openness. Different companies at different stages of evolution will have different requirements of leaders as they relate to this mix, so the Bremnus Big Five DNA is a generalized illustration. If you're a startup, your leader, who is likely to be the founder, will typically be very high in openness but may not be extremely high in conscientiousness, for example. The real answer to the question of what mix of personality traits makes a good leader is, "It depends on the company, where they are currently in their evolution, where they need to get to, and in what time frame." It is probably fairer to suggest what definitely will not make a great leader, and that is someone who is very high in agreeableness, very high in neuroticism, very low in openness, and very low in conscientiousness.

Certain personality traits have already been identified as being a strong predictor of job performance. Also, it has already been acknowledged that personality tests themselves are, in many ways, limited due to the self-scoring nature of the tests undertaken. Research suggests that personality is already assessed in interviews. For example, in a meta-analysis study by Cortina et al. (2000), they discovered that the interviews they observed all contained questions that measured some facets of conscientiousness, such as initiative, work ethic, and thoroughness. Also, Huffcutt, Conway, et al. (2001) found that one-third of all interview questions in forty-seven actual interviews measured personality. Finally, Morgeson et al. (2007) suggested that structured interviews designed to measure personality might be a better way to measure personality than self-report measures themselves. Conscientiousness was the most frequently assessed trait. Therefore, it may be the case that designing an interview process that encompasses questions that measure some of the more significant personality factors may, in turn, do away with the need to conduct separate personality tests, which are flawed in their self-score design anyway. This is exactly what we have done in the Bremnus leadership success model.

So there you have the Big Five personality traits. The fact that most of us don't know about them, and I include myself in that for most of the past twenty years, is really quite shocking. It's not that we necessarily should have known about them, but the value they bring in explaining so much about all of us, inside and outside of work, is so great that they should be studied and understood by anyone entering the workplace, in my opinion. It is certainly fair to say that, to date, we do not have a better way of explaining personalities. Sure, it's not the perfect explanation, but nobody ever said it is. Humans are so unbelievably complex as individuals, with so many factors affecting us growing up, with so many influences and so many human interactions, that we may never fully account for personality in its entirety. What we can do, though, is take more time to better understand and accept ourselves, our limitations, our possibilities, and our preferences, much of which can be better understood with the Big Five model.

What is certainly clear is the application of the Big Five traits when we look at candidate selection and interview processes. That is not to say we just give everyone a personality test. I don't actually believe that the words used to describe the Big Five are sufficient to get relevant enough information from such an approach. This is also why I don't think personality tests are useful in the hiring process. I think understanding the Big Five is incredibly useful at a macro level, but it is too low resolution to apply directly as an assessment method, especially when we can get much more granular with the right structure of questions. You only need to take one of the personality tests yourself to know that you can tell people what they want to hear based on the answers you give. In order to address such cheating, we have to move away from self-scoring and develop ways of observing the extent to which people exhibit each of the Big Five personality traits through other methods. This is part of what the Bremnus Method seeks to do. The great thing about leadership hiring, or even manager hiring, is that they have a history of facts to work with. Of course, candidates can be economical with the facts, but not if the interview is structured in the right way, or certainly it can be much more difficult for them to lie with the correct structure.

Let's consider an interview where the candidate's early life was tough. For some reason, they were very open and told us about a parent dying and growing up in six different schools, yet they ended up in an incredible university, and from there, they have progressed all the way up to C level in a Fortune 500 company. Do we need to run a personality test to assess the extent to which that person is conscientious? Clearly not. Would we need to worry about how agreeable that person was? Well, we could observe this by asking certain questions and spotting patterns throughout their career. The same applies to the rest of the Big Five. However, the example about the conscientious candidate doesn't give us enough information to distinguish between one candidate and another. This is magnified when we're hiring for Fortune 500 companies at a senior level because, in this case, who isn't going to show that they're conscientious? They will all be conscientious, and the small difference between their levels of conscientiousness will be neither significant nor relevant for the most part, so we do need to think beyond the Big Five traits, or at least look at them differently.

INTUITION AND BIASES

When you first approach the subject of intuition, it's a tough one to get started on. There are so many definitions of what intuition is to begin with. Then, once you establish that intuition is real, you run into clashes with heuristics and biases, and you'd be forgiven for just giving up and never trusting your intuition. In fact, many scholars, even to this day, think that we shouldn't be using intuition when making decisions. One such organizational psychologist stated words to the effect: "There is conclusive evidence indicating that decisions based on intuition are almost always biased (and therefore less effective) than those based on data or actual evidence." I won't quote who said this, but he may be referring to the early work carried out by Tversky and Kahneman (1974), which refers to heuristics, or mental shortcuts, as being flawed, but heuristics are only one type of cognitive structure that relates to intuition. More on this later.

You can make your own mind up after reading the evidence on whether you, as a leader or hiring manager, should utilize intuition that has been refined over many years. However you reach your conclusions, like with all evidence and constructs in psychology, you have to take a step back, review the literature, how it came to be, how the constructs are defined, and how reliable and valid they are. Then you have to consider real-life and whether there is a peaceful and practical place for the theory to meet with reality.

"Don't let the noise of other's opinions drown out your own inner voice. And most important, have the courage to follow your heart and intuition. They somehow already know what you truly want to become. Everything else is secondary." (Steve Jobs).

"All of my best decisions in business and in life have been made with heart and intuition – not analysis. When you can make a decision with analysis, you should do so, but it turns out in life that your most important decisions are always made with instinct, intuition, taste, heart." (Jeff Bezos).

Here we have two of the most successful people to ever walk this earth speaking about how they use intuition to make their decisions. Perhaps they got lucky, or perhaps they are just very good when it comes to intuitive thinking and execution. It wouldn't be the first time we can't explain why some people are incredibly gifted at certain things. Think of artists and musicians, for example. What makes them so incredible, and why can't I sing or paint the same way? We don't necessarily know why, but the differences are very clearly expressed in their work. Is it, therefore, possible that there may be varying degrees of competence that are unexplained when it comes to leadership and decision-making? I believe it is possible, as evidenced by some of the incredible leaders that have existed in all facets of society over the years.

I don't think anyone, for a second, is suggesting that intuition is always right. For example, in 1993, Apple launched what was effectively the first iPad, the Apple Newton. It was a complete flop. It was probably more of a case of timing and technology not quite being advanced enough, but no doubt intuition played a part in their decision to launch that product. For some psychologists to just strike down the utility of intuition because they're not always right or because there's a fine line between intuition and biases is like saying that any psychometric experiment with a correlation coefficient of less than one renders it invalid. That would, in other words, render nearly every single significant measure of behavior completely invalid. Thankfully, over recent years, many more studies have been done on intuition, and we're starting to get closer to a place where reality and theory speak a similar language.

The effective use of intuition has even been seen as critical in differentiat-ing successful top executives and board members from lower-level managers and dysfunctional boards (Agor, 1986). Ralph Larsen, a former chair and CEO of Johnson & Johnson, suggested: "Very often, people will do a brilliant job through the middle management levels, where it's very heavily quantitative in terms of the decision-making. But then they reach senior management, where the problems get more complex and ambiguous, and we discover that their judgment or intuition is not what it should be. And when that happens, it's a problem; it's a big problem." (Hayashi, 2001).

Classical analytical decision-making suggests that we should observe all potential outcomes, work with the data, measure which outcome may be most favorable based on the desired outcome, and decide only once all potential scenarios and relevant parties have been consulted. That's fine for scenarios where time is on your side and all required information is readily available, but that doesn't work in moments when decisions have to be made almost instantaneously.

Herbert Simon, a Nobel Prize winner, introduced the concept of bounded rationality to explain why it is impossible to make any important decision by gathering and analyzing all the facts as there are simply too many facts and too many combinations of facts. Instead, what enables us to make good decisions is intuition in the form of a very large repertoire of patterns acquired over many years of practice. Without those patterns, decisions wouldn't be made. For example, think about traders watching swing movements on their monitor and deciding whether to double down or get out. What about a police officer with someone walking towards them with one hand in their pocket and not obeying an order to stop? How about a candidate sitting in an interview having been presented a scenario with not very much information and being asked how they would respond? The intuitions these scenarios rely on are not very well understood by those of us that subconsciously rely on them every day.

The subject of intuition has fascinated me for years. I remember once, in an interview for a job, I was asked, "How do you know when a candidate is a great candidate?" I pondered the question and came to a conclusion in my mind that after many years of headhunting, "I just know." Of course, that answer would not have been satisfactory, as you can't "just know," or so I thought. The answer I gave instead was something like, "It depends on the client and the role. I would need to know who they would be working for, what that person is like, and fully understand the type of candidate they typically like to hire. It's less important what I believe and more important to understand how the client would define a good candidate." In truth, that was approximately true as many times I've seen clients hire candidates that really surprised me. In retrospect, I believe many of those surprising hires were made because the hiring manager wasn't even sure what they were looking for. Perhaps they'd just "know when they knew," which I never used to believe in, but now, after researching intuition, I believe that people can at least think they "know when they see it," as there are a lot of subconscious influences at play.

DUAL SYSTEM THINKING

The renowned Nobel Prize laureate, Daniel Kahneman, was interviewed at "Our Crowd Global Investor Summit" in 2019 and said, "You're better off if you collect information first and collect all the information in a systematic way and only then allow yourself to take a global view and to have an intuition about the global view" (Our Crowd, 2019). He then went on to speak about work he did 63 years ago when he modified the interviewing process for the Israeli army. He spoke about how the key modification was to delay intuition until all of the information was collected when they would then be in a position to form any kind of global view.

It was Kahneman who also wrote the book "Thinking Fast and Slow" (2011) which describes how we think about and arrive at decisions utilizing two different "systems." What became known as System 1 and System 2 thinking was expanded upon in a paper published in Perspectives on Psychological Science (Evans & Stanovich, 2013). This "system" method was met with a lot of critique from the scientific community in that it wasn't really a precise definition, and also that, for example, "System 1" thinking is actually made up of a whole number of different brain functions and therefore cannot be called one system. This is the typical debate psychologists get into when trying to define things. Anyway, the outcome of this 2013 paper, which sought to answer some of the criticism, proposed a "Type 1" and "Type

2" model. Yes, to you and me, this is exactly the same thing as "System 1" and "System 2," and the semantics regarding these definitions are of little importance to us. Conceptually they are talking about the same thing.

Type 1 refers to the automatic thinking parts of the brain, which involves implicit learning. Think about learned actions that, over time, become intuitive. If you think about the first few times you ever drove a car, it was anything but intuitive. You were probably petrified and excited all at the same time. You were undoubtedly overwhelmed with all the instructions you had to master simultaneously. You had to make sure your seat belt was on; you had to look in the rearview mirror, put the car into drive or reverse, and then focus on staying alive and ensuring all innocent pedestrians survived your journey. It was a lot. After a while, that turns into intuition, and before you know it, you're disobeying all the rules by checking your phone as you drive.

Kahneman characterizes System 2 as "the conscious, reasoning self that has beliefs, makes choices, and decides what to think about and do." (Kahneman, 2011). It has also been described as "cognitive decoupling: the ability to distinguish supposition from belief and to aid rational choices by running thought experiments." (Evans and Stanovich, 2013). It is the conscious chaperone of Type 1 thinking, constantly monitoring Type 1 actions and overriding any instincts it recognizes as wrong. It is more analytical and slow in reaching decisions, relying on all available information rather than internal impulses.

In the driving example from before, even though the driver may have developed their driving skills to the point where they do it on automatic pilot, or Type 1, whenever they encounter potential danger, like passing a large truck on a windy, wet day, this is when Type 2 thinking kicks in to make sure it is taking in all available information to make choices that would otherwise be intuitive. This is what the unconscious bias theory doesn't take into account. It assumes that our Type 1 thinking is so flawed that we need to focus on retraining that system from scratch. Good luck with that approach. A much quicker, more effective way to combat unconscious bias is to work on system 2, which is really what we do anyway, as evidenced by the decisions being made in large corporates and other companies on a daily basis.

DEFINING INTUITION

What is described above goes some way to providing the simplified context that helps understand the exploration of intuition in full. Dane and Pratt (2007) defined intuitions as "affectively-charged judgments that arise through rapid, non-conscious, and holistic associations." In another similar paper by Hodgkinson et al. (2008), they went on to describe what is meant by these terms, and in doing so, we are able to build quite a specific picture of what we're referring to when describing intuition.

"Affectively charged" refers to the feelings that are associated with intuition, like "gut feeling," for example. Agor (1986) notes that as executives make intuitive judgments, they often experience excitement and harmony.

"Nonconscious" refers to the fact that intuition occurs outside of conscious thought. Jung, for example, defined intuition as "that psychological function which transmits perceptions in an unconscious way" (1933). We already know this from our evolutionary biological instincts, which originate outside of the experiential processing system, like pulling back your hand from a hot stovetop when you didn't realize it was still hot.

"Holistic associations" refers to the linking of disparate elements of information and making holistic associations unconsciously based on previously known patterns or cognitive structures or, in other words, mental processes.

UNCONSCIOUS BIAS

From what's been happening in the corporate and HR world for the last two decades, it is clear that "unconscious bias" is a well-used term but perhaps better described as well-misused. When it comes to candidate selection, we're now told that we must eliminate our unconscious biases or risk hiring through one of many corrupt lenses that we allegedly all see through and cannot control.

You may recall playing the kids' party game, telephone, when a word is whispered from one kid to the next, and what started as "birthday cake" ends up being "birdie cage." Over the past hundred years, unconscious bias has gone through a similar filtering system of childlike naivety and carelessness. Instead of unconscious bias, we've ended up with a proverbial birdie cage.

The birdie cage largely stems from the work done by Khaneman & Tversky (1974) and Banaji & Greenwald (1995), who both wrote about some of the negative consequences of utilizing heuristics, or cognitive shortcuts, to make decisions. However, the work done by Herbert Simon (1947) and later by Gerd Gigerenzer (1996) demonstrated that heuristics are a necessary cognitive tool in deciding under times of uncertainty when we don't have all the information we need.

The only part of a century of research that seems to have ended up in the LinkedIn and HBR headlines is that our biases are corrupt, and we must get rid of them. It's just not that simple. This is only part of the story, a narrative made out of the crumbs of the whole story, which hasn't been told until now.

Today's Corporate Definition

A bias is a strong feeling or inclination toward or against something or someone. Once companies hastily learned that we're all prejudiced and our unconscious biases are to blame, they rushed to hire consultants to advise them about this apparent plague of our implicit thoughts. Just look at what one of the world's largest and most successful companies, Microsoft, trains their employees to believe. Microsoft is not the only guilty party – most prominent global companies will have rolled out similar training. What follows is taken directly from their publicly available unconscious bias training.

"Unconscious bias is defined as stereotypes, prejudices, or preferences that cause us to favor a person, thing, or group in a way deemed unfair. They are implicit attitudes, behaviors, words, or actions that we exhibit in our personal lives and the workplace. We all have unconscious biases. They are mental shortcuts that help us navigate our day effectively and efficiently"

(Microsoft, 2022).

No wonder we are confused. First, they write that unconscious bias causes us to favor a thing or group in an unfair way. That's consistent with how we're being taught to view unconscious bias, despite it being wrong, or at least not altogether accurate. Then they write, "They are mental shortcuts that help us navigate our day, effectively and efficiently." That is a definition of heuristics, not unconscious bias.

So, which is it? They're mental shortcuts that help us navigate our day effectively and efficiently, or do they cause us to favor a thing or group in a way that's unfair? The truth is, as you'll read shortly, heuristics are shortcuts our brains take to reach decisions under conditions of uncertainty. As a result, our biases learned from previous experiences will influence our conclusion when we don't have enough information, knowledge, or time to make an informed decision.

Microsoft was off the mark in the initial statement that unconscious bias leads us to favor things or groups unfairly. This is the negative narrative on unconscious bias that's been hijacked by higher education and adopted, without question, by the corporate world to blame something intangible for the actions of those who consciously discriminate.

The historic lack of diversity in our companies is a multi-dimensional problem with many contributing factors. Singling out unconscious bias has been a distraction that has slowed progress. It's not the smoking gun we have been led to believe it is. So how did we go from birthday cake to birdie cage? What follows is a summary of the scientific literature on the subject.

Early Influence – Thorndike and Polya

It wouldn't be fair to get into the research without mentioning some of the earlier work done on the broad topic of biases. Unconscious or implicit bias wasn't used at the time, but these early 20th-century scientists were most certainly talking about the same subject.

In 1920, Edward Thorndike, an American psychologist, was the first to use correlation analysis to show how people judge others based on seemingly unrelated criteria. He asked servicemen to rank their fellow officers based on several traits and attributes, including intelligence and physique. The soldiers who were identified as being taller and more attractive were also rated as being more intelligent and better soldiers. Thorndike called this the "halo effect" (Thorndike, 1920).

In 1945, a Hungarian mathematician, George Polya, was a professor of mathematics at Stanford University. That year he wrote a book called "How to Solve It," which went into great detail about heuristics and problem-solving. How do we know he was influential? Well, he taught Herbert Simon, who you will soon learn changed everything when it came to how we utilize heuristics in decision making in real life under certain conditions.

Heuristics Undefined - Herbert Simon

Herbert Simon is most famous for his theory about economic decision making which he first outlined in his 1947 book, "Administrative Behavior - A Study of Decision-Making Processes in Administrative Organizations" (Simon, 1947). In this book, he introduced the concepts of "bounded rationality" and "satisficing," which led him to win the Nobel Prize for Economics in 1978 for his work on decision making.

In his book, he proposed that, to date, traditional economic decision-making theory assumes we are entirely rational beings with unlimited information, unlimited time, and unlimited cognitive abilities at our disposal. This is the classical economic model of rational thinking. However, we are often deciding under conditions of uncertainty, and we are limited by the information we have available to us, time, and our ability to think and solve problems.

Simon summed up bounded rationality perfectly in his Nobel Memorial Lecture in 1979 when he said, "The classical model of rationality requires knowledge of all the relevant alternatives, their consequences and probabilities, and a predictable world without surprises. These conditions, however, are rarely met for the problems that individuals and organizations face." (Simon, 1979). In other words, our rationality is *bounded* by our cognitive limitations, the information that's available to us, and time constraints. Instead of making the 'best' choices, we often make choices that are satisfactory, which he called "satisficing," a combination of two words: satisfy and suffice.

"Because administrators satisfice rather than maximize, they can choose without first examining all possible behavior alternatives and without ascertaining that these are, in fact, all the alternatives. ....They can make decisions with relatively simple rules of thumb that do not make impossible demands upon their capacity for thought. Simplification may lead to error, but there is no realistic alternative in the face of the limits on human knowledge and reasoning" (Simon, 1947).

The" rules of thumb" he writes about are what we now call heuristics. The last sentence in the quote is significant: "Simplification may lead to error, but there is no realistic alternative in the face of the limits on human knowledge and reasoning." The errors he writes about here result from our implicit or unconscious biases. However, those unconscious biases also lead to the right choices when the choices turn out to be correct. He doesn't write that they "do" lead to errors but "may." This is, for me, where we find the first accurate representation of what biases are. They are not some automatic, unconscious prejudiced instinct that's hardwired into us all.

Having biases is hardwired into us, but the biases themselves are not. These biases are our backup decision-making influences we default to when we are forced to make decisions without knowing everything we need to know and are constrained by time and our cognitive limitations. These are the conditions that nearly all leaders work in most of the time.

Think about any other kind of bias. Let's take religious and political bias. If you grew up a Christian, for example, and as an adult, you decided that Judaism was a religion you wanted to pursue, in time, your religious biases would change. If you grew up in a family that supported the democrats, but then as an adult, you felt more compelled by the message of the republicans, your resulting biases would change.

Think about candidate selection for a moment. We can't just plug their entire history into our mental hard drive and make exact calculations regarding their suitability for a role. We will only ever have the hour or multiple hours we're interviewing them and whatever other information we can find to make a decision. That decision will always be made under uncertainty and subsequently be prone to our biases. However, even that is a very narrow and loaded view of the consequences of biases.

Let's take a hypothetical example of a global bank looking to hire a new Chief Financial Officer (CFO). Two people will interview the candidate. One is the CEO of the bank, and another is an intern in the first week of their internship. Neither of these interviewers has a detailed biography of the candidate's life. They only have one hour to make a choice. The CEO and the intern will rely on heuristics to make a decision.

Are we to believe that both interviewer's heuristics will lead to the same scale of errors, or is there any value in the experience of the CEO? Of course, it's unrealistic to propose that an intern will play a pivotal role in hiring a board-level executive.

Still, the point is that with experience comes knowledge and intuition. Intuition and biases cannot easily be untangled. They are both implicit actors, after all. With these, we move from a decision-making scenario of maximum uncertainty (the intern) to a decision being made with minimum uncertainty (the CEO). There is no maximum certainty scenario here as it's impossible to know everything there is to know, so it's a heuristic-based decision in conditions of uncertainty.

Over time and with experience, we can get much better at intuitively making decisions, which is the upside of heuristics. Also, when it comes to hiring for diversity, if we know we have to hire more diverse candidates, whatever that means, then it should no longer be subject to our unconscious biases, as, by definition, biases result from heuristics under conditions of uncertainty. If one of the conditions that are known in the interview process is that we have to hire more females, for example, then to overlook a female in favor of a male could no longer be blamed on unconscious bias; it would be explicit discrimination. The same can be said if a female was just hired because she is a female rather than a competent candidate. The prejudiced outcome is the same, but focusing on our unconscious biases does not tackle the problem.

Herbert Simon never used the term heuristic in this book in 1947, but he is clearly referring to heuristics when writing about rules of thumb and satisficing. He did start using the term later in his career. We know this because he was a student of George Polya, mentioned previously, at Stanford University. In Simon's memoir about his 1978 Nobel prize for Economics, he wrote, "Polya's widely read book, How to Solve It, published in 1945, had introduced many people (including me) to heuristic, the art of discovery."

Getting rid of our unconscious biases is impossible. It's also wrong to think that AI will help us eliminate our unconscious biases. In 1955, Herbert Simon and Allen Newell, his ex-student, and John Shaw, a programmer from RAND, built the world's first AI program (Simon and Newell, 1955). The Logic Theorist, as it was known, was the first machine in the field of heuristic programming and proved 38 of the first 52 theorems of the Principia Mathematica. It was presented at an event at Dartmouth College in 1956, where the term artificial intelligence was introduced to the world (coined one year earlier in a proposal submitted for a 2-month, 10-man study of artificial intelligence by John McCarthy (Dartmouth College) and his collaborators. Although computer science had been around for at least two decades at this point, this was the advent of AI.

In another event in 1957, Herbert Simon stated:

"In short, we now have the elements of a theory of heuristic (as contrasted with algorithmic) problem solving, and we can use this theory both to understand human heuristic processes and to simulate such processes with digital computers" (Simon, 1958).

The reason he was describing heuristic problem solving as a solution for AI is that computers, still to this day, don't have the computing power to calculate all possible outcomes for all problems. They have to use heuristics, which is what they do, and why Simon's research and findings on bounded rationality were so crucial to the development of AI. Simon distinguishes between "well-structured problems" as being those where algorithms suffice and "ill-structured problems," which are problems with no known algorithms.

Take chess, for example. In 1950 an American mathematician, Claude Shannon, calculated what came to be known as the "Shannon Number" (Shannon 1955). That number is 10, followed by 120 zeros. That's an estimate of the amount of potential chess moves a computer or human would have to calculate to capture all possible moves before making a decision. So, like humans, computers 'playing' chess work on decision trees of 10-20 moves ahead, thus reducing the computing power required. This is heuristics at play in computers.

Herbert Simon's work has been instrumental in understanding heuristics and biases. Yet, it has been, at best, selectively interpreted and, at worst, entirely ignored by the corporate agenda to blindly pin the unconscious bias tail on the diversity donkey. People seem to be completely ignoring the utility of heuristics and how they improve with experience. Also, how errors are reduced when information, like the need to hire more diverse candidates, is better known. We're being taught that our biases have corrupted our decision-making abilities and are always unfair. That's just not true. Furthermore, they're suggesting we should rely more on computers and AI, yet, thanks to Herbert Simon, computers also rely on heuristics to make decisions.

Heuristics and Biases - Kahneman and Tversky

In the journey towards our present-day definition of unconscious bias, we leapfrog from Herbert Simons' revelations to work done by two psychologists, Daniel Kahneman and Amos Tversky. In their 1974 paper, "Judgment under Uncertainty: Heuristics and Biases," we first saw the appearance of the term "cognitive bias."

"This article has been concerned with cognitive biases that stem from the reliance on judgmental heuristics." (Kahneman & Tversky, 1974).

Remember the Microsoft definition that confused heuristics with unconscious bias? They wrote a definition of unconscious bias and suggested they're unfair, and then went on to use a definition for heuristics to define unconscious bias. This paper by Kahneman and Tversky was the first time in history that heuristics and cognitive biases were mentioned together. Definitions are important.

In the paper, they wrote about how the average human does not always make rational choices, which is clearly an idea that's evolved from Herbert Simon's work. The paper opened with, "Many decisions are based on beliefs concerning the likelihood of uncertain events such as the outcome of an election, the guilt of a defendant, or the future value of the dollar" (Kahneman & Tversky, 1974). It then went on to describe three heuristics: representativeness, availability, and anchoring and adjustment. This was the first time certain heuristics were given a label.

Representative Heuristic

Kahneman & Tversky use an illustration where a description of a man is shared, and individuals are asked to assess the likelihood that this individual is in one of several different careers based purely on the description of the person. Those being assessed rank order the likelihood of this individual having different careers based on the degree to which that person is representative of, or similar to, the stereotype of that occupation (librarian, engineer, doctor, and so on). Clearly, this heuristic can lead to errors as not all information is known.

Availability Heuristic

The availability heuristic occurs because we can recall specific memories in our minds more easily than others. The example that Kahneman and Tversky gave is that participants asked if more words in the English language start with the letter r, or have the third letter, r. While most would respond with the former, the latter is actually true. It's just easier to recall words starting with r than words with r as the third letter.

Anchoring And Adjustment

"Different starting points yield different estimates, which are biased toward the initial values. We call this phenomenon anchoring" (Khaneman & Tversky, 1974). For example, let's say you're buying a new car. You see that the price at the dealer is $25,000. You didn't shop around. When you get there, you negotiate the salesperson down to $24,000. You think you got a bargain. You then drive by another showroom on your way home and see that this identical new car was on sale for $23,500. You formed your value judgment based on the initial price of $25,000, the anchor price.

The "summary" section of the paper reads, "These heuristics are highly economical and usually effective, but they lead to systematic and predictable errors. A better understanding of these heuristics and the biases to which they lead could improve judgments and decisions in situations of uncertainty" (Khaneman & Tversky, 1974). Remember what Herbert Simon wrote in his 1947 book, "Simplification may lead to error, but there is no realistic alternative in the face of the limits on human knowledge and reasoning" (Simon, 1947). They are all saying the same thing – heuristics are not only helpful but often necessary, and on occasion, they may lead to errors. Where the unconscious bias narrative has gone astray is in the isolation of the statement "lead to systemic and predictable errors" without any regard for "usually effective" or the fact that these are decisions made under conditions of uncertainty where not all information and options are known. This is extremely important in leadership decision-making, where so many decisions are made without all the required facts or sufficient time.

Hijacking Heuristics and Biases - Banaji and Greenwald

Now we're getting to the point where the birthday cake turned into the birdie cage. Psychologists Mahzarin Banaji and Anthony Greenwald introduced the concept of "implicit bias" in their paper, "Implicit social cognition: Attitudes, self-esteem, and stereotypes" (Banaji & Greenwald, 1995). This research led to the explosion of unconscious bias over the past two decades.

Their paper started by claiming it had come up with a new construct, "implicit social cognition," and then went on to define it as meaning that "traces of past experience affect some performance, even though the influential earlier experience is not remembered in the usual sense—that is, it is unavailable to self-report or introspection." That's not exactly news to anyone; our past experience affects how we think, even in unconscious ways. Remarkable.

What is interesting about that statement is that if our past experience affects our perceptions, then it follows that our existing experiences can also change our future views, so it follows that we can change our perceptions. Many of us knew this already, but if you read the headlines and articles on HBR and LinkedIn, you'd be forgiven for thinking we are all doomed and can't be trusted to make informed choices because our unconscious biases have forever corrupted our moral compass. That doesn't bode well for those who believe our beliefs are ingrained in our unconscious biases, and our only hope is to try and cover them up.

The paper concluded: "Much social cognition occurs in an implicit mode. This conclusion comes from a reinterpretation of many findings that indicate the importance of implicit operation of attitudes, and of the self-esteem attitude in particular, and also from existing and new evidence for the implicit operation of stereotypes. By adding this conception of the implicit mode to existing knowledge of the explicit mode of operation of social psychology's basic constructs, the scope of those constructs is extended substantially" (Banaji & Greenwald, 1995).

No, it's really not extended substantially. The paper was just a regurgitation of previous research by others into stereotypes, attitudes, and self-esteem. It even says in the paper:

"Of any newly offered theoretical construct, it should be asked: How does the new construct differ from existing ones (or is it only a new label for an existing construct)? The preceding paragraphs show that implicit social cognition, although strongly rooted in existing constructs, offers a theoretical reorganization of phenomena that have previously been described in other ways and, in some cases, not previously identified as having an unconscious component."

So attitudes, stereotypes, and self-esteem have never been identified as having an unconscious component? If nobody has ever identified attitudes, stereotypes, and self-esteem as having an unconscious component, it's probably because it's self-evident from their definition that they reside in our silent unconsciousness before manifesting in explicit behavior. Just in this one paragraph, they've suggested that it's new because they've reorganized and renamed existing constructs; the same paragraph where they wrote that one could not do that according to the rules.

This paper was published in 1995, and in 1994 the authors were playing around with the Implicit Association Test (IAT), which was made public in 1998. Perhaps they came up with the IAT, retroactively tried to come up with an interesting paper that could be passed off as both new and evidence for the necessity of the IAT, and then launched the IAT to prove the effects of "implicit social cognition empirically." Come on now.

The IAT is the test that, still to this day, purports to measure our unconscious bias as it relates to race, sex, age, and other prejudices. This isn't one of the many tests; it's the foundation upon which all contemporary unconscious bias commentary is built. Anyone can take the test. It was such a compelling breakthrough that even the famous author Malcolm Gladwell wrote, "The IAT is more than just an abstract measure of attitudes. It's a powerful predictor of how we act in certain kinds of spontaneous situations." (Gladwell, 2005). Sounds amazing, right? Not so fast.

When you take the test, it takes you through a series of questions that you could quite easily lie about if you felt so inclined. For example, it gives you various statements when defining how warm you feel towards European Americans and African Americans, with a choice to be neutral. You are then asked to use two keys on your keyboard (E and I), using the left key when you see a bad word pop up on your screen and the right key when you see a good word. You're then asked to select the left key when a good word or an image of a Black person appears and the right key for when a bad word or an image of a White person appears. Then they switch it, so the bad word is associated with a Black person and the good word with a White person. The whole measurement of this part of the test is the millisecond difference in response time when bad or good words are associated with Black or White people. If you're clicking Black people quicker when they're associated with the bad word, their theory is that you have a *"slight, moderate, or strong"* preference for White faces over Black faces. So, in other words, this test claims that depending on how quickly you react, you are either racist or not. Even if you believe you're not racist and your actions have never implied that you're racist, this test can "find the truth." You are then a candidate for unconscious bias training, where well-paid consultants will come to your office and train it out of you, or so the theory goes.

In an interview with National Public Radio (NPR) in 2016, Mahzarin Banaji said, "In the late 1990s, I did a very simple experiment with Tony Greenwald in which I was to quickly associate dark-skinned faces - faces of black Americans - with negative words. I had to use a computer key whenever I saw a black face or a negative word, like devil or bomb, war, things like that. And likewise, there was another key on the keyboard that I had to strike whenever I saw a white face or a good word, a word like love, peace, joy. I was able to do this very easily. But when the test then switched the pairing, and I had to use the same computer key to identify a black face with good things and white faces and bad things, my fingers appeared to be frozen on the keyboard. I literally could not find the right - the right key. That experience is a humbling one. It is even a humiliating one because you come face to face with the fact that you are not the person you thought you were" (NPR, 2016).

I've done the test on more than one occasion, and it isn't difficult to find the keys. There are only two of them (E and I). Perhaps Professor Banaji needs some unconscious bias training?

It's interesting to note there's now a rather confusing disclaimer at the end of the test, just after you complete it:

"These IAT results are provided for educational purposes only. The results may fluctuate and should not be used to make important decisions. The results are influenced by variables related to the test (e.g., the words or images used to represent categories) and the person (e.g., being tired, what you were thinking about before the IAT)" (Project Implicit, 2022).

So even they say the test should not be used to make important decisions and that the results may fluctuate. Despite this, the test is still up there, and Mazarin Banaji is certainly still promoting it. In her book, Blindspot, published in 2013, Banaji writes:

"Studies that summarize data across many people find that the IAT predicts discrimination in hiring, education, healthcare, and law enforcement. However, taking an IAT once (like you just did) is not likely to predict your future behavior well" (Banaji, 2013).

So, in other words, it's not reliable or valid if you take the test, but if many people take it, the results are reliable. Sorry, that's not how it works. That reminds me of the story of the Emperor's New Clothes by Hans Christian Andersen, except a ridiculous version. "Emperor, I know you think you're naked in this gold suit we stitched by hand for you [that doesn't actually exist], but if you buy many of them, you will no longer believe you're naked, and their splendor will be revealed."

What's happened since the IAT would be the equivalent of a scientist doing a made-up scientific paper on anger and then coming out with the Implicit Anger Test that is engineered to 'prove' everyone is angry based on the time it takes people to respond to phrases like "I would hit him" or "I would smile at him." Then everyone in the company is forced to go on anger management classes because they discovered that most of us are angry. If that sounds funny, that's exactly what's happened with unconscious bias and the IAT.

If only the IAT held the key to why discrimination still exists today. If only all we had to do was go to training and have our unconscious biases educated away from our unconsciousness. The theory of the IAT and its underlying suggestions looked very robust until it came time to go under the scrutiny of the psychometric standards of testing for reliability and validity, something which should have happened before it was even released. That didn't happen.

In 2015 Banaji and Greenwald wrote a paper with a title that could have easily read, "No, we know it's nonsense, but even a tiny correlation could mean something, right? Trust us; we're psychologists." The actual title was "Statistically small effects of the Implicit Association Test can have societally large effects." (Greenwald et al., 2015).

This paper then went on to respond to many meta-analyses (studies of studies) that have since been carried out regarding the IAT. In their conclusion of the paper, it reads:

"First, both studies agreed that when considering only findings for which there is theoretical reason to expect positive correlations, the predictive validity of Black-White race IAT is approximately r .20. Second, even using the two meta-analyses' published aggregate estimated effect sizes, the two agreed in expecting that more than 4% of variance in discrimination-relevant criterion measures is predicted by Black–White race IAT measures. This level of correlational predictive validity of IAT measures represents potential for discriminatory impacts with very substantial societal significance."

This work by Banaji and Greenwald perfectly illustrates how Thorndike's halo effect is alive and well. People believed that because these are 'scientific papers' written by 'credible' scientists, the IAT was the foundation upon which we would build more diverse and inclusive organizations. The truth is that it had no place being published in the first place as it did not meet the criteria of reliability and validity outlined in the guidelines provided by the American Psychological Association (APA, 2022). Yet because it was published and made headlines as being 'scientific' research, it spawned a billion-dollar training industry, and the rest is history.

Restoring Faith in Heuristics - Gerd Gigirenzer

Around about the same time that Banaji and Greenwald were working on their theory, a psychologist by the name of Gerd Gigerenzer, along with his colleague, Daniel Goldstein, were working on further developing the ideas first introduced by Herbert Simon on bounded rationality and satisficing (Gigerenzer and Goldstein, 1996). Their view contrasted with the doom and gloom presented by the likes of Banaji and Greenwald and, to a lesser extent, Kahneman and Tversky.

They came up with the concept of fast and frugal heuristics, particularly the "recognition heuristic" and "take the best heuristic." Their studies concluded that often "less is more" when it comes to making decisions. They showed how individuals with experience in a given field are better equipped to rank-order any cues offered to help them decide and choose accordingly.

Their research helped illustrate the work done some fifty years earlier by Herbert Simon, showing how and when heuristics can be more effective and how experience is an essential factor in minimizing the errors caused when making decisions in conditions of uncertainty.

Summing Up Unconscious Bias

Unconscious bias is the same thing as implicit bias, which stemmed from the work done on cognitive biases, which is grounded on the work done on heuristics. Heuristics are the shortcuts our brains use to make decisions when not all information is known, and we are limited in time and our cognitive abilities.

Heuristics are a necessary cognitive tool, so much so that we also teach computers to use heuristics in AI to lighten the required computational load for complex problems. When deciding under conditions of uncertainty and therefore resorting to heuristics, these heuristics can be at the mercy of our unconscious or implicit biases. We have long been taught that our biases are hardwired into our brains. However, the process of forming biases is hardwired into our brains, but the biases themselves can change.

Informed heuristics are significantly more useful than uninformed heuristics, and this isn't captured in the corporate world's interpretation of unconscious biases. The way to make diversity hiring more effective is not to remove all of our biases. We have to reduce uncertainty and create more "knowns." In other words, with a mandate to hire more 'diverse candidates' and a reliable periodic audit of such a process, we are no longer making judgments under the same degree of uncertainty. As a result, we are not at the mercy of heuristics and, therefore, not held hostage by our biases.

If the facts are known, and the facts, in this case, are that we need to hire more diverse candidates, then heuristics should not play a part. If heuristics don't play a role, then there are no unconscious errors in judgment (unconscious bias); there are only conscious 'errors in judgment. That's still the same problem, with the same results, but one we can aim to tackle differently than just covering up for these people while condemning the rest of the company with inappropriate labels of bigotry.

Anonymity Only Protects the Perpetrators

Yet because of these unconscious biases, we seem to be adopting recruiting processes that do the exact opposite of what they're meant to be doing. There's even technology now that omits information from resumes that may give an idea of age, race, sex, and other potentially discriminatory references. They believe that this will reduce unconscious bias. There are two major problems with this. Firstly, all candidates go on to get interviewed, which just shoves the problem along to the interview process. During the interview, it's not like unconsciously prejudiced inclinations turn off. Interviewers don't sit in an interview when a "diversity candidate" walks in and say, "Oh! We weren't expecting you. Well, thank goodness our resume selection was blind; otherwise, you may not have come this far. Now you're here, our unconscious prejudiced biases have miraculously disappeared. So tell us a bit about yourself?"

Secondly, having a blind resume screening process based entirely on merit is the right thing to do, but it's not the right thing to do for diversity. Diversity requires human intervention to ensure diverse candidates are included in a shortlist. Removing references to diversity indicators, like taking out names at the beginning of a hiring process, leads only to a meritocratic selection process, which is great for the best candidate but is not always a pro-diversity solution. For example, let's say you have 100 candidates, 50% are women, and 50% of those women are racially diverse. The rest are White males. If there are no diversity indicators, none of that information is known. Let's say that in doing a blind review of the resumes, you happen to end up with an imbalance of white males, then you're in a position where diverse candidates have been removed from the process before you even begin. Of course, in the same example, you may end up with an imbalance of diverse candidates, but you can't just leave it to the blind chance that this will occur, especially not when they are statistically underrepresented from the offset. I believe the chances of diverse candidates being accidentally omitted from a blind screening process are statistically higher than the chances of a diverse candidate being discriminated against in a known resume screening process.

You have to give the underrepresented groups a fighting chance by making sure they are represented, which means identifying who they are in the first place.

In 2022, with diversity hiring being so high on all corporate companies' agendas, with all of the measures in place to rebalance the inequalities that have existed for a long time, we really must consider much better ways of addressing these inequalities. Companies removing names from resumes implies that without such measures, their recruiters and hiring managers will be out of control with their prejudiced biases making choices on their behalf.

Consciously Overcoming Unconscious Bias

One thing that has to be considered in addressing these issues, especially in large companies, is the candidate selection process. Internal recruiters are usually the first people to screen candidates. Not always, but for any significantly sized company, it typically will be. Internal recruiters have an unbelievably time-intensive job where they are almost always stretched beyond capacity. When they receive 200-300 applicants per role, and they may be working on 20-50 roles at any given time, they're not always getting through all the applicants. Often they'll skim through the first 20-50 candidates, select three or four, send them on to the hiring manager, and then onto the next role. If they're only seeing 10% of the applicants, it's not obvious that the list will be proportionately representative of the whole group of candidates. What is certain is that not enough diverse candidates will be in that 10% as they're already statistically underrepresented. So the representation needs to change by forcing more diverse candidates into that initial group that will be seen, and the only way to do that is by knowing who the diverse candidates are in the first place. If discrimination is to be dealt with at the resume stage, redacting any race or gender indicators is not the way to do it. That's a proverbial band-aid on the knee for a punctured lung.

So what is the solution? Can we control our unconscious bias, or is it a more achievable goal to manage our conscious thoughts to better control a process?

I believe we have to focus on our System 2 thinking, which you may recall is characterized by Kahneman as "the conscious, reasoning self that has beliefs, makes choices, and decides what to think about and do" (Kahneman, 2011). In doing so, if we are to use technology to reduce resume bias, instead of making it a blind resume process that only results in any prejudices emerging in the interview process, let's use technology in a different way. In the example of the 200-300 applicants, candidates with diversity indicators should be highlighted and prioritized in the list, and recruiters must consider them based on merit and skill set. They must also be rejected based on merit and skill set.

There could be an audit owned by the diversity and inclusion (D&I) team that audits this process in the same way financial processes are audited. How do we de-risk the chances of a finance director stealing money? Do we start by assuming they're going to cook the books and therefore anonymize certain parts of the financial ledger to prevent them from committing fraud? Of course, we don't. What we actually do is get them to pass exams to qualify that they know what they're doing, then their books are audited on an annual basis. They're not offended by the audit. It's part of the job. Will there be finance directors that still steal money? Of course, there will be. There will always be criminals in all walks of life, but the overwhelming majority of finance directors want to do a good job and act as good corporate citizens and probably enjoy the satisfaction of seeing a clean audit on their work.

With this potential solution, the D&I team would access the candidate applicant tracking system (ATS), and recruiters could have a bi-yearly or yearly audit where some roles are selected, and the recruiters are asked to talk through their decisions. This would hold recruiters accountable, and for the overwhelming majority that do the right thing, this would be a welcome process to demonstrate their commitment to D&I through their actions. For any that fall short of expectations and are clearly making prejudiced decisions, there should be a zero-tolerance approach. Blind resume processes are literally turning a blind eye to the problem.

Diversity training should be about why it is important to the company and all its employees and how the company will take proactive steps to become more diverse. Unconscious bias training starts with implied accusations about how our unconscious thoughts manifest into explicit action. These are two different ways to deliver a similar message. Any unconscious bias training that starts with an IAT test says something completely different. A much better approach is to start with what we know scientifically about dual system thinking. Recognizing that diversity training can educate people's conscious thought processes to make sure we are well enough educated about the issues in order to be proactive in making the right choices and, when required, have our selection processes audited for fairness and consistency.

LEARNING WITHOUT LEARNING

Aside from our unconscious biases allegedly corrupting our everyday lives, there is another set of highly sophisticated, unconscious cognitive structures that allow experts to build intuition in another way: through experience and learning (Agor, 1989), relying on pattern recognition processes. Furthermore, back to Kahneman's Thinking Fast and Slow (2011), the unconscious mind doesn't just run riot in the conscious world. Explicit learning, or conscious learning, is what we all understand when we speak about learning. For example, Khatri and Ng argue that, for managerial intuition to be effective, it "requires years of experience in problem-solving and is founded upon a solid and complete grasp of the details of the business" (Khatri & Ng, 2000). This goes without saying. However, we are also developing our intuition through a process of implicit learning or learning without knowing that we are learning. In fact, researchers have found that knowledge acquired via implicit learning will be retained when an individual suffers from amnesia, even when more explicit knowledge is lost (Seger, 1994). This suggests that although explicit and implicit learning can occur simultaneously in a given context, implicit learning involves a different process of knowledge acquisition and storage. Reber (1989) has tied implicit learning to "intuitive knowledge" and argues that it is through implicit learning that individuals come to form the complex cognitive structures necessary for intuitive judgments and decisions.

For example, there is a game in Japan called Shogi, which, for simplicity, we can think of as a game like chess, but much harder with many more possible moves. A group of neuroscientists studied the brains of professional players using MRI scans and compared these to scans of amateur players (Xiaohong Wan et al., 2012). They identified an area of the brain called the caudate nucleus, part of the basal ganglia—a set of interlinked brain areas responsible for learning, executing habits, and automatic behaviors. "The basal ganglia receives massive input from the cortex, the outer surface of the brain. Ultimately these structures project back to the cortex, creating a series of cortical–basal ganglia loops. In one interpretation, the cortex is associated with conscious perception and the deliberate and conscious analysis of any given situation, novel or familiar, whereas the caudate nucleus is the site where highly specialized expertise resides that allows you to come up with an appropriate answer without conscious thought" (Koch, 2015). They found this area only "lit up" in professional player's brains. They concluded that this is the area of the brain linked to intuition as the professional players were mapping out their next moves based on previous experience, or in other words, using their intuition. To further validate the point about the proposed neuroanatomy of intuition, in a much-cited paper written by Lieberman (2000), he commented:

"This review proposes that implicit learning processes are the cognitive substrate of social intuition. This hypothesis is supported by (a) the conceptual correspondence between implicit learning and social intuition (nonverbal communication) and (b) a review of relevant neuropsychological (Huntington's and Parkinson's disease), neuroimaging, neurophysiological, and neuroanatomical data. It is concluded that the caudate and putamen in the basal ganglia are central components of both intuition and implicit learning, supporting the proposed relationship.

Implicit learning suggests a mechanism whereby sequential associations can be learned without the learner ever being aware of the learning process or its ultimate product. There are other cases when the representations formed by the basal ganglia result from intentional efforts to learn some set of associations. Over many repetitions, explicit knowledge is thought to recede from conscious access while the associations become compiled into more efficient representations in the basal ganglia" (Liberman, 2000).

We can see from the above that attempts have been made to understand intuition from a neuroanatomical perspective. These unbelievably clever people seem to suggest that there is an area of the brain that stores these "folders" of implicitly learned patterns and structures, which are then unconsciously recalled and projected onto new situations that lead us to make intuitive decisions. They're also suggesting that at some point in time, explicitly learned processes, once repeated, are stored in these same folders and form part of our learned process of intuiting.

INTUITION IN CANDIDATE SELECTION

I wrote before about holistic associations. Another way to think about these as they relate to intuitive thinking is by taking our stored mental maps of what we know and subconsciously projecting new situations onto these known maps. When we recognize most of the map, but not necessarily all of it, we make an intuitive decision based on what we at least already know. A good analogy is working with a jigsaw puzzle but without a reference picture. Let's say you have a 1000-piece jigsaw puzzle of a horse in a stable. When you're about 800 pieces in, you recognize what the end result is going to be based on the pieces you have already laid. For someone who is very intuitive or has done many horse picture jigsaws before, they may recognize what the final image will look like after laying down only 200 pieces. Either way, at whatever point the final picture is formed in one's mind, it will be formed long before the final piece has been placed. This is akin to the holistic associations when we subconsciously recognize certain patterns emerging.

Experts, or in this case, leaders, get better and better at this with the more experience they get, or at least they should do. This was essentially the theory proposed in Klein's (1998) recognition primed decision model, which sought to explain how people can make useful predictions. Furthermore, in an article written in Farnam Street, an online publication, Nobel Laureate Herbert Simon was quoted as saying:

"We have seen that a major component of expertise is the ability to recognize a very large number of specific relevant cues when they are present in any situation, and then to retrieve from memory information about what to do when those particular cues are noticed.

Because of this knowledge and recognition capability, experts can respond to new situations very rapidly– and usually with considerable accuracy. Of course, on further thought, the initial reaction may not be correct, but it is correct in a substantial number of cases and is rarely irrelevant. Chess grandmasters, looking at the chessboard, will generally form a hypothesis about the best move within five seconds. This initial hypothesis will be the move they ultimately prefer in four out of five cases. Moreover, it can be shown that this ability accounts for a very large proportion of their chess skill. For, if required to play very rapidly, the grandmaster may not maintain a grandmaster level of play but will almost always maintain a master level, even though in rapid play, there is time for almost nothing but to react to the first cues that are noticed on the board."

CONCLUSION

Let's first go back to the comment I made about an answer I would have liked to have given to an interview question I was once asked. I was asked when I knew a candidate was a good candidate, and I wanted to respond, "I just know." Now we know a little about intuition and know that it goes beyond heuristics, which can be misleading, and actually involves building experience and implicit learning; I believe we can be more confident in our decisions as leaders, or in this case, in selecting candidates.

To Ralph Larsen's point (former CEO of Johnson & Johnson), "But then they reach senior management, where the problems get more complex and ambiguous, and we discover that their judgment or intuition is not what it should be" (Hayashi, 2001); dealing with ambiguity and complexity are two of the defining factors of senior leadership success. Managers are typically told what to do and how to do it. They have mentors and leaders above them to help. When you are truly the leader in a company, you have your team to share facts and opinions, but you are ultimately dealing with a lot of unknowns, and much like with the speed chess players, you will often have to make decisions under a lot of pressure and time constraints. Therefore your intuitive decisions are called upon more than ever.

To Daniel Kahneman's point, "You're better off if you collect information first and collect all the information in a systematic way and only then allow yourself to take a global view and to have an intuition about the global view" (Our Crowd, 2019); in selecting candidates, the time to make a decision is not when they walk in the door, because "you just know." Rather, it is when you have finished interviewing the relevant candidates and then making a call on it. By then, you may be heavily reliant on your intuition, as all you've really been able to do during the interview process is gather some information. It is, therefore, crucial that you gather the right information in a systematic way and do so consistently across all candidates.

I truly believe that intuition is a lot like creativity. We cannot scientifically account for why some people are incredible at drawing, singing, or writing music, other than to say they are high in the Big Five trait, openness. That doesn't explain their talent. We can see their talent in their work, but we can't explain it. Also, such individuals do not produce the greatest work of all time, every time. They make mistakes, or they may occasionally produce work that is below par for them. I think intuition is the same in leaders and, in this case, in identifying and hiring leaders. People like Jeff Bezos, in my opinion, just have incredible intuition that is rare in itself. He probably can't even explain why his intuition is so good, but we can all see it in his decisions and his success. Of course, many other factors are at play, but intuition isn't something to just be ignored.

In selecting candidates for leadership roles, how do we recognize someone with the strength of intuition required to deal with such ambiguity and unfamiliar problem resolution? Well, we can look at the patterns of progress and success that any given candidate has demonstrated. How have they dealt with novel situations? How do they make decisions about ambiguous situations? What were the outcomes of these decisions that were made? How did they learn from some of the bad choices they made, and how did they grow as a result? We can't even ask them outright about intuition because it's so misunderstood that they may, at that moment, second guess that we are looking for someone who only makes data-driven decisions. Therefore, it is even more important to just get deep into their chronological story in a way that allows you to observe patterns of how they dealt with novel situations in the past.

Only by following such a detailed process of fact-finding will you be in a position to rely on your intuition to make an informed candidate choice. You can do so by following what appears to be the scientific explanation for how intuition works in the brain. Take the maps of knowledge you have, which is your experience of hiring, when it has worked well in the past, the types of people who typically do well in your company, and finally, your knowledge of the people in your company this person will have to get on with to succeed. You then take the little information you have now gathered about each candidate. This knowledge is then overlaid onto your maps of previously acquired knowledge and experience and projected forward into the unknown. These are your "holistic associations." Which of these candidates feels like they will perform best against the projected unknown future state? There is your answer.

Intuition is not just thinking you know based on your inherent misinformed biases. If cultivated and understood correctly, you can harness your intuition in a healthy way. It requires building experience over a number of years, making mistakes and correcting them, and always working with as much information as you can gather before reaching any conclusions that feel right.

As far as biases and candidate selection are concerned, if we solve the problem that exists when screening candidate resumes, then we have only solved the first problem. The main problem comes in the interview process, where any underlying prejudices will most certainly surface. In Chapter 9, we will look at the process to manage this effectively, but in summary, it comes down to having a consistent process that gets deep into candidate stories, where people are evaluating the same answers and using a universally understood method of evaluation. This can't eradicate biases altogether, but that should never have been the goal in the first place.

THEORY AND CANDIDATE SELECTION

Ask anyone around you, "What is the most effective method for selecting the best candidates?" and you will receive a multitude of answers. Ask enough people, and you will start to see the same answers coming up again and again. Does anyone actually know for sure what the best way to recruit is? Well, it depends on what you're recruiting for and at what level, but there have been some scientific studies conducted to try and answer this question.

In 1998 a really interesting paper was published by F. Schmidt and J. Hunter, which was a meta-study named "The validity and utility of selection methods in personnel psychology: Practical and theoretical implications of 85 years of research findings" (F.Schmidt, J.Hunter. 1998). Of course, a lot has happened since 1998 when it comes to identifying and selecting candidates. Back then, there was no LinkedIn, and online video hiring and AI were still a long way off. However, relatively speaking, little has changed regarding the methods used to evaluate a person's candidacy for a role. The basic premise of this research paper is that because of its special status, GMA can be considered the primary personnel measure for hiring decisions, and one can consider the remaining 18 personnel measures as supplements to GMA. That is, in the case of each of the other measures, one can ask the following question: When used in a properly weighted combination with GMA, how much will each of these measures increase predictive validity for job performance over the .51 that can be obtained by using only GMA?

PERSONNEL MEASURE	VALIDITY (r)	MULTIPLE R	GAIN IN VALIDITY FROM ADDING SUPPLEMENT	% INCREASE IN VALIDITY	STANDARDIZED REGRESSION WEIGHTS	
					GMA	SUPPLEMENT
GMA tests	0.51					
Work sample tests	0.54	0.63	0.12	24%	0.36	0.41
Integrity tests	0.41	0.65	0.14	27%	0.51	0.41
Conscienciousness tests	0.31	0.6	0.09	18%	0.51	0.31
Employment interviews (structured)	0.51	0.63	0.12	24%	0.39	0.39
Employment interviews (unstructured)	0.38	0.55	0.04	8%	0.43	0.22
Job knowledge tests	0.48	0.58	0.07	14%	0.36	0.31
Job tryout procedure	0.44	0.58	0.07	14%	0.4	0.2
Peer ratings	0.49	0.58	0.07	14%	0.35	0.31
T & E behavioral consistency method	0.45	0.58	0.07	14%	0.39	0.31
Reference checks	0.26	0.57	0.06	12%	0.51	0.26
Job experience (years)	0.18	0.54	0.03	6%	0.51	0.18
Biographical data measures	0.35	0.52	0.01	2%	0.45	0.13
Assesment centers	0.37	0.53	0.02	4%	0.43	0.15
T& E point method	0.11	0.52	0.01	2%	0.39	0.29
Years of education	0.1	0.52	0.01	2%	0.51	0.1
Interests	0.1	0.52	0.01	2%	0.51	0.1
Graphology	0.02	0.51	0	0%	0.51	0.02
Age	-0.01	0.51	0	0%	0.51	-0.01

Table 5: Predictive Validity for Overall Job Performance of GMA Scores (F. Schmidt, J. Hunter. 1998)

Table 5, taken from the report, shows nineteen different ways companies have been known to assess candidates. The recruitment decision-making methodologies were ranked in order starting from highest to lowest. They are ranked with a validity score (r), roughly translated as "relative effectiveness in comparison to the others." Then, they were scored (Multiple R) for combining the results of GMA tests with the relevant other predictive measures. So, for example, when a structured interview is combined with a GMA test, the validity score goes from 0.51 to 0.63. If it's easier to think of it as a percentage of reliability, you can consider it going from 26% to 40%. What this chart tells us is that GMA tests and structured interviews are the best predictors of success as a collective consideration. What the chart doesn't tell us is that these numbers are averaged over different levels of jobs, so parts of it are not entirely relevant for senior-level hiring. For example, you're not going to give a senior leader an IQ or GMA test if it is evident from their twenty-plus years of experience in progressively more senior roles that they will have a sufficiently high enough level of cognitive ability. They couldn't have gotten to where they are without it.

As part of the meta-analysis, one of the studies conducted for the US Department of Labor with a data set of 32,000 people (Hunter, 1980) showed that the GMA for senior roles was 0.58 instead of 0.51. Again, this shouldn't be a surprise to learn that the more senior up an organization someone goes, the more likely it is that higher GMA scores will be observed. For example, it is fair to assume that if someone worked hard to get a master's from any credible university and then joined a graduate training scheme of a Fortune 500 company, that by the time they were being considered for any kind of promotion or job elsewhere, there was an assumed level of GMA. Therefore you wouldn't have to test this individual's GMA when considering them for a senior-level role. The GMA test may be better used in hiring entry-level people who had not, for whatever reason, attended university.

Conscientiousness, unsurprisingly, has a very positive correlation with strong work performance. Its strong presence in Table 5 reinforces the theory that those who are more conscientious, with high GMA, are likely to perform better. This may be because they spend more time on tasks, have a strong propensity to complete tasks, and perform their role to a very high level of satisfaction. Therefore, in discounting the methods that may be more suited to less senior hiring, these results are consistent with what we already know: The most reliable selection process is one that recognizes high GMA as a fundamental predictor of potential workplace success. This is followed by the use of structured interviews, with focused attention given to levels of conscientiousness.

I haven't included work sample tests or integrity tests in this summary. Work sample tests, for me, aren't part of the discussion here. They would be used to test someone's typing speed or how many denim pockets they can sew on in ten minutes, or other non-leadership-type tasks. Regarding the integrity tests, as they do feature quite high on the list, it is worth at least mentioning that they typically fall under overt or covert integrity. Sackett, Burris, and Callahan (1988) defined two types of integrity tests: "Overt integrity tests" and "Personality-based measures." Overt integrity inquiries about a candidate's attitude towards things like theft and absenteeism. On the other hand, covert integrity is measured with personality style tests and largely measures conscientiousness.

Arguably, someone in a senior-level position should still undergo overt integrity tests, especially in light of some of the scandals that have happened in the corporate world over the past decades, like Enron and the Madoff Ponzi scandal. However, people interviewing for leadership roles are typically granted the courtesy of assuming, given their tenure in other organizations, that they have a relatively sound level of overt integrity to prevent them from stealing much more than a company pen. Besides, these overt integrity tests are open to the same abuse as self-assessment questionnaires favored in personality tests. In other words, if you're going to ask someone, on a scale of 1 to 5, how they would rank their integrity, nobody is going to score themselves a 1 with a footnote saying, "I'm a compulsive liar who steals. Don't hire me."

Of the other methodologies listed, some are appallingly weak predictors of success and offer virtually no upside when used in conjunction with other methods. Again, these are generalized from several different studies across different job seniority, so with consideration of potential exceptions, it's fair to say that things like age and graphology (the study of handwriting, still used in some countries) have very little to no validity when it comes to predicting job performance. That being said, the separate issue I have identified in the hiring process is not which methods to choose but the methods' structure. For this reason, we will look at interviewing methods, questions, and what needs to change in the following chapters.

HR PRACTITIONERS

A study by Rynes et al. (2002) sought to find out how closely aligned the beliefs of HR practitioners are with some of the better-known research into different areas relating to HR. In this study, 959 respondents with an average tenure in HR of 14 years answered various questions relating to different aspects of the HR discipline. Unsurprisingly, in the area broadly referred to as "staffing," less than half of the respondents got the answers right on average. I'm not surprised because I've felt for a long time that people in companies have just been doing what they've always done, asking questions in interviews that lack structure and comparability, which are often not fit for purpose.

The most valid employment interviews are designed around each candidate's unique background.	FALSE 70% (6%)	Meta-analytic evidence that structured interviews (where all candidates receive the same questions) have higher validities than unstructured ones (Schmidt & Hunter, 1998; Wiesner & Cronshaw, 1988).
Although people use many different terms to describe personalities, there are really only four basic dimensions of personality, as captured by the Myers-Briggs Type Indicator (MBTI).	FALSE 49% (23%)	There are five basic dimensions of personality— the "Big Five" of Conscientiousness, Extraversion, Openness to Experience, Agreeableness, and Emotional Stability/Neuroticism (Digman, 1990). Except for Extraversion, these are not the traits assessed by MBTI.
On average, applicants who answer job advertisements are likely to have higher turnover than those referred by other employees.	TRUE 39% (13%)	Meta-analytic (e.g., Conard & Ashworth, 1986) and primary study evidence (e.g., Decker & Cornelius, 1979; see Rynes, 1991, for a review).
Being very intelligent is actually a disadvantage for performing well on a low-skilled job.	FALSE 42% (12%)	The validity coefficient for intelligence is always positive. Hunter (1986) and Schmidt & Hunter (1998) estimate the corrected validity coefficient for unskilled jobs to be .23. (Comparable figures are .40 for semi-skilled, and .58 for professional-managerial jobs.)
There is very little difference among personality inventories in terms of how well they predict an applicant's likely job performance.	FALSE 42% (30%)	The validity of personality measures as predictors of performance will depend to a large extent on the degree to which they tap important "Big Five" personality dimensions, particularly Conscientiousness. So, for example, Big Five personality measures are relatively good predictors of performance, while the MBTI doesn't even claim to predict performance (Gardner & Martinko, 1996).
Although there are "integrity tests" that try to predict whether someone will steal, be absent, or otherwise take advantage of an employer, they don't work well in practice because so many people lie on them.	FALSE 32% (34%)	Even if applicants or employees do distort their answers, validity of these instruments is still substantial. A large meta-analysis suggested that the overall corrected validity coefficient for integrity tests (across all types of performance measures) is .41. Counterproductive behaviors such as theft or absenteeism are somewhat better predicted (.47) than overall job performance (.34).
One problem with using integrity tests is that they have high degrees of adverse impact on racial minorities.	FALSE 31% 50%	A recent study based on four large-sample databases showed "trivial" differences (less than .15 standard deviations in all cases) across Caucasians, Asians, Native Americans, and African Americans (Ones & Viswesvaran, 1998).

Table 6: HR Survey Results By Rynes et al., (2002)

In Table 6, you can see what some of the questions were, along with the correct answer and then the percentage of respondents that got the answer right, along with the percentage of those who were "uncertain," in brackets. This doesn't represent every person in HR, and there will be many exceptions.

However, this was not a study to ascertain how good HR people are at their job but rather to find out how well-aligned practitioners are with the literature. The conclusion is that interviewing and candidate selection are so fragmented and broken that the very people in a company identified as the experts also can't reach a consensus on some of the basics.

THE INTERVIEW

We have already studied a lot of the theories when it comes to intelligence, personality, emotional intelligence, and so on. However, the theory on interview structures must at least be understood if we are to reach any kind of objective, informed conclusions about how best to interview people. The academic literature on interviewing is quite scarce. Unsurprisingly, there isn't any particular theory that demonstrates the best approach to interviewing with the key questions that will always give us a consistent outcome. I went into this research with low expectations of what I would find and was predictably disappointed. However, some interesting research validates a lot of what we already know. This leaves sufficient enough gaps in the knowledge for us to explore new structured ways of working to improve the outcomes of a scientifically unsound process – the candidate interview.

INTERVIEW STRUCTURE

There is overwhelming consensus from the literature that structured interviews are superior to unstructured interviews. Huffcutt and Arthur (1994) defined structure as "The degree of discretion that an interviewer is allowed in conducting the interview." Structured interviews follow a set framework with pre-determined questions that are asked consistently across all candidates, with standardized ways of scoring the results. On the other hand, unstructured interviews follow more of a conversational style with no set structure, questions, or consistent measures. A study by Wiesner and Cronshaw (1998) found that structured interviews were far more valid than unstructured interviews, with a validity score of .63 compared to .20.

Similarly, a study by Mc Daniel et al. (1994) found that structured interviews, regardless of content, are more valid (.44) than unstructured interviews (.33) for predicting job performance criteria.

Structured interviews have stronger psychometric properties because structure links the decision process to job-related factors and limits the influence of extraneous information, such as disability, gender, or race. At least seventeen studies have been conducted on this topic since 1996. Race, gender, and disability were the most frequently examined group differences (McDaniel et al., 1994). Unstructured interviews have been criticized for their low reliability, low validity, and susceptibility to different biases, such as race, gender, and disability (Arvey & Campion, 1982). Because interviewers conduct unstructured interviews in an idiosyncratic way and have discretion in what they ask and how they evaluate responses (Dipboye, Wooten, & Halverson, 2004), the content and evaluation process in unstructured interviews may be more reflective of the interviewers' implicit theories of the job requirements than the actual job requirements (McDaniel et al., 1994).

According to the Harvard Business Review (2016), "While unstructured interviews consistently receive the highest ratings for perceived effectiveness from hiring managers, dozens of studies have found them to be among the worst predictors of actual on-the-job performance — far less reliable than general mental ability tests, aptitude tests, or personality tests. Why do we stick with a method that so clearly does not work when decision aids, including tests, structured interviews, and a combination of mechanical predictors, substantially reduce error in predicting employee performance?"

This is perhaps one of the most important reasons to focus on when conducting structured interviews. As the evidence shows, unstructured interviews are susceptible to preexisting biases, which in today's corporate world is not only not acceptable, but actively petitioned against. Fundamentally, without structure to the interview, we are not in a position to evaluate like for like or evaluate people fairly based on the company's culture and the job requirements. Furthermore, structured interviews have been shown to provide incremental validity over personality tests and cognitive ability tests because they are weakly related to each other (Berry et al., 2007).

It has also been suggested that structured interviews can be designed to measure different constructs and behavioral traits such as GMA, problem-solving skills, and ethical behaviors (Huffcutt, Conway, Roth, & Stone, 2001). In the study by Huffcutt et al. (2001), they identified seven categories of constructs: mental capability, knowledge and skills, basic personality tendencies, applied social skills, interests and preferences, organizational fit, and physical attributes. A summary of their findings can be found in Table 7.

CATEGORY AND CONSTRUCT	Low Structure		High Structure	
	n	%	n	%
MENTAL CAPABILITY	25	19.2%	30	14.4%
General intelligence	15	11.5%	5	2.4%
Specific ability	1	0.8%	0	0.0%
Applied mental skills	6	4.6%	22	10.6%
Creativity and innovation	3	2.3%	3	1.4%
KNOWLEDGE AND SKILLS	15	11.5%	18	8.7%
Job knowledge and skills	3	2.3%	11	5.3%
Education and training	4	3.1%	2	1.0%
Experience and general work history	8	6.2%	5	2.4%
BASIC PERSONALITY TENDENCIES	48	36.9%	70	33.7%
Extroversion	8	6.2%	13	6.3%
Conscienciousness	19	14.6%	36	17.3%
Aggreableness	7	5.4%	3	1.4%
Openess to experience	0	0.0%	6	2.9%
Emotional stability	12	9.2%	9	4.3%
Other personality traits	2	1.5%	3	1.4%
APPLIED SOCIAL SKILLS	23	17.7%	71	34.1%
Communication skills	7	5.4%	19	9.1%
Interpersonal skills	11	8.5%	32	15.4%
Leadership	3	2.3%	17	8.2%
Persuaing an negotiating	2	1.5%	3	1.4%
INTERESTS AND PREFERENCES	7	5.4%	8	3.8%
Occupational interests	5	3.8%	8	3.8%
Hobbies and extracurricular activities	2	1.5%	0	0.0%
ORGANIZATIONAL FIT	3	2.3%	8	3.8%
Values and moral standards	3	2.3	8	3.8%
PHYSICAL ATTRIBUTES	9	6.9%	3	1.4%
General physical attributes	6	4.6%	2	1.0%
Job-related physical attributes	3	2.3%	1	0.5%

Table 7: Differences in Construct Frequency Between Low and High Structure Interviews (Huffcutt et al., 2001)

Interestingly, these findings are consistent with the literature already reviewed. As you can see, the outstanding numbers here are GMA or "mental capability" as it is referred to here; the Big Five personality traits, and in particular, conscientiousness, and EQ, or certainly a broader construct of EQ: "Applied social skills." The other interesting outcome of this study is the difference between structured and unstructured interviews and what they focus on. As you can see from Table 7, they managed to capture some key differences. Highly structured interviews focus on applied mental skills, direct job knowledge, social skills, and organizational fit. On the other hand, less structured interviews appear to focus more on GMA, background credentials (education, training, and experience), agreeableness, emotional stability, and physical attributes. In other words, as previously discovered, non-structured interviews are way more susceptible to personal bias and preconceived judgments on the interviewer's part.

Now we understand the constructs outlined to assess in the interview, what does the academic literature tell us about the structure of the interview itself? Campion et al. (1997) identified 15 separate components that influence the effectiveness of a structured interview. These are outlined in Table 8.

| | Structure Dimensions | | |
| | Content | Evaluation | |
Structure Components	Mean (SD)	Mean (SD)	p-value*
1. Job analysis	4.77 (.43)	2.67 (1.24)	<.0001
2. Same questions	4.27 (1.14)	3.20 (1.54)	0.02
3. Limit prompting	4.37 (1.00)	3.03 (1.27)	0.003
4. Better questions	4.73 (.52)	3.47 (1.36)	<.0001
5. Longer interview	4.13 (1.04)	3.03 (1.33)	0.001
6. Control ancillary information	3.50 (1.41)	4.10 (1.03)	0.09
7. No question from applicant	3.90 (1.40)	3.03 (1.33)	0.02
8. Rate each question	2.30 (1.34)	4.87 (.35)	<.0001
9. Anchored rating scales	2.33 (1.27)	4.90 (.31)	<.0001
10. Detailed notes	2.47 (1.38)	4.47 (.68)	<.0001
11. Multiple interviewers	2.63 (1.30)	4.47 (.97)	<.0001
12. Same interviewer(s)	2.93 (1.39)	4.33 (.99)	<.0001
13. No discussion between interviews	2.20 (1.47)	4.56 (.82)	<.0001
14. Training	4.23 (1.04)	4.73 (.52)	0.01
15. Statistical prediction	1.70 (1.15)	4.77 (.67)	<.0001

Table 8: Expert Mean Ratings of Structure Components Across Content and Evaluation Dimensions (Campion et al., 1997)

The first seven components relate to the structure of the interview itself, and the rest relate to the evaluation elements of the interview, or in other words, what methods they use to assess the data they're gathering during the interview.

"Regardless of the reliability of either type of interview, interview reliability can be increased by increasing the number of interviewers" (Schmidt et al., 2004).

This research indicates that, in theory, the best approach to interviewing is to have a set structure where questions are predetermined, structured and scorable in a consistent way, where multiple interviewers do the same interview and compare notes, but only after all the interviews are done. From a practical standpoint, interviewers have to be able to share some information with each other in between interviews. For example, if someone has a terrible first interview, there's no point in them continuing in the process and wasting valuable company resources having other executives conducting further interviews. However, it is possible to have a relatively unbiased interview process if, for example, as a company, you have agreed to have two interviewers conduct a thorough interview process beyond the initial screening. In such a case, each interviewer will follow a structured process with a pre-designed scorecard, where the answers may be shared simultaneously in a report following the interview. More on this can be found later in Chapters 8 and 9.

It will be no surprise to anyone that what we ask in the interview significantly impacts the validity of the interview itself. While it may not be a surprise, the questions that people continue to ask leads me to believe that they're not entirely sure what they're asking, why they're asking it, or what they expect to be able to measure from the questions they're asking.

From an academic research perspective, scholars have attempted, somewhat successfully, to break down the types of questions that we're all familiar with. For example, in a meta-study by McDaniel et al., they observed a distinction between situational and job-related questions (McDaniel et al., 1994). Situational questions are those where a scenario is posed to the interviewee, and they're asked to comment on how they would deal with such a situation. They assume that intentions predict future behavior (Latham,

1989). Job-related questions assess past behaviors based on job-related experiences and are often referred to as behavioral or competency questions. These often start with "Give me an example of a time when...." Behavioral questions rely on the premise that past behavior indicates future behavior (Janz, 1982). A study by Day and Carroll (2003) found that behavioral questions are more related to experience, and situational questions are more related to cognitive ability. This is another unsurprising outcome, yet it doesn't address the fact that talk of past experiences can be faked. The irony is that the faking of such experience has been positively linked to cognitive ability, as previously mentioned.

"In sum, the reviewed studies seem to suggest that when situational questions and behavioral questions are carefully designed to assess the same characteristics, they tend to measure different constructs, with situational questions primarily measuring job knowledge or cognitive ability and behavioral questions primarily measuring experience and perhaps some personality facets. Researchers commonly recommend the use of both question types, in part because situational questions and behavioral questions tend to measure different constructs and may complement each other (e.g., Campion et al., 1997;) to increase overall criterion-related validity and also because they allow some variety in question format" (McDaniel et al., 1994).

On the face of it, it makes sense that an interview would be made up of both types of questions. However, asking hypothetical questions about how someone would deal with a situation in the future does not necessarily mean that is how they would deal with that situation. All their answer tells you is how they say they would deal with the situation, and the reality could be very different. Therefore these situational questions must be assessed with a certain degree of caution.

CONCLUSION

The academic literature lays out strong arguments for the part that GMA and personality traits play in individuals succeeding in the workplace. Being intelligent enough to learn and solve problems won't come as a surprise to anyone. Having the right mixture of Big Five personality traits to lead, build relationships, and drive performance and motivation in others, also seems to be well established in the literature. The polarizing opinions on how to effectively define and measure EQ, coupled with questions about it being anything more than personality and IQ, leaves it in a less certain place. However, I think that EQ, regardless of its questionable definition or validity, is valuable in helping people connect with language that conveys how they should conduct themselves in the workplace.

Why is all of this even relevant anymore to how we go about hiring people? As indicated in the first part of this chapter, even HR, the guardians of our knowledge on everything people related, are not as connected to the theory as one would assume they should be. Therefore, it is fair to assume that any other executive in a company is likely to be at best equally ill-informed and, at worst, utterly clueless.

Understanding the usefulness and limitations of why the academic theory behind GMA, the Big Five, and EQ are important is critical in establishing an objective center of thought upon which to build informed opinions. Without such an understanding, our opinions are simply uninformed, which means we're left guessing and continuing doing what we've always done when it comes to interviewing, which in my opinion, has largely been a collection of bias and guesswork. Obsessing over the academic merits and demerits of these constructs, how they're measured, the validity of such measures, and even how they're defined is an ongoing argument we should leave to the scholars who dedicate their lives to studying these. It is for the rest of us, the practitioners, the leaders, and those of us who work outside of academia, to apply the underlying theory in a practical sense, to use what is sensible, and discard what is as yet unresolved.

It makes sense that despite GMA being the greatest predictor of job performance, it is not in itself enough to predict success. It makes sense that someone with a super high IQ does not automatically imply they will be a great leader. It makes sense that such an individual will also need the right personality traits and emotional intelligence to mobilize their IQ in a meaningful way. Based on the research, how do we best qualify someone in or out as a good potential candidate? It seems that high GMA coupled with the right combination of the Big 5 personality traits and structured interviews, is enough to identify the good candidates. That's the theory anyway.

Let's consider almost any global Fortune 500 company and who they will typically have working there. They will have hired the best graduates, taken them through training programs, then promoted them up through the hierarchy while also recruiting from other firms at various levels. By the time anyone working there is in a leadership capacity, it is fair to assume, based on their academic background and previous promotions, that they will all score sufficiently well on IQ. That renders the IQ test, or any other cognitive test, unnecessary at this level.

The issue here is that we now have a level playing field. All of the candidates are of sufficiently high IQ and general cognitive ability, which makes any differences in such measures meaningless. This is both good and bad. It is good because we've pre-qualified every candidate working at a certain level in a certain set of companies. It's bad in that the largest indicator of job performance, GMA, no longer becomes a differentiating factor. Instead, we have to rely on other measures to make an informed assessment.

It's less obvious that an individual will have the right combination of the Big Five. So, we can safely assume that we don't need to give a middle manager working in a top 10 financial institution an IQ test, but will it be useful to give them a personality test? Based on the research covered here, I believe that a straight-up personality test, in the traditional sense, is unnecessary. It may be helpful and somewhat insightful, but they're all flawed in one way or another. More to the point, people in mid-senior level roles have work experience, and their behaviors will be demonstrable in their historical actions and even in their engagement style in the interview itself. We learned this in the quoted studies by Morgeson et al. (2009) in the section on personality and interviews. Therefore what may be more effective than deploying cheatable personality tests is a structured interview process with questions that focus on experiences where personality traits and EQ can be observed and cross-referenced for factual accuracy.

The theory tells us that structured interviews are superior to unstructured ones. Most of these theories were developed before the current issues of diversity and inclusion were being recognized and prioritized to any significant degree. Therefore, now more than ever, we need to focus on structured rather than unstructured interviews to avoid the influence of underlying biases as much as possible. That's not to say we're going to eradicate any biases, but we certainly have a clearer path forward when choosing which of the two approaches is more appropriate. Furthermore, the evidence tells us that having multiple interviewers assessing candidates on different occasions, and asking the same questions can lead to better validity across the board. Having different people do their version of what they believe is the right way to interview people, as in the case of unstructured interviews, provides no basis to reach any informed consensus.

It is evident that having structured interviews with pre-determined questions, asked by and scored by different people on separate occasions, is the best scenario for minimizing bias. Furthermore, if personality questions can be incorporated into the interview, which has been shown to have more validity than a simple Likert scale self-score personality test, then we can also remove the need to have a separate psychometric test, the results of which may be misleading anyway.

As previously stated, no interview process is perfect, but that's not to say we cannot devise the best possible approach based on all the research we have, both academically and from practical experience. All of the above facets will be brought together and considered when we discuss the Bremnus model and Extraview interview process in Chapters 8 and 9. Most of what you will read aligns with the research done by the scholars, but in my view, they have missed some of the finite details that one can only learn about "on the job." They've also failed to provide a practical solution to the identified problems, so this is what I'll attempt to do in the remainder of the book.

II

THE ART

PREPARING TO LAND LEADERS

If you ask anyone when the interview process starts, be they a candidate, the HR manager, or the CEO, they will invariably tell you that it starts when you have the right candidates to interview. If you intend to build high-performing teams, this is not the way to look at it. An interview is a two-way event. The candidate is there to try and win the job, and the company should also be viewing it as an opportunity to win the candidate. This differs greatly from what we typically see in many companies, where the interview is a one-way process to qualify if a candidate is a fit.

The interview is the final destination of any hiring process. It happens only after a vacancy is established, a job spec is written, and a selection process has been agreed upon. Typically this will involve a series of interviews with various individuals in the company, followed by an HR interview. During the preparation process, with the candidate being the focus, a lot of preparation is often overlooked. If you interview a candidate who is truly a star for the role, how prepared are the interviewers to give the candidate a positive and challenging interview experience? How well aligned are each of the interviewers in terms of what is asked, what is measured, and what the desired outcomes are? This part of the preparation is often seriously lacking. The preparation seems to be more focused on qualifying out the poor candidates than it is on making sure the process is robust and efficient enough to attract and land the best candidates. The difference between these two approaches is subtle but significant. It's significant because selling the company and why your company is a great place to be is so important to the candidate. However, in many cases, the interviewer is so focused on testing the candidate that they fail to properly articulate why someone would want to join the company in the first place.

In my experience of working with senior executives in companies, often they don't know what they're doing when it comes to interviewing. From not selling the company and the opportunity enough, or coming across in a way that does not best represent the company, or just asking questions for the sake of asking, often these interviews lack structure. Before going on to design an effective interview process with impactful questions, the company needs to get itself aligned to deliver a consistent message to articulate the company vision, goals, and values and how they translate down through the organization. Hiring managers need to be tested and trained to conduct a proper interview. Not just what questions to ask, but role-play interviews, and if possible, record the role plays so they see how they conduct themselves in the interview. Do they even know how to sell the company and articulate why this is a good place to work? Please don't assume they will just because your company has some inspiring values. The best way to find out is to speak to people, especially hiring managers, and ask them, for example, "How do you pitch the values of our company to a candidate you're interviewing?" I bet over 80% of people you ask, who interview people regularly, will not be able to give you a concise answer. Not knowing how to interview and articulate the company's vision and values is largely one inward-facing issue, along with the interview being too much about qualifying out candidates rather than pitching the company.

EMPLOYER BRANDING

Just getting to the interview stage takes a great deal of focus on employer branding. How good do you want the list of candidates to be? Does your company want the best candidates in the whole market or just the best candidates on the market who happen to be looking for work? That's not to say that candidates looking for work are less qualified than those currently employed. That's often a mistaken observation that people make when they talk about unemployed candidates and passive candidates. Passive candidates are currently working, not actively looking, but may be open to hearing about opportunities if someone proactively contacts them. It's not for me or anyone to say if an unemployed or passive candidate is better. What cannot be argued is that if you broaden the search of candidates to include those who may not be actively looking, you have a wider talent pool to choose from.

Attracting the best candidates in the first place is what employer branding is all about. This includes many facets, and the whole subject of employer branding has been extensively written about already, so this will not be a deep dive into the detail in this regard. Employer branding is really about the company culture, how the company is perceived compared to its competitors, how they treat people, what their values are, and generally speaking, what it's like to work there. What are your company's values and goals, and how do these transcend the organization and manifest in specific goals and targets for teams and individuals? These are the fundamental basics that have to be sufficiently good enough so as not to prevent candidates from even considering an interview.

Employer branding is easy to define but difficult to master. You can't please everyone in the company; any time there's a promotion opportunity, someone internally will get the job, and others will not. Perhaps someone from the external market will get the job, so none of the internal candidates will get it. Now with the various online employee rating websites, anyone with an ax to grind about their current or past employer is free to go on and use the power of the stars to make sure their voice is heard by someone.

Companies should be working very hard on employer branding, with constant dialogue throughout the organization to find out what is going well and what could be better. Also, a constant dialogue with the external market about what is going well at other companies and what people who work there feel could be better. This can be done by collating all the data from interviews at all levels of the organization. If you want to hire the best people, you certainly need to be at least as attractive as your best competitor when it comes to the fundamental basics of employer branding, otherwise, why would these candidates even want to join? This brings us neatly onto finding out how prepared the hiring leaders and managers are to take on the big responsibility of landing leaders.

LOOK IN THE MIRROR

It is important to have inspiring leaders and managers in place to help attract talent into the organization. When managers may be exceptional but not inspiring, they must be trained. There has to be a top to bottom view on this. Think about the question for a moment, "Why do you want to come and work at X company?" This is a standard interview question, so you'll often get a standard answer - rehearsed. As someone who interviews candidates, have you ever considered what you would say if they were to ask you back, "Why should I come and work at X company?" Now, granted, they're unlikely to say that, but for sure, the hiring manager should be ready to answer this because the hiring manager should be acting as an ambassador of the company and, at the very least, know and be able to articulate what is great about working for their employer.

It is a relatively safe assumption to make that one of the four to ten candidates you're interviewing for the job will be the candidate you want. You won't always know who that is coming into the interview, so you have to be prepared to sell to every candidate like they're someone you really want to join the company. Perhaps you won't feel like pushing the company so much to everyone, but you should always be ready for the ideal candidate interview.

Often when I sit down and ask a hiring manager to tell me why a candidate would want to come and work at their company, it's amazing how uninspiring their answers are. Often it's as dull as, "Well, we have great benefits," or meaningless statements like, "It's a really dynamic work environment." What does dynamic even mean? Do we all share a common understanding of its definition, or is it just one of those words we hope will add some gravitas to our statements? As a general rule of thumb, if my response to your answer is "Yes, well, so do your competitors," then you may need to consider a different reply.

This is something you can try now for yourself. It doesn't matter if you're the CEO or someone reading this book at the beginning of their career and looking to preempt what hiring managers may look for as you grow through your career. Go and ask five to ten of your colleagues this:

"What would you say to a stranger who asked, 'Why should I come and work at this company?'"

You'll be surprised. In addition to the potentially lame or uninspiring answers mentioned above, the other answer that should concern you is silence. It will happen. As a business leader, the above wrong answers should worry you. It means your business has failed to communicate a shared vision and goals across the company. Without purpose and meaning, your team is at risk of being headhunted by other firms who have thought this through, communicated with their people, and listen to their team's feedback.

It's such basic stuff but utterly missed by many well-known organizations. Get back to basics. Communicate with your teams. Start with sharing the vision at a macro level, and engage teams in identifying a sense of purpose of their own. It's actually a positive exercise to do with teams and direct reports. Get your team together and come up with a shared sense of vision that relates to the broader company goals and vision. This will connect your team with that shared sense of purpose and get them speaking about it, which can reinforce the kind of behaviors that energize people about the company and where it's going. One of the other great benefits of engaging in such an exercise and feeding it back up through the organization is what you'll find out from such an exercise; insight about your colleagues, your team members, how people view the company, and subsequently what can be learned about what changes need to happen. This needs to be a two-way dialogue with information getting fed back up through the organization.

In doing such an exercise, out of every ten answers, most will likely fall into the category of wrong answers previously identified. Therefore you need to work together in teams to identify the truly unique things about your company, its story, its vision, and its culture. Then these items can be refined every year, but these items are what should be used constantly in pitching the company to potential candidates. A story, a vision, a set of beliefs, and a common goal that has been crowd-sourced by your employees is about as powerful a marketing tool as a company needs to have to attract and retain new talent. As a company, you cannot lose by undertaking such a process of self-identity and purpose. For example, let's consider a situation where your team uncovers many things wrong with the business and its identity. These are incredible catalysts for change. If your team has identified them and they get the opportunity to be part of the solution, then you will have a team of people who are incredibly engaged and bonded with a common sense of purpose. This can only be a good thing. If, on the other hand, your team assessment identifies the fact that there is a clear vision for the company and the team, well understood at all levels, then in confirming this to be the case, you have also taken the opportunity to discuss these benefits, thus reinforcing the message. Also, the team in this particular scenario should be able to very clearly articulate an answer to the question, "Why would someone want to join this company?"

So what would a good answer be? Well, let's say you're the hiring manager. Think about a scenario where you were thinking of leaving, and you were interviewing at a company you admire. What will you want to hear when you ask the hiring manager why someone would want to join them? This will not be your answer, but rather, this is an indication of what is important to you in a company. If certain things are important to you, then chances are these things will be important to others. If enough people in the company are asked and enough individual responses are gathered, you will certainly be able to form a clearer picture of what your employees actually want, not just what you think they want based on what was dreamed up on a company values retreat.

As a candidate, I'd want to hear about things that were unique and specific to that company. I'd want to hear stories that reflect how the company is living its values and how it is collectively working towards its goals. The emphasis here is on the word story, as stories talk to people. Not things many companies have, like subsidized meals or X weeks holiday. This comes back to the point about aligning the organization with the goals and vision of the whole company, and that energy and focus permeating through every layer of the company.

So a good answer may be, "We are at a really exciting juncture in the development of our company. Five years ago, the CEO set out a plan for us to grow into these markets and for us to be recognized as a leader in this field. We've already made our way up to the number three spot in this market, and the whole company is working hard to deliver our CEO's vision. It's a great journey to be on. Just two weeks ago, we went through a new funding round that is going to allow us to expand at a faster pace than we initially thought, and we're just really excited to be in a position to be bringing on new people who share in our belief in getting to the number one spot."

Now, that's not a perfect story, and it's extremely unlikely to be your company story. It doesn't have to be, but it has to be a story about what's going on in the company that the candidate can potentially get excited about. This is a story about what is happening in the company, why it's happening, and how it's an amazing journey to be part of. Well, that's great in theory, but what if you're hiring for a government organization that's not growing like crazy, or you're hiring someone to lead a company that has recently had a lot of bad press?

Well, for the government example, what is the function of that government department, and how does it relate to the country's well-being? How do you articulate a connection that people can get excited about? Why does the government department exist, and what is its purpose? The answers to these questions should help to create a kind of narrative that can be communicated in the interview process. Someone out there will be excited about it. The right candidates will be excited about it.

For the organization that's been experiencing bad press recently, there's an opportunity to be part of the solution. So many candidates I speak to in leadership positions are not status quo "run the business" type of leaders. Certainly, the most inspiring leaders I've met are the transformation stars who have incredible stories about turning around businesses. I'm thinking of one person in particular as I write this. He works in the telecom sector and has been an executive board leader in five globally recognized telecom businesses in the past 14 years. He has zero interest in joining a company and just picking up the reins. He seeks proverbial crime scenes to clean up. He wants it to be messy, to have failed enough times that the company may not think it can be done. People like this like to be challenged in new ways, and often taking an organization through a transformation from bad to good is an attractive opportunity. Certainly, it's the case that the right candidate will be excited at this prospect, and again it's about creating a narrative that is well communicated throughout all levels of the organization where people share, to the degree that it's possible, some common sense of purpose and goals.

TRAIN LEADERS TO LAND LEADERS

The art of the interview is covered in Chapter 9, so I am only briefly touching upon it here, but the training of hiring managers is an essential part of the process. Laid out in Chapter 9 is a step-by-step structure for getting the most out of the interview. Even the best interview process and its outcomes are unscientific, given the idiosyncratic nature of what and who is being assessed, but that's not to say they cannot be well-structured and thought through.

In my experience, based on feedback I get from candidates, it doesn't matter how senior someone is; they may still be bad at interviewing or may certainly have space for improvement. One may argue that they have been interviewing the same way all their life, and they know what to look for, and they've achieved enormous success in their career, partly due to how well they choose their team. That's great, but what if you could have been even better at selecting the right people? What if you could have hired even better people out of the hundreds or thousands of people you interviewed? What if some of the people you hired scraped through because you started with the assumption that they were good and didn't challenge them, and then they joined such a great team that any shortcomings would have been covered up anyway?

I remember a time in 2018 when a partner at a global investment bank asked a candidate what I believe to be the weakest question in recruiting:

"What are your strengths and weaknesses?" Is she in a position to boast that her ability to interview is exemplary, as evidenced by her career that led her to be promoted to partner at an investment bank? Absolutely not. She's worked at this investment bank for most of her career. Of course, the candidates coming through the process and ending up hired will be good. That's not to take away from her achievement of becoming a partner at an investment bank; that's an incredible achievement. However, she didn't get all that way in her career because of her challenging and creative approach to candidate assessment. The point is, for those very desirable companies, the interview process is not enough to turn a candidate off as "Everyone wants to work at X company." You see it with companies like Google, where people in the past were prepared to answer such silly questions, the answers to which will have had zero meaningful impact on their suitability for the job, but it didn't matter as "Everyone wants to work at Google."

However, most organizations are not on the list of the 500 most desired companies in the world and so aren't afforded the luxury of believing their interview process doesn't need to change or be tweaked because "Look at who we can hire – our interview process must be good." Most companies need to at least start by believing that the candidate may be interviewing elsewhere, and therefore, every impression counts. Well-structured, challenging, and well-thought-through interview processes will inevitably reflect well on the hiring company. This is a huge mistake that companies make when trying to structure interview processes. I suspect the conversation may go something like this:

HR Manager (HRM) "Let's look at how the best companies in the world are interviewing, and let's just copy them. Google asks how many ping pong balls will fit in a school bus, so let's ask, I don't know, how many Apple AirPods can you fit in a Tesla? Tesla's are cool, Apple is cool, and you know, we want to be cool, so this is a cool question, no?"

Hiring Manager (HM) "But what is the answer?"

HRM "Well, it doesn't matter. You see, it's about how they approach the question."

HM "Right, but do we hire someone because they get close to what we think the right answer is, or do we hire someone who just has the coolest answer?"

HRM "I don't know, what do you think?"

It's a huge mistake just to copy what the most desired companies are doing in the interview process because most companies won't have the luxury of choosing from a pool of brilliant candidates who have already passed very tough technical tests and will no doubt be from the best universities. Many of these questions are utterly useless predictors of success, other than to potentially predict their problem solving or creativity skills, which will already be evident in the technical tests, and certainly shouldn't be assessed based on only one question. Companies must strive to have the best interview process that is rigorous, challenging, structured, and consistent across the organization. It should also be one where the candidates feel very well treated throughout the whole process.

The structure and order of questions outlined in Chapter 9 are designed in such a way that minimizes the candidate's ability to lie and also maximizes our ability to identify competency trait patterns. This differs greatly from traditional interviews, where competency questions are asked directly, and the candidate can pick and choose which part of their career history to base their answer upon. It is safe to say that if in your company, competency and behavioral questions still feature as the main or a significant part of the interview process, you may want to reconsider how you train your hiring managers in how to interview.

To understand the extent to which your managers may need to be trained, you will first have to develop a basic template and approach to interviewing, and I consider the process outlined in Chapter 9 to be just that. The ultimate goal is to ensure all hiring managers up and down the organization are well enough trained to best represent the company in an interview. This means they all understand the values, the culture, where the company is going, and why they enjoy working there. It also means they know the questions to ask, the order in which to ask them, and the outcomes that can and can't be measured.

You will learn very quickly how much training hiring managers need by sitting in on interviews with them. What are they asking? How are they asking it? How aligned are their statements to the company's vision and goals? Based on their interview style, would you regard them as positive ambassadors for the company? Was the interview thorough enough with enough of the right challenging questions so that the hiring manager could likely form an objective opinion about the candidate? If hiring managers are falling short on any of these factors, these are all things that can be trained. If, after reading this book, you feel like the structure and questions outlined in Chapter 9 may not be entirely useful, it should still act as a catalyst to start thinking seriously about how your company is presenting itself to the candidate world and what changes may need to be made.

AGREE ON WHAT YOU NEED

In trying to establish the type of candidate you're looking for, in addition to any job spec or job ad, it's helpful to start by asking a series of questions that can collectively be referred to as the "success profile." A job spec or job ad is there to tell the candidate what they may be doing in the role or why the company may be a good place to work. It doesn't tell the internal hiring team, which could be made up of representatives from both HR and the business, exactly what they're looking for or why they need it. So the success profile is there to define better who you're looking for, why you're looking for them, and where you think they may come from. Below are some questions you may want to consider in exploring what the success profile may look like.

Why is this role important?

It's an obvious place to start, but it's not a question typically asked when putting together any job spec. What is important about the role is the whole definition of its purpose. As an e-commerce manager, the role may be important as it is "instrumental to the success of our 12-month strategy to migrate to a new e-commerce platform that will allow us to improve the customer experience." This differs greatly from a typical job description that would likely state a long list of technical requirements. Also, knowing why a role is important helps to frame the pitch to candidates about why they may consider joining the company.

What will they have to deliver in year one?

What is this person actually going to be doing? Not the long list of tasks we normally see in job specs, but what are their four to six key objectives? What will they deliver by the end of the first year to demonstrate they've succeeded in hitting their objectives? These should be tangible objectives. This is also more useful and inspiring to a candidate than the typical job spec containing phrases like "must have strong communication skills." I still see that all the time in management and leadership job specs. Why does that reference to communication skills still exist? Communication skills are a prerequisite to all jobs. Do people who make such references in job ads really think that a candidate is going to be reading through it, get to the line about communication skills and think, "That's a shame. This leadership role in a global bank was perfect for me, except on top of leading a team of 800 people, they also want good communication skills. Oh well, never mind, onto the next job application." It's ridiculous that we continue to include such basic prerequisites that don't need to be mentioned.

What is the person likely to be doing currently?

This has to be spoken about between the business and HR, so everyone is on the same page. We all may know what we believe we're looking for, but there is often surprising dialogue when it comes to an understanding of what the hiring manager is looking for.

What may look like a fit but definitely won't be?

This question seeks to better define what is required, or at least what candidate background will be ideal. It is a useful question to ask in the conversation to define the role because the hiring manager and the recruiter may have different views on what a relevant background may be. Therefore, by discussing what backgrounds will be very close but not quite right, both parties can better understand what the perfect candidate profile may be.

What could potential outlier candidates be doing currently?

Any diversity conversation's focus is typically centered around gender, race, sexual orientation, age, and others. This is what the focus should be, of course. However, we can also think of diversity as widening the pool of talent beyond where candidates typically come from. Later in the book, I share an example of a board-level candidate that joined a global bank in a very senior position that came from the aerospace industry. She had no previous banking experience but was an incredible leader of a global organization. The more creative we can be in exploring this question, the better. After all, what is exciting for a candidate about coming from one competitor to another to do the same role? Not much. However, if a candidate can come from another industry, and that move is technically possible, the chance for them to learn and grow in a completely new environment is very exciting.

What are the top 10-20 companies we would want to see candidates from?

The answer to this question will mean the recruiter, either internally or externally, has an opportunity to put together a target list to headhunt from. There will obviously be some competitors in this list, but depending on the role and company, the list may be much broader. Instead of relying on posting an advert on a job board to find this leader, the recruiter should map out and identify all potential candidates in the target companies.

In considering the current team dynamic, what kind of leader are we looking to hire?

When hiring leaders or managers, companies can fail to prioritize the existing team dynamic and what type of leader is required to optimize the team to achieve their delivery objectives. All too often, companies focus on the broader cultural identity and finding a fit for the company rather than a fit for the team. Sure, they may be the same, but often, especially in an internationally diverse company, not every team will be at the same level of maturity, have the same state of harmony, or be in the same stage of a delivery life cycle. For example, you may have one team that's just running a steady-state division of the business with a team of close people who work together well, and all they need is someone to come in and keep it working well without too much disruption. On the other hand, you may have another team, for example, customer services, which has high rates of attrition, low levels of customer satisfaction, and two leaders within the past year who were both terrible. The requirements of leadership in these two different scenarios are completely different. It's not always about company culture;

the team objectives and the existing team dynamic are much more pressing indicators of what the candidate requirements may be.

If it's a replacement, how did the previous incumbent excel?

If you're replacing someone for whatever reason, hopefully, because they've been promoted into a bigger role, you have a great benchmark to work with, for good or bad. There may be elements of their style and approach that didn't work so well. However, in defining what they did do very well, part of the new hire requirement is already done. What is it about this leader or manager that worked? How do you account for their great performance? What does their team say about why they were so effective at managing them? Remember, it is not safe to assume that a broader company culture definition, and this individual's fit, is why they performed so well. Each team is different in terms of the dynamic created by its unique members, where they sit in their organization, and where they are at in their objectives life cycle. Therefore, the conversation should focus on exactly how this person's success is defined, rather than on how successful the company's culture is and how much this person exemplifies the company culture.

If it's a replacement, in what ways should the new hire be different?

Even if the outgoing leader or manager was incredible and delivered record-breaking results, what could they have done differently to improve things? The chances are they were not the perfect leader. So what is it about the team dynamic, or what is it about the future direction of the team or company that requires the new person to be different? Perhaps the outgoing leader built the company from zero to its current state, and now a steady-state leader is required rather than a high-growth entrepreneurial leader. Perhaps it may not be about steady-state, but just hiring a leader who has demonstrated taking a company from 1000 to 20000 people where the previous leader has just been outgrown. By focusing on what needs to be different, you can get closer to having a well-considered and refined person profile.

If it's a replacement, in what ways should they be similar?

At first glance, this question looks like the question, "How did the previous incumbent excel?" However, it's seeking something slightly different. Referring to the previous question, how the previous incumbent excelled may not be what now needs to be similar. They may have taken the company through a significant period of hyper-growth, or perhaps they were responsible for taking a new product or service from inception to launch. Their replacement might be managing the team through a new period where a different approach or style is required, so the skill set that made the previous person excel may not be the same skill set that's now required for the team to continue to excel. Therefore, it is important to take this different approach just to get as close as possible to understanding what the ideal profile may look like moving forward.

Unfortunately, it will not always be the case that someone is being replaced. I use the term "unfortunate" because it's much easier to define and refine what is required based on what you know to have worked in your company, in this team, in the past. On the other hand, a brand new role that doesn't yet exist in the company is an incredible sign that growth is happening. I'm pretty sure most leaders would want this problem where growth is creating new roles that have never been done before, so they're faced with the difficulty of defining the profile with nobody to benchmark against.

If it's a new role, based on other people in the company, what do we know we need?

It's often hard to articulate exactly what profile of a person we need coming into a new role. Often the descriptions are too general and vague or perhaps not entirely well thought through. Therefore, if we start by observing the behaviors and styles of other people in the company that succeeded, we are in a position to better articulate exactly what we believe we need.

If it's a new role, based on other people in the company, what do we know we don't want?

Taking all of the experiences of people who haven't done so well in the company before can help shape a profile of what is definitely not required in this role. It can even just be in observing the objectives of the role or team itself that can help identify what is not required, which is often just as important as knowing what you want.

So what does all of this look like in practice, then? Well, what we come up with is a success profile. This isn't a job spec or a job ad; those are both separate documents that will look entirely different from this one. This is the success profile used only for the purposes of recruiting. Sure, some of the content of the job spec and job ad will be similar, but the three different documents should not be confused. A job spec may be a more detailed document listing the role's objectives and other additional information.

On the other hand, a job advert should be like any other advert. It should be written in a way that attracts people to submit their details to find out more. It should also be written so that potential candidates are very clear on how they should define themselves as suitable. A job ad is not a job spec, yet if you were to read nearly all job ads currently on job sites, you'd be forgiven for thinking that most companies just don't know the difference. They're often long, tedious lists of tasks and lists of what the candidate must have, most of which are implied by the role itself.

If I'm reading a job ad for a Sales Director, I don't need to be told that part of the requirement is good communication skills. If I'm reading a job ad for a Salesforce Architect, I don't need to read a list of the tasks that a Salesforce Architect performs. I already know what a Salesforce Architect does every day; I am one already. If I'm that Salesforce Architect, I want to read about what exciting project I may be working on, how you treat your people, if I may have the opportunity to travel or meet clients, or what I can be expected to achieve in terms of promotion if I deliver on my objectives. I want to know why I should leave my current job to come to work at your company.

The way job ads are currently written, it would be a bit like watching a Pepsi ad at the half-time break of the Super Bowl. In the ad, some dull-looking guy walks up to the screen and shows the can of Pepsi. He says, in a monotone voice, "This is a can of Pepsi. To drink it, you will first of all need to be thirsty. Then, you will open it like this. When you drink it, it will be fizzy. The taste is best described as, I'm not really sure, Coke, but different. To drink it, you put the opening to your mouth and tip it back. The liquid will flow into your mouth. When it's finished, you will know because the can will be light."

Now, how ridiculous would such a Pepsi ad be? Well, if it was done in a comedic way by Will Ferrell, some may find the irony entertaining, but there are better ways to advertise products, and there are definitely better ways to advertise jobs.

What follows is an example of what a success profile may look like for a Sales Director role for a technology company. You don't need to know what all of the terms mean, but you will see this is not a lengthy document. It may result from lengthy discussions, but the aim is to have a concise list of key points that will help anyone who reads this understand exactly what a successful profile should and should not look like.

SUCCESS PROFILE

Why is this role important?

This role is critical to growing our company as they will be responsible for bringing in $25m in new business in addition to running a $125m sales operation.

What do they have to deliver in year one?

Deliver $25m in new sales.

Grow the team from 200 to 230 people.

Implement a new commission structure.

Fire the worst 10% of performers.

Grow the business beyond the US into the UK market.

What is this person likely to be doing currently?

Running a significant multi-regional SAAS sales team of at least 100 people.

What may look like a fit but definitely won't be?

Someone working in hardware technology sales.

What could potential outlier candidates be doing currently?

Running a multi-region sales team in the cloud technology sector or other software products.

What are the top 10-20 companies we would want to see candidates from?

Our ten biggest competitors and the top 10 mid-tier SAAS companies in the US.

In considering the current team dynamic, what kind of leader are we looking to hire?

One that is different from the existing tough autocratic leader. Someone who can lead from the front, train, and support best-in-class salespeople.

IF IT'S A REPLACEMENT

How did the previous incumbent excel?

Driving sales by being all over the details and managing the team very closely.

In what ways should the new hire be different?

They should be more of a coach/mentor type of leader rather than an authoritarian one. They will be a great listener with strong empathy and an inclusive coaching style. We have to fix the morale of the team.

In what ways should they be similar?

Laser-focused on sales growth.

IF IT'S A NEW ROLE

Based on other people in the company, what do we know we need?

It's not a new role.

Based on other people in the company, what do we know we don't want?

It's not a new role.

EXECUTE WITH URGENCY AND CONVICTION

In preparing to land leaders, the process has to be well thought through so the candidate has a seamless candidate experience. In my experience working internally and as an external executive search partner, it is time management and poor execution of the recruiting process that loses great candidates. Of course, most of the candidates you interview will not be right as only one person gets the job. However, for that one person that does get offered the job, if they truly are a star candidate, you better hope that your process was so seamless and their experience was so great that when you offer them, one of their negative considerations was not the experience they had as a candidate. For this to happen, all candidates need to be treated as if they're the next hire because you won't know, coming into the process, which one it's going to be.

There should rarely be an excuse for a bad candidate experience as these things can be prepared for in advance. However, companies are still terrible at managing this process. When you move from the long list of candidates to the shortlist, and you decide that these are the four people you want to interview, every stage should be planned out at that moment, and the process should happen over two weeks or three weeks maximum. No doubt there will be exceptions when certain meetings can't happen, but it shouldn't be dragging on for one, two, three, or more months.

It really doesn't matter how senior the role is. The further up the organization one goes, the more of a priority hiring becomes, so everything should be planned. Diary time should be blocked out for interviews at the start of the year, each quarter, each month, and each week. It should be blocked out first thing in the morning, at lunchtime, and as late in the day as possible, as these are the times candidates are most likely to get away from their existing employers without raising too many eyebrows. You don't have to just block out time hoping that someone may be interviewing. That is clearly not a good use of your time, but there should be a minimum expectation that you'll conduct X interviews per month, given the company's hiring goals and expected attrition.

Who is going to be conducting the interviews? Who else? Is there any potential eventuality that will lead to someone else having to also interview the candidate? How many interviews will they have? How many will be over the phone, via video call, or in-person? Once they're in-person, can all interviews be scheduled on the same day? There are other questions to ask here, but the aim is to be in a position to say to a candidate something along the lines of:

"I'm delighted to say that you are on the shortlist of four candidates we'd like to meet, so congratulations. This is going to be a four-stage interview process. First, you will have a phone interview with the hiring manager, which will be 30 minutes. If that works out, the next stage will be face-to-face with the hiring manager. If that works out, the third stage will be a meeting with HR, and finally, a meeting with the hiring manager's boss. The final two meetings we aim to do on the same day. We will then be in a position to make a written offer within five days from your final interview, pending any checks and follow-up questions you may have."

If you're not ready to say something along the lines of the above, you should consider holding off on starting the hiring process. I've lost count of the number of times a process has started with good intentions, and then it stalls in the middle for a whole host of reasons, and then the candidate just loses interest. Why would they maintain interest when the company can't make its mind up about completing a hiring process? What does this say about how the company makes other decisions and what the candidate may be walking into? This process of the interview and the efficiency that all candidates should observe throughout is the easiest part of hiring to get right, yet it remains a fractured process in so many companies.

CONCLUSION

Preparing to land leaders should be treated with no less rigor and deep consideration than preparing to launch a new product. One can only imagine the process and time that went into launching the first iPhone in 2007 and every iPhone since, for that matter. When Apple can sell ten million units in their first weekend as they did after a launch in 2014, they're not just hoping everything is fine. Sure, things can still go wrong, but they get it as close to perfection as they do through meticulous planning, testing, and development.

I'm not suggesting that planning to run a hiring process needs a similar degree of focus and intensity, but rather, the DNA has to be there. Organize, test, and re-test until something is right; coordinate people and timing so things can work to schedule. All of the points discussed in this chapter can be addressed before any candidate even picks up the phone for a first interview. Before any interviews happen, some basics should be covered. Train hiring managers how to interpret the vision and goals of the company and make them meaningful in their team; put together a success profile that is meaningful and impactful; train interviewers to conduct interviews properly and schedule the process, so the goal is to give the candidate the greatest interview experience of their life. Why shouldn't the goal be to give the candidate the greatest interview experience of their life? It's certainly possible, not least because so many companies appear to only make an effort to give candidates the most mediocre interview experience of their lives. Hiring managers should inspire, be deeply connected to the company's vision and goals, and make hiring their priority. We haven't even gotten to the art of the interview yet. That's way less binary than simply picking up some organization skills and learning a few questions. All of this can be trained and perfected before a candidate begins the interview process. What are you waiting for?

WHY ALL COMPANIES ARE BAD AT INTERVIEWING

In many ways, recruiting for leadership roles is easier than recruiting for entry-level positions. Over time, an individual has an opportunity to build up a track record, for good or bad, and patterns have an opportunity to establish themselves. The other great thing is you can see where this person has worked over the years, how long they stayed there, how progressive their career has been in terms of growth, and so on. In other words, there are more clues regarding how successful a potential candidate may or may not be based on their career experiences. Think about recruiting graduates. Comparatively speaking, they don't have any work experience, or certainly very little to speak of. So you're faced with looking at academics, extra-curricular activities, achievements outside of the classroom, and indicators that may predict success but ultimately don't give any guarantees.

We need a better system to accurately predict outcomes, as anyone can cheat in an interview. Interviewers are subject to such strong bias that the answers given are often assessed based on preconceived notions by the interviewer about that person's suitability. There's no escaping from the fact that people will prepare for interviews, rehearse answers, objectively review their resumes and finesse their stories about what went right and wrong. Candidates should be doing this; why wouldn't they? However, the process of interviewing is not an exact science with predictable outcomes. So, when we don't have a perfect way, we have to identify the best way possible, given the inherent limitations of interviewing. So why are all companies bad at interviewing? We're starting here with the recognition that no interview process will be perfect. Lies will be told, biased judgments will be made, answers will be rehearsed, and the interviewer is likely to go off on tangents that will lead to judgments made that have nothing to do with how well the candidate can do the job. Let's look at some of these issues in more depth before identifying the solutions outlined in the remaining chapters.

PROBLEM 1 - THE INTERVIEWER

Just asking a series of unrelated questions does not make someone an interviewer. The structured behavioral competency interview is where this is often most obvious. An interviewer has a checklist of questions and asks a series of questions that they may not be in a position to evaluate, given how misleading and patchy competency interviews are in the first place. Interviewers no doubt learned their interview skills from the interviews they've been on in the past rather than from any meaningful or useful structured interview training.

Candidates only have one story. Everything the interviewer needs to know about the candidate is contained in their story. What makes the difference is how much of the stories the interviewer can extract and analyze in a meaningful way. There's no need for these difficult trick question interviews. The candidate's story will be more honest and fluid if the interviewer directs the line of questioning to flow between each stage of the candidate's life. Of course, people can still lie. However, you can minimize the candidate's opportunities to lie. You can start by not asking completely abstract questions and instead be very specific in leading them through their career, getting deep into details about the key moments in their career and life.

A candidate should never fail an interview. Perhaps they may not qualify for the job, but they shouldn't be failing the interview itself. By failing an interview, I mean they crumble under the pressure of the interview and get stuck. That won't happen if they're made to feel comfortable in the interview, and you ask them about things they know about: their life and career. If you're all over the place asking them to recall unmemorable events randomly, as in many competency interviews, they will make mistakes. I recall many amazing candidates with great careers completely failed an interview because the interviewer was terrible. Do you recall a time when you had a terrible interviewer and walked away feeling like your background wasn't well represented in the interview? That's usually not your fault.

In "The Source Of Truth," written in the Harvard Business Review (HBR 2019), it states: "The first problem with feedback is that humans are unreliable raters of other humans. Over the past 40 years, psychometricians have shown in study after study that people don't have the objectivity to hold in their heads a stable definition of an abstract quality, such as *business acumen* or *assertiveness*, and then accurately evaluate someone else on it. Our evaluations are deeply colored by our own understanding of what we're rating others on, our own sense of what good looks like for a particular competency, our harshness or leniency as raters, and our own inherent and unconscious biases."

According to HBR, this phenomenon is called the *idiosyncratic rater effect*, and it's large (more than half of your rating of someone else reflects your characteristics, not theirs) and resilient (no training can lessen it). In other words, the research shows that feedback is more distortion than truth. Clearly, this is some worrying research. We are apparently incapable of holding shared definitions of competencies or being able to evaluate people based on these competencies. Forget competencies for a moment; we can't even agree on what A, B, and C represent when it comes to performance. You may be aware of companies talking about A, B, and C players. Some even use these references as part of an interview process. How do we know the interviewer and candidate are even speaking about the same thing? I've never bought into the A, B, C player narrative as there are too many moving targets for it to hold value.

Are they universally classified, or is it within a company relative to their peers? If it's relative to their peers, what are the criteria? Does it change when more A or C players are added because the median will definitely change? Look at the academic world. Being an A player in a mid-tier university won't even make you a C player in an Ivy League school. They at least have SAT scores to underpin some assumptions. In the corporate world, how are we classifying these? Besides, how does a B player know they've hired a C player? Isn't it part of the job of a leader and manager to develop people, and therefore it's okay they hire C players? Aren't grads technically C players compared to those with two years of experience until they're trained? If a B player only hired C players, wouldn't their resulting performance be a C and therefore not make them a B player? Does a B player technical manager only hire C player coders? Will they really be that silly if they're looking to climb the ladder?

I feel like the only utility for this type of narrative is in explaining, in part, why poor leaders manage to climb the career ladder in the first place. I don't think it should be used as any kind of measurable part of an interview. Let's say I work in a global bank. I may be an A player individual contributor who gets my first promotion as a reward for being an A player. For example, perhaps I'm a great computer engineer or a great salesperson. As a new manager of five people, I may then be a B or C player as I haven't yet developed the experience, but I have a team made up of two A players, two B, and one C, which is enough for me to look like a competent manager. Therefore I'm promoted again a year later, even though I'm not an A player-manager. Now I'm really out of my depth and a C player leader, but I have a team of ambitious people mostly made up of A's and B's, so I keep my job and may even be promoted again. As a C player leader, I will keep hiring A's and B's so I'm not found out. I'm not going to hire C's as then I have a team of terrible people that expose my incompetence. Why would I do that? If it's because I'm insecure and incompetent, then the best way to hide that is to have a better team, not a worse one. This is why I don't believe this "B players hire C players to look good" narrative. C player managers can get into management by being an A player individual contributor but cannot grow without a team that is more competent than they are. In my opinion, the degree of complexity in unwrapping this narrative renders its application in interviews useless. Let's go back to the competencies.

If the interviewer asks a candidate about a specific competency, that interviewer has to have their own interpretation of that competency. The candidate will also have their interpretation of the competency, and do we just have to hope they're speaking about the same thing? We may never reach common ground in understanding the interpretations of what certain competencies are, but what we can do is reduce the error caused by the idiosyncratic rater effect. For example, instead of asking the candidate about specific competencies directly, the interviewer can observe the competencies in the process of asking very focused and detailed questions about each role. I'll share more on this process in Chapter 9, but this way, you only have one interpretation of these competencies - the interviewer's interpretation. In this proposed method, the candidate is merely talking about their work experience in detail, closely directed by the skilled interviewer, with no mention of the competencies themselves, yet in their stories, the competencies will be quite apparent. For example, the candidate may tell several stories demonstrating an unusually high level of determination. The interviewer can make this observation without asking questions like, "Give me an example of a time when you demonstrated your determination to finish a task."

Secondly, by assessing fewer competencies. Not so few that we're missing chunks of valuable data, but instead of fifty, in the Bremnus model and Extraview interview method, we have four success factors and twelve traits. Not all competencies will be relevant at all times. By condensing many into a few that are more easily understood and interpreted, we can further reduce the potential for human error. More importantly, we're not negatively skewing the results with competencies that are not significant decision influencers. Finally, in having two or more people interview and ask similar questions, we may not necessarily reduce human error, but we will at least have different relatable viewpoints to combine and aggregate.

However, we can't have everything. As unique individuals, we still have to be able to exercise our right to an opinion. Opinions are shaped by individual life experiences, culture, and many other things, but we must start somewhere. We can't just leave our opinions to the objectivity of so-called perfect questions, as would be the case if Amazon's Alexa was the interviewer. This is why the development of AI in interviewing is concerning to me. Not all of it, but the parts pitched as a solution to the bias problem in recruiting are frankly alarming. We need to know who the diversity candidates are to ensure they are hired. For example, technology that takes out references to gender and race on resumes is not doing diversity candidates any good for reasons I've outlined previously.

The next problem with the interviewer is they haven't been properly trained to interview, or the training they've received has been in an interview method that is not fit for purpose. I've seen it happen many times over the years when hearing feedback from candidates. Often I'll hear about a ridiculous question that's been asked that could not possibly have provided the interviewer with any meaningful, useful feedback. Or even worse, I'll have three different candidates all interview with the same person, and when I ask what questions they were asked, they all give me completely different answers. How can one interviewer make an informed judgment on a candidate if they are using different questions to assess each candidate's suitability for a given role? It's not possible.

There was a really interesting study done by Richard DeVaul et al. (1987) called "Medical School Performance of Initially Rejected Students." This came about as Texas legislators tried to figure out a way to deal with the shortage of physicians. Their solution was to increase admissions to medical school by 50 people beyond the initial 150 selected. That meant the 50 people came from a pool of potential students who hadn't previously made the grade. Furthermore, only seven of the 50 had even received an offer from another school, so it's fair to assume that Texas medical school was not the only rejection some of these candidates initially received. Two incredible discoveries came from this study. Firstly, the difference in the eventual pass rate between those initially rejected and those who got in the first time was zero. What does that tell us? The interview process that each candidate went through, where they were quizzed on factors outside of their academic qualifications, was completely useless as a predictor of success. In theory, the medical school could have gotten the same results if they just made it a lottery for any students who met certain academic criteria. The second interesting finding from this study was, "It serves in most schools as an effective recruiting device. Students at UTMSH were surveyed to determine what influenced them to select the particular school. A majority stated that the positive effect of the interviewer(s) was of major importance in their decision" (Medical School Performance of Initially Rejected Students, 1987).

Yes, this was a study done in the 1980s with medical students as the subjects, but it accurately conveys that bias happens on both sides of the interview, which is very important. The interviewer is also being judged by the candidate. How impressive are they? How convincing are they? How well do they know the company? How tough and relevant are their interview questions? You have to make sure the interviewer representing the company does so with similar preparation as the candidate must undertake in getting ready for an interview.

The other issue with the interviewer is they're not prepared to be inter-viewed themselves. It's unlikely the candidate will interview them, but the interviewer needs to be fully prepared to answer questions and sell the company and the opportunity. Whatever part of the organization you currently work in, if you or your colleagues cannot answer the following questions with succinct and consistent answers, known throughout the company, how can you expect to land the star candidates?

1. How are the company values visible at different levels of the organiza-tion?

2. What am I likely to get in a career here that I can't get at your best competitor?

3. How would you describe the company culture?

4. Why did you join the company, and why are you still here?

5. What frustrates people most about working here, and what's being done about it?

6. Where would you want to work if it weren't here and why?

I will often ask these questions to a client that I'm recruiting for. The thought process that an interviewer has to go through to answer these questions forces them to think more broadly and deeply, which in turn prepares them for so many other related questions that may come up. Not only that, but they're then equipped to articulate what is great about the company. Let's explore each of these six questions in more detail.

1. How are the company values visible at different levels of the organization?

This question assumes the interviewer knows what the values are in the first place. In my experience, it is likely they don't, at least not without checking their company website. If the values listed don't make sense or don't accurately reflect who the company is, this is a great place to start to work on this with your colleagues. In today's workplace, people value purpose and want to know they're working towards one. Values are no longer the shortlist of funky words that the marketing team dreamed up to fill out space on your company website. This is an integral part of attracting great talent. Know your values and learn how they manifest in each area of the company.

2. What am I likely to get in a career here that I can't get at your best competitor?

When I ask this, I usually get terrible answers. Typically the answer will end up being a list of things that aren't even unique to this company. We're not looking here for, "Well, we have great benefits, and we get a pension plan." What really makes you unique as an employer? You may well be working on some of the most interesting solutions to problems in your industry, but so are your two best competitors. What else is it that's unique that candidates can't find elsewhere? These things need to be thought long and hard about as if you can't articulate them, there may not be any, and if there's nothing unique, how can you expect people to join? Why do they join? Maybe it's the culture? Well, there you go. Culture is arguably unique in any company; it has to be. The unique combination of people you have working in your company will never exist anywhere else. So it's best to think hard about this, and if culture is the only thing you can come up with, ask yourself this: What are people likely to get at my top competitors that we can't offer them here? If you don't know what your top competitors offer, why not?

Knowing what your competitors can offer that you currently aren't is a great starting point to level the playing field and make your company more competitive. And don't wait to rely on HR to come up with the answers. They're too busy dealing with the many things you've asked them to do very cheaply, like recruiting, to have time to gather such data. Sure, get HR involved, but also be proactive in working with the rest of your leadership team. Get them to find out. Get their teams to find out by joining groups on LinkedIn, chatting to their ex-colleagues, and doing whatever they can to identify this information.

3. How would you describe the company culture?

I often get very dull and predictable answers when I ask this question. If someone is describing something in a dull and predictable way, you can be sure it's not something that's going to get candidates excited. I'm sure your culture is dynamic, fun, and inclusive, but what does that mean? When I ask this question, I like to hear the stories that are told in response. Such a response may start with something like, "Sometimes, culture is hard to define in words, so I'd rather give you an example of what our culture is like."

Then you give anecdotes about what happens in your company that best represents the culture. It may be the collaborative nature of teams that come together once every two months to work in the community on environmental issues, or it may be the monthly hackathons your team has with their international colleagues where they come together to solve problems. It could be anything, but rather the usual adjectives used to describe culture, answer the question with stories. Put yourself in the candidate's shoes and speak to yourself as if you're the one in the hot seat being interviewed and wanting to hear why you should be joining this company.

4. Why did you join the company, and why are you still here?

Just think about that for a second as you're sitting there or standing reading this. Why did you join the company? What was it about the company that made you want to join? Was it the right decision? How could it have been better? How have things changed since you joined, and why do you now stay? Sure, it will be the money, the stability, the benefits, and so on, but what's great about the company that keeps you and others there? This is the kind of thought process and questions you should go through internally to reach the point where you have positive energy and the words to articulate your answers.

5. What frustrates people most about working here, and what's being

done about it?

Again, this is another question for the internal dialogue. It's a chance to get it all out in your mind before having to share any of it with a candidate. It's a bit like a candidate preparing for "What are your strengths and weaknesses?" Sure, you will want to be honest, but you may not want to share all of the truth for whatever reason. Even if the exercise of thinking this through only helps you better frame some of the challenges that you or your colleagues can impact, it's worthwhile.

6. Where would you want to work if it weren't here, and why?

This question helps do a couple of things. Firstly, it gets you in the mindset of the candidate looking to join your company. Nothing else gets you in that mindset like this as you're forced to analyze what you love about competitors or other companies. It may get you thinking about what is important to you in a role and a company, and then cross-referencing these important factors with what exists in your company and what still needs to be changed.

The whole process of getting prepared will get you ready to sell the role to candidates you want to hire, and the exercise itself can do so much more. If you're reading this and you're a manager or even more senior, and you're not in HR, you don't have to wait for HR to take the initiative here. Think about these questions, discuss them with colleagues, hold workshops, and get the debate going. This is a free and inclusive way to get people at every level in your organization involved in the pulse of the company. If you already have incredible values and a well-defined culture, that's great, but things can change.

What employees need and want can change, but employees wanting to feel valued and involved will remain consistent, so keep this in mind. You can even run an anonymous email campaign for your team or the whole company to get them to answer these questions and analyze the feedback. There's no better way to understand what your team and colleagues think than to ask them. I don't see it being done enough in companies. You'll know immediately if it's done enough by asking at least three people these questions and seeing how different the answers are.

You may acknowledge that these are some good ideas, and you may even stop to think about how you can integrate them into your team, or at the very least, you may test yourself to see if you have good answers. This is serious, though. In my twenty years of recruiting, I've rarely been blown away by a set of answers someone has given me to these questions. Even if I've been impressed by certain individuals, by the time I've asked two of their colleagues, it's back to square one. Think about candidates that don't prepare for interviews. We've all interviewed them. Did you ever offer one of them a job or recommend to your colleagues that they deserve a further interview? This is no different. It's unlikely a candidate will ask you these questions, but you better be sure that if you want to hire someone outstanding, you will need every tool available to land them, and this is the simple stuff – just be prepared.

PROBLEM 2 – THE INTERVIEW STRUCTURE

Timeline

One of the main issues I face in working with clients is the actual timeline of the process. Clients often start by saying they need a superstar, and they needed the superstar to start yesterday. Then I agree on a process including X number of interviews with certain people and timelines, and then I get to work. I find a superstar. Sometimes I find more than one. The client acknowledges they're a superstar. The candidate interviews with the three people I've been told they will meet. Then the process goes on hold. Then I find out there are two more people that want to meet the candidate. Then I find out they're thinking of an internal candidate for the role. Then they change the job spec of the person they're looking for. Things happen and change, but not to the extent and frequency I've observed in my career. Things need to tighten up.

It's about the candidate experience. That's what matters here. Unless it's a one-person startup, the company will have hired before. Even if it is a one-person start-up, the chances are that one person will have hired for another company before. A recruitment process should never begin until you are ready to finish the process, assuming you get a great candidate through the door. If you are interviewing a truly great candidate, there is always a chance that you won't be the only one. You must be at least as good as whichever company you compete with for the candidate. This is the easy stuff. Get organized to run a process from start to finish. Who is part of the interview process? Who has the final say? When a verbal offer is made, who needs to take what action to get the offer letter to the candidate? Is there any way to expedite that process? How long will the process take from start to finish? What will we tell candidates to expect from each stage of the process, and how many stages will there be? Can any of the stages be combined and conducted in one day? All these questions should be considered before going to market to find a candidate. Again, you are competing for talent. If you want the best out there, get the basic easy stuff right first, and not being prepared will not cut it.

Memory Recall Versus Problem Solving Questions

We have already looked at this from an academic research perspective, observing the difference between situational and behavioral questions. For example, situational questions are: "We have this scenario at our company. Talk me through how you would deal with it?" Behavioral questions explore the candidate's past behavior and experiences with questions like, "Give me an example of a time when you experienced conflict with one of your team and how you resolved it?"

Neurologically, when given the opportunity to, we grow more in our areas of greater ability. Think for a moment about extremes like child music prodigies who get noticed aged four playing the piano. By age nine, they're reciting classical pieces on the piano as if they are a professional adult concert pianist. Or consider physicists who start out being great at math from a young age and grow to work as a professor at one of the world's great universities. Partly due to genetic inheritance and the uniqueness of our early life, our brains are wired uniquely. Individually we all have areas of our brains that are dense in synaptic connections and neurons, while other areas may be less developed. According to brain science, people grow far more neurons and synaptic connections where they already have the most neurons and synaptic connections. In other words, each brain grows most where it's already strongest. "As Joseph LeDoux, a professor of neuroscience at New York University, memorably described it, 'Added connections are therefore more like new buds on a branch rather than new branches'" (Buckingham and Goodall, 2019). Through this lens, learning looks a lot like building, little by little, on the unique patterns already there within you. Therefore, someone who happens to be great at memory recall may do very well in an interview, or at least they will recall real memories very well in an interview. That's not to say those recalled memories will be sufficiently impressive to convince the interviewer that they are the best candidate for the role.

On the other hand, someone who may have a far more developed creative area of the brain that is just not good at memory recall at all will potentially struggle with such questions. The caveat is that the creative person may be able to imagine and describe fictitious situations that supposedly occurred in their career. Such a "memory" may be too old to be challenged by anyone, but too good an answer to discount the candidate from the hiring process.

The other issue with memory recall questions is that the memories must be significant enough to be recalled. Otherwise, they may have been overwritten by other memories, much like you use the same hard drive in your computer to delete and replace information. Per Sederberg, a professor of psychology at Ohio State University, put it quite simply when he said, "A memory of a lifetime is like a big city, with many roads that lead there. We forget memories that are desert towns with only one road in. You want to have a lot of different ways to get to any individual memory" (Ohio State University, 2017).

Big events stick in our minds. If you're old enough to remember when the Twin Towers fell, you'll likely recall what you were doing that day. In the work context, you will probably be able to recall your biggest achievement, your biggest disappointment, the greatest boss you ever worked for, and the most stressful situation you've had to deal with at work. However, when a specific question is asked, such as, "Recall a time when you had to quickly change project priorities. What steps did you take to initiate change?" How do you respond when any such events may be so insignificant in your career that you can't remember? Behavioral competency questions could be renamed the "how good is your memory" part of the interview.

On the other hand, with problem-solving questions, where a hypothetical situation is proposed, and the candidate is asked how they would deal with that situation, the candidate is, of course, going to try and give their best answer. Their best answer may not accurately reflect what they would actually do. Instead, it may be what they believe the interviewer is looking for, based on a whole number of factors that lead the candidate to weigh up and guess their answer.

PROBLEM 3 - THE QUESTIONS

Interviewing in nearly all companies I've worked for or studied, many of which are Fortune 500's, is best described as chaotic guesswork. We've all read about the ridiculous questions that cannot possibly have any measurable outcome and the justifications for these questions, which are, in my view, even more ridiculous. We've already touched upon the over-reliance on competency questions and how they are essentially memory recall questions. What about different people in the interview process asking whatever questions they like and forming opinions largely based on their preconceived ideas? Furthermore, what about interviewers basing their decisions on many things other than the answers to their questions. The list goes on and on. It is chaotic guesswork.

Look online, and you will find no shortage of interview questions to test various aspects of a candidate's experience, performance, and style of engagement. On LinkedIn, there is a special guide with over 100 questions relating to various competencies. On Indeed.com, there are also numerous questions that you can pick out to test different categories. These guides remind me of some basic language learning books that give you a bunch of questions you can ask, but without any preparation for how the locals may respond in their given dialect and what that response tells you. Imagine yourself walking through the streets of Shanghai as an English-speaking tourist, and you've learned some of the basics, all gained from one of those little tourist language guide books. You barely learn "Turn left" and "turn right," and you've just asked a local for directions to the local bus station, hoping they are going to say in a robotic voice, like they're speaking to a three-year-old, "Go straight, then turn left, then turn right. Bus station." What they actually say, in their local dialect, at high speed, is:

"Ah, so you want to go to the bus station? I get it. So what you want to do is, walk over there to the traffic lights and take a left. About half a mile down that road, you'll see a gas station. When you get there, take your third left and keep walking until you get to a small shoe shop called Comfortable Feet. Just round the corner from there, you'll see the bus stop."

They say all that in Mandarin, and all you can say in return is, "Thank you." It's just useless having a set of questions when the answers aren't going to help you.

We've been asking the same old questions for years and getting the same old answers. The degree to which an interview question is relevant and measurable or susceptible to interviewer bias has rarely been questioned. People who haven't interviewed before tend to seek advice from HR or peers regarding which questions to ask, and those with many years of experience "just know what they're looking for," and have all their favorite questions ready to go anyway. Are these the right questions, though? Why do we believe these are the right questions? What do these questions tell you about the candidate and their ability to do a job? How is this answer useful? How can you measure the answers compared to other candidates' answers? Can the answers be objective enough to compare in a meaningful way? Do we even need to be able to compare and measure responses? These are difficult questions, and it's no wonder we haven't sought to tackle them and instead have chosen to revert to the same way we've always done it. If it's not broken, don't fix it, right? To believe it's not broken, or act like it's not broken, is not the lens through which to view this problem. What if it could be improved, and what if the candidate's experience could be better? Wouldn't you be curious to find out how? We're going to go on to the solution in Chapter 9, but for now, we need to get to the bottom of what is wrong with the questions we're asking today. This is a very complicated issue, and it's no surprise we continue to bury our heads in the sand and keep asking what we've always asked. To illustrate the complexity of the issues we're faced with, I've summarized below much of what is wrong with the questions we ask in interviews today:

• Interviewers aren't questioning what they're asking. If they were, we'd be asking different or fewer questions.

• The answers we get from the questions we're asking cannot be accurately measured or compared in most cases. Sometimes it's not necessary to measure, like when we're looking to build a story that we can then ask further questions about, for example. However, for the most part, like-for-like comparisons are difficult.

• For any qualitative answers, the interviewer will often base their opinion on the extent to which they agree with the candidate's opinion.

• For any quantitative answers, people can lie, and often, answers are impossible to fact check.

• For competency-based interviews that require memory recall, not everyone can remember every situation they're asked to recall an example about.

• For competency-based interviews, candidates can lie if they can't think of a real reason.

• For hypothetical-based interview questions, someone is responding about what they "would do in that situation." That's not to say they would do that, and again, they can lie about what they say they would do.

• Interviews are inevitably biased towards what the interviewer thinks they're looking for.

• Interviewers are often terrible at interviewing.

How can we unravel this mess and put it back together in a way that can better predict the outcome of interviews and get us closer to the truth in the first place? It's complicated, right? We have already established in Chapter 5 that between structured and unstructured interviews, structured interviews win hands down in the ability to lead to more consistent and predictable outcomes. That's not to say the outcomes are reliably predictable, but they're less unreliable than unstructured interviews. To recap on the difference: structured interviews follow a set structure with predetermined questions, typically asked and scored by more than one person on separate occasions. The theory is that if several different people ask the same questions and score them accordingly, there will be less bias towards or against a candidate, and the interviewers will be less likely to recruit versions of themselves or people they just happen to like. That bias is not completely eradicated with structured interviews, but it is minimized to a far greater extent than can be achieved by one person asking a bunch of random questions that follow no structure whatsoever. Therefore, it's safe to say that we can focus on structured interviews as the basis for problem identification and also as a basis to solve this problem, which we will do in Chapter 9.

(IN)COMPETENCY QUESTIONS

I haven't referred to these questions as competency questions because incompetence describes this line of questioning more accurately, in my opinion. According to the dictionary, incompetence is "The inability to do something successfully," and competency questions fail on so many levels to qualify candidates in an interview, hence why I refer to them here as incompetency questions. I should add that it's not the concept of understanding a candidate's level of competence through asking questions that I take issue with. Rather, it is the traditional behavioral competency-based questions that are the problem.

Figure 10: Job Ad From 1970

Behavioral competency interviews, as we have come to know them, were created in the 1970s. To put this in perspective, Figure 10 shows a job ad from the same decade. It reads, "Girls, you can be somebody. Doctors, lawyers, executives"…wait…"are looking for us to send them CTC secretaries… It's a great feeling, girls. You can be somebody who is really needed." Clearly, that's not a job ad that would go down well today, over fifty years later, yet we're trying to make our companies more diverse and inclusive using an interview method created in the sexist seventies.

Competence is the ability of an individual to do a job properly. Competencies in the workplace are meant to be a set of defined behaviors that provide a structured guide enabling the identification, evaluation, and development of the behaviors in individual employees. The term "competence" first appeared in an article by R.W. White in 1959 as a concept for performance motivation. Some scholars see competence as a combination of knowledge, skills, and behavior used to improve performance; or as the state or quality of being adequately or well qualified and having the ability to perform a specific role. For instance, management competency might include emotional intelligence and skills in influence and negotiation.

Competency questions, also referred to as behavioral questions, seek to elicit answers about how someone dealt with a particular situation in the past while at work. A popular framework for developing structured behavioral interview questions is the STAR method. STAR stands for "Situation, task, action, result." It was also created and first used in the 1970s. The basic premise of this model is:

· **Situation**: What was the situation the candidate was in? A question may begin with, "Tell me about a time...."

· **Task**: What was the task the candidate needed to accomplish? For example, "...when you were faced with multiple competing deadlines."

· **Action**: What were the actions the candidate took to accomplish this task? For example, "What did you do and...."

· **Result**: What were the results of these actions? For example, "...how did it turn out?"

Thus, the complete behavioral interview question presented to the candidate would read, "Tell me about a time when you were faced with multiple competing deadlines. What did you do, and how did it turn out?"

This STAR method, albeit very popular, is rendered useless by the underlying answers it seeks to find. Ask for examples, sure, but "Can you give me an example?" should follow from something they tell you about their experience. Asking for an example of a competency allows for the candidate to pick the best example from any job they've ever done. This does not imply the extent to which that person is generally competent in that regard.

For most general competencies, any candidate who has bothered to look up "competency questions" will have come up with a few examples, anticipating such questions. If asked to demonstrate one competence in one example out of a whole career, what does that tell you about the candidate? That they are abundant in that competency and that if they've been able to share an example, no matter how weak or insignificant, they "pass" that question? It's a ludicrously ineffective way to assess competencies.

The issue is that competencies are not normally demonstrated to any reliable degree in just one example. We have to look for patterns of competencies rather than just examples of them chosen randomly from any stage in their career. Getting a candidate to choose an example from some time in their career is too easy. We also have to make the interviews more engaging and better flowing, focusing on roles one by one so it's not entirely obvious to the candidates which competencies we're seeking to identify. I will come on to cover all of this in Chapter 9.

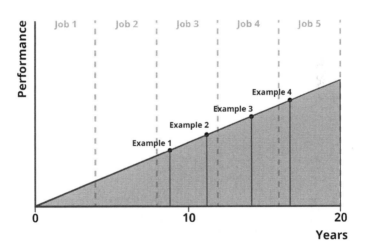

Figure 11: What Competency Interviews Believe They May Be Capturing

To illustrate, Figure 11 represents a hypothetical persons' career who has been working for twenty years, and at that point in their career, they are being interviewed for a new role. For the sake of simplicity, their twenty-year career has been broken up into five different jobs of equal tenure. What job this person does or what companies they worked for are unimportant to this illustration. It shows what someone conducting a competency interview may conclude they are observing. The dark area is an abstract representation of the perceived performance of the candidate over their career, according to the answers they are receiving to the competency questions. The interviewer picks a competency, asks for an example, and the candidate gives their best answer. These answers are plotted on the diagram as examples one, two, three, and four. Their position represents the time in the candidate's career that those examples came from and the assumed performance of the candidate, as graded by the interviewer, based on these examples.

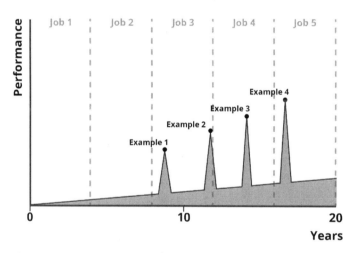

Figure 12: Everything That Is Wrong With Competency Interviews

What is often happening in competency interviews is that mediocre candidates whose actual performance, illustrated here by the shaded area in Figure 12, can give amazing examples because despite a mediocre career, they either have one good example of each competency from a whole twenty-year period, or they are just good at making things up, and therefore, give great answers. As the interviewer is skimming through a series of competency-based questions, they are not getting into enough detail about each of the roles to spot patterns of competence or lack thereof. Instead, they are forming opinions based on a series of great examples, which may not even be real. Worse still, they may be basing their view on a series of bad examples when a good candidate just hasn't been able to remember some of the unmemorable moments the interviewer is inquiring about.

Almost anyone in any profession could patch together an amazing history based on the few examples they may have or examples they completely make up. If all the interviewer is doing is targeting specific competencies and not diving deep into their story with very specific questions, key information will be missed, and worse still may end up with a misleading story. This problem is further exacerbated by the interviewer telling the candidate exactly what competency they're looking to find out about. The candidate then has a chance to assess what they believe the interviewer may be looking to hear and respond accordingly. This differs greatly from asking them questions that guide them deep into each role, where the interviewer is drawing informed conclusions about the presence of certain competencies, or not as the case may be.

Competency interviews have little to no requirement for real interviewing skills, certainly not as I would define them. I would define real interview skills as "The ability to direct a candidate through a series of related questions that seek to form as complete and honest a representation of a candidate's history as one can hope to achieve, given inherent interview limitations." The biggest inherent limitation of an interview is that the candidate can lie. Also, it's like meeting a potential partner for an hour and deciding at that moment if you're willing to spend the next two to five years with them. Not "maybe see them again," but make a commitment where you're going to be with them for eight hours a day, five days a week, potentially for years. That brings all kinds of pressure and expectations on both sides.

Short-term memory is stored sequentially, but long-term memory is stored and retrieved by association. This is why when you forget something, you try to mentally retrace your steps to spark that associative memory.

There's a model of long-term memory retrieval which started as the semantic network model (Quillian, 1967) and has evolved into various similar iterations, including the associative network model (Wickelgren, 1981). It proposes a logic-based structure of memory representation and retrieval. According to this theory, memory is a network of nodes or cognitive concepts like objects, events, and ideas that are interconnected by pathways. When someone is thinking about a node, it is "activated," and "excitation" spreads from that node along the pathways, activating other closely associated nodes.

Think about the word banana for a moment, which represents a node. When you focus on the word banana, your brain may start to think of words, concepts, places, or personal memories directly relating to the word banana. So you may think about the color yellow. That would be another node with a pathway between banana and yellow. You may think about a banana milkshake. That would be another node. You may think about when you last had a banana, which would be a personal memory, but still a node. So when the banana node is activated, it excites the pathways which, for you, hold the strongest links to that one node. Any associations encountered more frequently in your past are likely to be stronger, and the excitation process will illuminate these memories more strongly.

Once activated, a node retains the excitation as long as it is receiving attention, after which the excitation will dissipate. So, for example, let's say that when you thought about milkshakes in relation to the banana, you now start focusing on milkshakes. You're focusing on milkshakes now because it triggered a very strong memory from drinking a banana milkshake when you were last on holiday. The milkshake node now becomes your focus, and the branches from the banana start to fade, and in place, the focus on the milkshake is exciting other pathways to memories relating to that holiday. This is the excitation based on what you're focusing on coming into play.

How does this apply to interviewing? Well, let's take two different approaches to interviewing. The first approach is the competency interview, where a competency is selected, and one directed question is asked about that competency before jumping to the next question. The second approach is the Extraview interview, where a candidate's one and only life story is chronologically explored, bit by bit.

With the competency interview, we can forget about the aid of nodes and branches to help recollect information because we're attempting to spark memories in the brain using very unmemorable cues. If one's career was hypothetically made up of 1000 interconnected nodes, with competency interviews, we would go from asking about node number 94 to then asking about node number 794, before coming back to ask about node number 217, before skipping to node 857, and so on. We don't have the benefit of proximity between nodes in order to aid in the memory recall process by the excitation of strongly connected nodes. These memories we're being asked to recollect are so faint that we can't even recall the node, never mind the associated pathways and nodes. With the Extraview interview method, we're starting at node one and working through to node 1000. In doing so, we are helping the candidate to fill in all of the blanks by exciting the nodes in the closest proximity.

Example

If the competency interviewer was interested in finding out about a time when a leader had to manage a difficult employee and how they dealt with it, that candidate has to mentally trudge through an index of 1000 hypothetical nodes from their career, which are not all indexed or labeled in a way that makes them easy to recall based on such a cue. They may or may not identify an example in time, and even if they do, the pressure on them will build as they sit there staring into space, trying to recollect such an unmemorable event.

Instead, let's consider the Extraview method, where the candidate is taken chronologically through their career with macro and micro questions helping them navigate from node to node. In that conversation, each question will excite the pathways deeper into each previous role, so a complete story is accessed, and along with it, anecdotes of situations with difficult employees.

You can do this exercise yourself. If I were to ask you where you were working on December 11th, 2018, how would your brain process that? Would it immediately try and recollect where you were on December 11th, or would it instead go, "I left Coutts in summer 2019 and had been there for three years, so I was at Coutts," or something like that? As soon as I then ask you to tell me about the best and worst hires you made while there, you'll immediately start recalling people in your mind. You won't remember everyone that worked for you, but you'll be able to rank order the best and worst, at least partially. Memories will start to flood in as you see images of these people in your head. You then index the best and worst people you hired. When the interviewer then asks you to tell you some more about the worst hire, you then start to recollect some of the stories. As you start filtering how you're going to present those stories, the memories keep coming. You present your story in the best light possible. The interviewer then asks how things ended with the candidate who really let you down. You then immediately recall the story of how that all ended because you've built up several mental cues that brought the story into full resolution.

With the competency interviewer, they may not even have got to this particular story as they'd given the candidate carte blanche to choose any moment from their whole career. However, with the Extraview method, for each role, this depth of storytelling is prompted by the structure and proximity of the questions. Therefore, by the end of the interview, the interviewer has gathered a large catalog of telling anecdotes that helps them form a view about how the candidate deals with difficult employee engagements at each stage of their career, rather than just having one example, which may be too insignificant to even recall as in the case of the competency interview.

The conclusion is that if you conduct competency interviews, you just allow the candidate to dip in and out of their career history at will, choosing the greatest moments or making the moments up. The bottom line is candidates have one history and one story. To get the best from candidates and to give them the best opportunity to present themselves fully and fairly, you have to get very deep and specific about each role. It helps them remember through the association of facts, and it will help the interviewer to spot trait patterns and reach a more informed conclusion about their candidacy. We will revisit this when reviewing the solution in Chapter 9.

To give you a sense of how bad this behavioral interview epidemic is, here are some guidelines taken directly from the Society For Human Resource Management (SHRM), the largest membership organization of its kind in the world, with a reported 300,000 members in 165 countries. For competency-based questions, they suggest having a five-point Likert scale, with the definition of each number being broadly described below:

"**5- Far Exceeds Requirements:** Perfect answer. Demonstrates competency accurately, consistently, and independently. All points were relevant. All good examples.

4- Exceeds Requirements: Demonstrates competency accurately and consistently in most situations with minimal guidance. Many good examples.

3- Meets Requirements: Demonstrates competency accurately and consistently on familiar procedures and needs supervisor guidance for new skills. Some good examples.

2- Below Requirements: Demonstrates competency inconsistently, even with repeated instruction or guidance. Few good examples.

1- Significant Gap: Fails to demonstrate competency regardless of any guidance provided. No good examples."

Below are four examples of their questions, along with some commentary on why I find them falling short of being fit for purpose.

"**1. Describe a time when you needed to work as part of a team on a project or initiative. What was your role on the team, and what actions did you take to contribute to the team in that role?**

Rating Scale: Candidate's response indicates that in a similar situation, he or she could be expected...

1 - To fail to offer information about his/her part on the team.

2 -

3 - To offer advice on various pieces of the project or initiative.

4-

5 - To discuss contributions with the team and come to a consensus on the best approach to meet all needs."

Comment: As previously mentioned, one of the problems with nearly all competency questions, for me, is that they're too specific. Sure, being specific about experience is a good thing, but only when there's a journey in the conversation from the big picture to the specific question. The issue with this, and nearly all competency questions as we've come to understand them, is that they are part of a battery of questions that suffocates the interview format of any conversational direction that would make life for everyone involved a little more interesting and productive. With this question, the interviewer assesses the candidate's ability to work in a team or lead a team, and they ask the candidate to pick one example. So based on this one example, is the interviewer expected to conclude that this is how that person works in teams in general? They may have ten, twenty, or thirty years of experience. Getting this granular is just a complete miss regarding the bigger picture.

The worst thing about this question is the definitions in the rating scale. It's so prescriptive that someone can either get a one for failing to offer any information at all, to a five, which states, "To discuss contributions with the team and come to a consensus on the best approach to meet all needs." What if their role on the team was not to reach a consensus but to lead and drive change, or something that didn't require reaching a consensus? What if their role on the team wasn't a leader, and the leader had a particularly autocratic leadership style, which is part of the reason the candidate is looking to move? Do they fail this question because they weren't allowed to contribute much to the team discussion? Are they no longer considered a good team player because their answer wasn't sufficient enough?

How could this question be better posed? Well, it all depends on the context, the seniority of the candidate, the role they're interviewing for, and the roles they've been doing. That's another reason why these specific behavioral questions don't work. If you're going to design a set of interview questions that will be reused across many different roles that cover broad terms like "team contribution," the questions have to start more widely. In Chapter 9, we'll look at how you get better results with a more engaging interview process by breaking it down into facts and stories, with a model that favors competence over experience. The short answer is, rather than asking about one example and making an assessment on that basis, the interviewer should ask general questions about each role. Then they should go deeper with other questions that help to identify patterns of behaviors, not just single instances.

"2. Give an example of a time when you had to change project priorities quickly. What steps did you take to initiate change?

Rating Scale: Candidate's response indicates that in a similar situation, he or she could be expected...

1 - To be too busy to initiate change.

2 -

3 - To change what s/he was doing to address the immediate need.

4-

5 - To seek out relevant stakeholders to assist in change initiation and priority order."

Comment: I assume this question aims to seek out information about how someone initiates change, how responsive they are, and how they mobilize other people in the organization to impact change. One can assume from the rating scale that if, according to this prescriptive model, the candidate tells a story about how they sought "out relevant stakeholders to assist in change initiation," they've done really well. What if the candidate is describing a situation where it sounds like the change in priorities was initiated because the original priorities were due to poor judgment on their part? Does the interviewer score them a five because they were correct to shift their priorities, even though it was from previously miscalculated priorities on their part? This is what I mean about the questions being too specific. They're so specific that the answers may satisfy the rating scale, but they don't paint a fair picture, for good or bad, about the underlying competence they're trying to assess.

"3. Think of a time when you had to build credibility with stakeholders. What actions did you take?

Rating Scale: Candidate's response indicates that in a similar situation, he or she could be expected...

1 - To fail to take action.

2 -

3 - To answer stakeholder questions and provide background information.

4-

5 - To identify and assist in implementing solutions to help the organiza-

tion become more effective."

Comment: The underlying question is, "How do you build credibility with stakeholders?" An interviewee scores top marks here by showing that in a similar situation, they "could be expected to identify and assist in implementing solutions to help the organization become more effective." Really? What is the difference between scoring a three and scoring a five here? By the looks of the grading system, the difference is influence. If they score a three, they simply developed their credibility to the point where the stakeholders will listen to what they have to say, whereas, with a five, they will be allowed to help implement solutions. What's worse, failing to take action (1) or taking action that is clearly so bad that it's not acted upon (3)? One could argue the latter is worse. At least the person who scored a 1 knew just to stay quiet. Because they stayed quiet, does that mean they will fail the test for building stakeholder credibility?

"4. Think about a time when you have encountered an ineffective process or transaction. What steps did you take following this discovery?

Rating Scale: Candidate's response indicates that in a similar situation, he or she could be expected...

1 - To ignore the problem.

2 -

3 - To analyze the process internally.

4-

5 - To investigate and make recommendations based on industry standards."

Comment: I assume this question touches upon integrity and initiative. This is one of those questions that is so specific, yet the incident could have been so insignificant that it may just not be remembered. As previously mentioned, stronger memories form deeper neural pathways and thus can be remembered more readily than those memories that get overwritten by other newer memories due to "lack of disk space." What if the memory was so insignificant that the interviewee simply couldn't recall it? Will the candidate be marked down even though all of their experience and growth, as evidenced by their resume and stories they've been sharing, tell you they hold integrity in the highest regard and readily demonstrate taking initiative?

In the above examples, I didn't even mention that people can lie and make up stories to suit the question. Some may think, "Well, they can follow up with references and find out from other people." Really? You're going to fact-check all the answers to 50 different questions, some of which ask about experiences recalled from ten years ago when a minor conflict was resolved because of their actions. Do you think their boss is going to recall those instances? Besides, it doesn't matter. The point is, this is a super inefficient, flawed, and frankly dull way to interview people. These examples are from the largest HR membership organization in the world. This is not a point to ridicule SHRM, but rather it best represents the fact that we continue to do what we've always done and aren't asking enough questions about the questions we're asking.

In my opinion, the all-time worst interview questions are, "What are your strengths?" and "what are your weaknesses?" These questions are still being asked. What does the interviewer do with the answers to these questions? Do they collate them and compare the lies people put forward as their weaknesses to see who has the most manageable weaknesses? Are they scored based on merit and imagination? How do they discern a candidate's ability to do a job by asking such a question? What do they hope to do with the candidate's weaknesses? How do they grade the extent to which a weakness will be an insurmountable challenge compared to someone else's weakness? Can they even rely on a candidate to tell them where they fall short? Have you, as an interviewer, ever stopped and thought about these questions in depth?

All too often, we get a trained answer that does not impact the process. Are interviewers expecting to hear the truth like, "My weakness is getting up in the morning. That's why I was fired. I lost count of the times I didn't make it in before 11 a.m. My strength is recognizing my weaknesses, although I'd say another weakness is not taking action to remedy my weaknesses. This is something I'd work on if I were hired, but until I am, I am determined to do nothing about it. Oh, that's another strength – determination. Can I use that one instead? I'm determined to overcome my weaknesses after I start work. There you go. Good, right?"

Will the answers to such questions be a pass or a fail? What are the criteria for passing and failing? Your own opinion as to what is a good strength and a bad weakness, or maybe how good or bad you believe their answer is compared to the other candidates? This does nothing to qualify a candidate in or out. Sure, those who fail may not be put forward, but people at the mid to senior level don't typically fail such questions. These are interview questions that, if someone is taking any time to prepare for the interview, they will have practiced their answers and be ready for them.

One of the problems is that the candidate is asked to provide an answer to a question that the interviewer cannot fact-check, so what is the best answer to give? What is the interviewer looking to hear? As I mentioned previously, a partner from a global investment bank, who was a global HR divisional leader, asked these questions in the 7th round of a 13 round interview process. She actually asked, "So what are your strengths, and tell me a bit about your weaknesses?" When I heard this, I just thought, "Here is someone who is almost certainly earning one million dollars or more per year, tasked with running the people organization of part of an investment bank, and they're taking time out of their busy day to interview a candidate, and this is all they've got?" I would have hoped to have been more inspired by such a senior person, a leader in the industry of HR, who I would have assumed would be asking some very challenging questions. This is just one example.

Some people who believe these are good questions will probably say, "It tests their self-awareness and brings to light areas they can improve, and it allows them to share their plan of action to combat their weaknesses." Or they may say, "In highlighting their weaknesses, we can put together a personal development plan for those with great strengths but just have one or two areas for development." I don't believe for a moment that this is the best test for self-awareness or that this question is simply being asked to put together a great development plan. It's asked because they haven't thought through the whole interview, and these are the questions they've always asked, and the team is great, so "we must be doing something right." Well, what if you can be doing better?

How does that conversation even go when they give you a 'perfect answer'? The candidate says, "I'm really good at leadership and winning the hearts and minds of the people and driving change that leads to better productivity and customer service. My weakness is I'm really disorganized, but I have a fantastic secretary who keeps me right." What does the interviewer do with that information? Run to their colleague after the interview, all excited, and say, "Claire, listen, you're not going to believe this. I've found the perfect candidate. You know we were looking for a change agent who could really charge up the team and deliver better customer service? He said almost these words. He even said 'change.' Can you believe it? He's our guy. And guess what? His only weakness is that he's disorganized. Jane is a fantastic assistant; she can totally take care of him. Let's get an offer out." Now I can't imagine this has ever happened, but that is how silly these questions are, in my opinion. Please, no more strengths and weaknesses questions. "But what else are we going to ask?" We'll come to this in Chapter 9.

PROBLEM 4 - HOW WE JUDGE THE ANSWERS

Many years ago when I worked for a recruiting company, I was asked to get involved in recruiting recruiters for our team. My boss would come out of the interview room, call me over, and often say something like, "I really like this guy. Have a chat with him and see what you think?" So first of all, I already know he really likes him. How am I now meant to undertake an interview with a candidate that I know is being favored by my boss? Is it my role to come back to him and confirm I also like him so as not to upset my boss, or is it the case that my boss is testing me and wants to hear what I really think? I always assumed it was the former, which is not a great position to be in, as I either have to like the candidate and agree, or probably, just to be safe, dislike the candidate yet still agree. In the end, I would always give an honest opinion. Either way, there was never any formalized way to evaluate. It was just, "See if you like the guy?" What does that even mean? Do I interpret what that means based on my understanding of the word "like"? Do I assume he means that I should assess whether he'll be a good culture fit, whether he's an ethical recruiter, whether he's a very high-performing recruiter, or a combination of all of these?

From my experience working with Fortune 500 companies, it is certainly more structured than it was back in my early recruitment days. Nevertheless, a lot of the structure seems to be for structure's sake itself, rather than any well-considered purposeful process where questions have been well thought through, and objective opinions can be compared fairly. Anyone responsible for interviewing in any capacity really only needs to sit down and think through their process, if there is one, and for each question, they typically use, ask: "Why am I asking this? Is there a better question to ask? What am I going to do with the answers I'm given? How will I compare these answers to the answers I get from other candidates?" If you can do so in a truly objective way, you may find yourself doing some interview question spring cleaning.

Beyond the limitations of interviewers and the traditional competency-based approach to questions, there is another issue to consider. What may appear to be poor or wrong answers may not always be the smoking gun you were looking for. For example, if someone is honest enough to tell you they were once fired, what does that actually tell you? They're susceptible to getting fired and should be overlooked for any role moving forward? Don't be so quick to judge. Steve Jobs was fired from Apple in 1985, only to start another company that was eventually bought by Apple, and he ended up back in the driving seat in 1997. He sold a large amount of stock in 1997, so much so that Apple's price dropped by 12%, and he convinced the board to fire the then CEO and hire him into that position. Jamie Dimon, the CEO of J.P. Morgan since 2005, was fired from his job at Citi by the Chairman and CEO at the time, Sandy Weill. In an interview with The New York Times in 2010, Sandy is reported to have said that he fired Jamie because he was too ambitious and wanted the CEO role, but Sandy wasn't ready to step down. In 2019, Steve Easterbrook, the CEO of McDonald's, was fired for breaking company rules by having a relationship with another staff member. In his four-year tenure, McDonald's stock price doubled. Does that mean he'll never work again, or should not be selected for any future leadership role?

He broke the rules, granted, but he will undoubtedly learn from this lesson.

The point is, even when we get the answers we may have been looking for but perhaps didn't want to hear, we can't just take every small detail and warp it into a negative viewpoint. In situations like these, the context and bigger picture must be considered. This is why it truly is a skill to interview someone. First of all, you have to get beyond the lies and the half-truths, but then you need to know what to do with the information when you get it because it's just not as straightforward as putting a black mark against their name. It has to be viewed with perspective and the bigger picture; otherwise, great candidates may fall through the cracks.

PROBLEM 5 – IS EXPERIENCE EVEN IMPORTANT?

In an interview with Y Incubator, the very successful startup accelerator investment company, Mark Zuckerberg was asked, "How do you assess someone's raw talent?" His response: "I think what's important is not to believe that someone has to have specifically done the job that they're going to do in order to do it well" (Y Incubator, 2016).

Throughout my career, interviewers often say that a candidate didn't have the right experience. Most often, that's perfectly valid feedback, but it depends on the context. You can't hire a theater nurse to do heart surgery any more than you can hire a burger flipper at McDonald's to work in a Michelin star restaurant, certainly not without a significant amount of training. This would be technical training, though. However, when it comes to leadership or management roles, while experience in leading or managing is important, the product or service that the company provides is less important. I've had firsthand experience of a client in a global bank, specifically wanting to hire someone with no banking experience. This was a supply chain finance leadership role. What the person does is less relevant, but needless to say, they wanted someone to come from the client-side outside of banking, who truly understood the client, and it turned out to be a great strategy for them. Another example, again in banking, but this time in technology. Not a hire I had anything to do with, but one of the big investment banks hired a CIO

THE CEO'S GREATEST ASSET

from the aerospace industry. She had no experience in banking, but she was a highly competent leader.

There is a valid argument for hiring people without experience but with competence in certain cases. The clearest example of this is in hiring graduates. Usually, they have no experience in the relevant field, aside from perhaps an internship, yet they get hired for their competence, intelligence, and how they have performed in their life to date. High-performing individuals are high-performing individuals. If people can demonstrate emotional and intellectual intelligence with patterns of competence being evident, and if they can demonstrate that they're a high-performing individual in many other ways, experience becomes less of a necessity. This also feeds in well to the need to hire a diverse slate of candidates. People with different experiences can often bring a new approach or different viewpoint on things. Of course, from a technical perspective, you cannot hire, for example, someone with only Python coding experience to code in a completely different language, but we're not discussing the technical aspect of roles here. This is leadership or management hiring. Roles that require people to come in, formulate a strategy, get the right people on board, execute, and deliver on goals. People bringing fresh ideas to the table with different backgrounds can add tremendous value and shouldn't always be overlooked in favor of "experience."

Furthermore, someone can have experience in a particular role, but that doesn't always make them better than someone with no experience in that particular role. Someone who is sufficiently intelligent and competent can do very well in a role where that person has no experience. We see this with entrepreneurs all the time. Look at Mark Zuckerberg. Would anyone in the world have hired him while he was still at Harvard to become the CEO of a social media company? No way. But he's smart and competent, and it's an understatement to say he succeeded in that role. Someone with lots of experience in a particular role with outstanding performance didn't get there without being intelligent and competent.

So we have to keep an open mind when hiring new managers and leaders. Experience doesn't always equate to performance, not least because someone who has done the exact role before may not be as motivated as someone who may see it as a fresh challenge. The suggestion here is not to go out and hire someone who's been running a chocolate factory to be a regional director for a luxury clothing brand, but rather industries where there may be broader synergies. Someone who has been a regional director for a luxury watch brand, for example, could make a great director for a clothing brand. Their customers are very similar, it's retail, the team dynamics are the same, and the overall structure of the business with the supply chain and so on will be very similar. In this instance, we need to keep an open mind and not discount a luxury watch director because they don't have fashion experience. Bringing experience from related industries but with different products potentially gives the candidate a significant enough career change to be exciting again, without it being so different that the candidate and the hiring company are at risk.

PROBLEM 6 – INFLUENCING OTHERS DURING THE PROCESS

If you're the final decision maker in an interview process, it goes without saying that you will have a degree of influence over others during the process. A key mistake in the interview process is having debriefs after every interview. Of course, you have to be able to share some opinions as otherwise, several different people will be interviewing terrible candidates when they could have been excluded from the process after the first interview. That communication should only really be, "I think we should progress this candidate to the next phase," or not, as the case may be. Any discussion about why they're great or what was on their scorecard will only influence any future interviewer, for good or bad.

Also, you may want to communicate with other interviewers areas of questioning you would like them to pursue if you spotted something that requires further investigation or a second opinion. However, sharing scorecards and deep detail about ratings during the process does not help minimize candidate bias or maximize a productive candidate discussion and debrief. In Chapter 9, you will read about a process that is designed to minimize unnecessary influencing, where scorecards are submitted as close to anonymously as the hiring process allows, so a final report is created, ready to share with the key decision-makers who will be responsible for making or signing off on the hire.

PROBLEM 7 – REFERENCE CHECKING

It may be a stretch to refer to reference checking as one of the seven problems. You should be doing background checking and reference checking, but this is more of a cautionary note. For me, taking references is a bit like thinking of marrying someone and then getting that person's ex to give a reference to help you decide whether you will marry them or not. What if their ex left them, and it wasn't their decision or choice for the partner to leave? What if their ex-partner had been the most amazing partner to them, but because of their decision to move on, the ex turned sour and couldn't utter a positive word about them even if they were paid to? On the other hand, what if they are still the best of friends and got on well, but the potential new partner was just too unhinged for the ex to see a lifelong romantic future together? Perhaps the ex couldn't deal with them anymore but wanted them to be happy, so the ex gave a good reference.

Many years ago, while recruiting in Canada, I was advised that when interviewing, I should ask for the names of every manager, and importantly, I should get them to spell the name. Asking them to spell the name was supposed to strike the fear of God into the candidate so they would feel obliged to tell the truth as they "knew it was going to come out anyway" when the interviewer would follow up and call the referees. At the time, I just thought, "This is the kind of transparent amateur approach that would work on five-year-old kids when you tell them they have to be honest because if they don't, the mattress monsters will bite them in their sleep." Besides, even if the interviewer does follow through and call all these references, let's think about how that process will go. Assumingly in this scenario, the candidate gives the interviewer the name of their previous bosses, and perhaps the interviewer even asks to set up the call. If I'm the candidate, I'm immediately going to email all of the referees with something like:

"Hey, John,

Long-time no speak. In checking your LinkedIn profile, it seems you're doing great – congratulations on your progress there. I'm currently in the running for this great new role, and they'd like to follow up on references with all my old bosses. Sarah Davies will be calling you sometime on Thursday, so I just wanted to give you the heads-up.

It will be great if we can connect before the call, but in case you don't have time, to jog your memory, all they know from me is that I was the Sales Director there and that I had a team of 20 people when I joined, 30 when I left, and that I grew the revenues by 180% in my three years there. I'm not even sure if they will ask anything else, but I really want this role, so I'd appreciate any positive words you may have to say.

Best regards,

Gavin"

The whole process of setting up reference calls and having the chance to prep referees can invalidate the whole interview process, or certainly the reference checking part of it. The chances are it's going to provide nothing meaningful to the process. I know that when I get calls to reference people who have worked for me over the years, I never give a bad reference. To be fair, I've never had someone work for me who got fired for stealing or any criminal activity, so I haven't had to contemplate such a situation. However, I've had people working for me who I fired or weren't up to par. For the most part, people who have worked for me in the past have either been great, and we get on well, and I wish them well, or they didn't do so well, and it didn't work out, but I still wish them well and want them to succeed in life. I remember a time in 2003 when I fired someone for under-performance, and it was clear to me a couple of weeks after inheriting her as part of a new team that she just wasn't going to work out. It was a terrible experience having to fire her as she burst into tears and acted like her life was over. I remember about three years later, I received a LinkedIn message from her, saying along the lines of, "You told me this wouldn't be for me, but I've been happy working for this company for three years, and I've done really well." I couldn't have been happier for her. Her email probably wasn't intended to make me happy, but it genuinely did. It was a good person who wasn't lazy, and things just weren't going to work out for her at this company, but she did well elsewhere.

Also, there are situations in life that affect people and their performance. Someone close to an employee could die, or perhaps they could be going through a terrible divorce, which renders them partially useless in the workplace for an undefined period. I've experienced such situations with people that have worked for me. One in particular that I remember had gone completely off the rails after a family bereavement. He was given as much time as he needed before actually starting back. After a couple of months, he came back too soon, then started being late all the time, calling up drunk, saying he was sick and just unable to hold down the job. In the end, after a long period, he was fired for one too many incidents that couldn't be tolerated in the workplace. He then went on to take the time out that he needed before going elsewhere to work. Knowing that he'd sorted himself out, there's no way I would have given him a bad reference upon his return to work, despite his terrible performance for many months.

So with references, you have to follow them up, and of course, you want to find out as much information as possible. However, references are just another opinion about how someone has done in their career. Furthermore, that opinion may be heavily influenced by the extent to which the referee had a positive working relationship with the candidate, or not as the case may be. If someone has been an absolute rock star their whole career, but one referee gives a bad reference from a few years back because they didn't get on so well, what will you do with that information? Pass on the candidate because Johnny McSomeone said he didn't think he'd be good at the role? Sure, investigate further, but just as we look for patterns of success through the Extraview method of interviewing, rather than single instance competency questions, it should be patterns of negativity rather than single instances that warrant a pass on a candidate, except in exceptional circumstances.

In my experience, the most useful references have come from people who have worked with the candidate in the past, with the reference being sourced confidentially through people in my network. It is certainly the case that the opinions of referees handpicked by the candidate should be considered with as much credibility as a four-year-old's response to the question about when quantum computing will render binary encryption useless. With a properly constructed interview process, with built-in fact-checking and cross-referencing, and with observations about significant patterns of success and progress being noted, references should be weighed up accordingly and with a degree of caution.

CONCLUSION

With all of the issues: the interviewer, the structure, the questions, how we judge the answers, whether experience is even important, influencing others during the process, and reference checking, it is clear that there's a lot of work we have to do to improve the whole interview process and experience. It is also clear that it's just a very complicated set of problems. In my observations of working with many companies over the past twenty years, I believe we tend to overthink the process and over-interview. I believe this happens because we don't fundamentally trust the process, and deep down, we know that we don't really have a good grasp on how this process should work. If we did, we wouldn't keep hearing about all of the bizarre questions. We certainly wouldn't just continue to rely on the very shallow and useless competency-based questions that typically form part of the HR interview in larger companies.

Ultimately, interviewing is a process to try and learn as much about a candidate in a short time, seeking to predict how well they may do compared to other candidates for a given role. I don't think we have to make it as complicated as we have been, and for sure, we need to be stopping, taking a step back, and asking a series of questions about our interview process:

1. Are the hiring managers trained to interview people in terms of selling the company, the role, and qualifying candidates based on pre-agreed criteria?

2. Are the questions we're asking fit for purpose, and if so, what purpose

do they serve?

3. Does our interview process have mechanisms in place to minimize the potential for candidates lying and for hiring managers to make as unbiased decisions as possible, given the inherent limitations?

4. Is the candidate experience going to be optimized by the structure of our interview process?

I haven't had an opportunity to analyze all Fortune 500 companies and others, but I am certain that all companies will fail to answer one or more of these questions. I strongly believe they'll all fail at the first question. If you think your company is the exception, try asking your colleagues some of the questions outlined at the beginning of this chapter and see if you're happy with the answers. If you're not, don't worry, as the remaining chapters will help give you some structure to get closer to the perfect interview process, or at least a version of one that is closer than you may be today.

WHAT TO LOOK FOR - THE BREMNUS MODEL

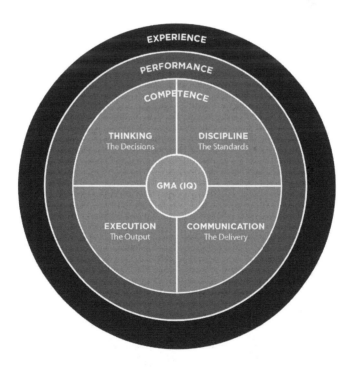

Figure 13: The Bremnus Leadership Model Assessment Considerations

Figure 13 summarizes the foundations of what we should be looking to assess during leadership candidate interviews. This has been refined over eight years with 1727 specific interviews and combining this experience with all of the academic research summarized in the science section. This model states that at the core of any good leader is strong general mental ability (GMA), which we covered in the science section. Then we have the competencies or key success factors that make a great leader we should look out for as we interview. These have been condensed and broken down into the actions a leader takes in approaching everything they do: the decisions they make, the standards they keep, the output, and how it's delivered or communicated. These success factors and the extent to which a leader demonstrates them drive performance, which, over time, I argue below, is of greater importance than the final ring in this diagram: experience. As I previously wrote, experience is, in my view, a misunderstood necessity when identifying and qualifying good candidates. Just because a candidate has more experience, it does not necessarily mean they will perform better. For me, patterns and evidence of performance are far more important than experience. There are some important caveats to this statement, which I will address later, but in essence, performance is closer to the core of this model than experience for a reason.

GMA, PERFORMANCE, AND EXPERIENCE

To recap, it's been shown that people with high cognitive ability are better at problem-solving, are more trainable, and, therefore, can progress quicker. Across the board, they are better equipped to be effective contributors to achieving company goals. I'll return to the competence part following this section as there's a lot to discuss.

Regarding performance and experience, I already touched on the fact that, in my opinion, performance is more important than experience. There are two main caveats to this statement. Firstly the seniority cannot be more than one level down from the level of seniority of the job. For example, a high-performing director of operations could step up into a COO role, but someone reporting to that director, like an operations manager, would not qualify. In this case, the performance versus experience argument suggests that you may want to consider a high-performing director of operations over someone who has been in a COO role for years but hasn't stood out performance-wise. The second caveat is for roles with very specific technical expertise, where clearly experience is a lead factor in a hiring decision.

This hypothesis relates to academic findings that link IQ to general mental ability and how those who are good at certain cognitive tasks tend to be good at all cognitive tasks. In the science section, we learned about the studies done in the early part of the last century where it was found in studying school kids that those who were gifted academically seemed to do well across a large number of subjects. I've observed the same phenomenon in twenty years of studying executive performance and interviewing many senior candidates. This has especially been evident in the financial services sector, where I focused a large part of my work. Large prestigious, well-known financial institutions, whether a bank, an asset manager, a hedge fund, or others, typically hire the best candidates from the best universities. To get into the best universities these days, it's not enough for candidates to only be gifted and hard working from an academic standpoint. They have to excel in other areas too. Often it may be sport, music, or other endeavors. The point is that they have come through quite a rigorous selection process by the time they are hired into a bank on a graduate scheme. These people typically have no banking experience other than perhaps an internship over the previous summer. However, the banks don't fall apart and implode because they've just hired thousands of graduates who don't know what they're doing. These people are highly trainable, as evidenced by their academic qualifications, and they go on, for the most part, to perform really well.

The issue for them is that to then climb the career ladder; they're now competing with the best high school candidates who went to the best universities, who got onto the best grad programs, who are now up for a promotion competing against the best of the best people at their level. This intense competition continues until they're deep into the organization, having reached the lofty heights of managing director or partner, depending on how the given institution labels its most senior positions. They're then in a position where they may be rotated around the bank, in different divisions, different countries, different regions, in different roles, to then prepare the best of the best for the C-Suite roles – CEO, COO, CFO, CHRO, or whatever it may be.

This is one great example to illustrate that performance is more important than experience. This doesn't relate to technical positions. You can't hire a building architect to go into a software architect position. You're not going to hire a regional retail director to lead a hedge fund. You're not going to hire a graduate who, on their first day, will be running a team of 1000 people. However, within a framework of like for like competence, it has been shown, for example, that a CIO of an aerospace company can become the CIO and COO of a global bank.

In PWC's 22nd Annual Global CEO Survey, published in 2019, and put together from 1,378 CEO interviews conducted in late 2018, one of the questions they asked was, "Which of these is the most important to close a potential skills gap in your organization?" 14% of respondents chose the answer, "Hiring from competitors," whereas 18% of respondents chose the answer, "Hiring from outside the industry." Now, granted, we don't know the exact details of the skill-sets being referred to, but clearly, an appetite exists for going outside of the industry and bringing in different people to help innovate and affect change. Incidentally, the most important factor identified was "Significant retraining/upskilling," which 46% of the respondents chose.

Where a different lens may have a positive impact or drive change in a slightly different direction, this is where performance is more important than experience. This fact really cannot be overlooked. In today's competitive corporate environment, where status quo management will not suffice when your competitors are innovating and trying new things, you must consider and think hard about what is important. Do you really want a candidate who has done this very job already for the past five years, who will have ingrained beliefs about how it should be done, and who frankly may find doing the same thing at a different company boring? Or do you want to consider someone who has demonstrated time and time again the competence to lead yet will be energized by the new challenge and will inject energy into the team and the culture by taking this on? So, whenever you hear, "Yeah, but they don't have experience in.....," really stop and think about whether that's a bad thing. Perhaps it may be an advantage, assuming that individual has demonstrated strong performance levels in their life and career to date.

There's another great example, referenced in Harvard Business Review (2016), which reads:

"Take Tom Murphy, former CEO of Capital Cities/ABC, and the late Jim Burke, former CEO of Johnson & Johnson, who tapped Lou Gerstner to take the helm of IBM in 1993. IBM was failing at the time, and the outgoing CEO had already announced its imminent breakup. Directors Murphy and Burke spent a month visiting customers and industry experts worldwide, listening to their issues to better understand what was happening externally. What they learned convinced them that the company's problems were more business-oriented than technological. They didn't rule out CEO candidates from the tech industry, but they saw that tech company experience was not the most important thing. As the business press hotly debated which technologist the board would ultimately choose—a *New York Times* article titled 'Help Wanted: Computer Skills a Must' named John Sculley from Apple, Ben Rosen from Compaq, and George Fisher from Motorola as likely options—the IBM directors turned elsewhere. The pivot they were looking for was a mix of proven business acumen, customer orientation, and the ability to make a large organization more decisive and accountable.

The position was first offered to Jack Welch, the celebrated CEO of GE, whose business acumen and ability to deliver results were legendary. When he declined, they asked if GE would buy IBM. No again. Then they turned to Larry Bossidy, a Welch disciple who had demonstrated the skills they sought as vice chair at GE and as head of AlliedSignal. After he rejected them, they reached out to Gerstner, a marketing whiz who had delivered a decade of profitable growth at American Express. Having left Amex when he hit a ceiling there and not quite liking his new post as CEO of RJR Nabisco, Gerstner was game for the challenge. And as history shows, he rose to it."

There have been many examples of this ever since, where competence and delivery experience in other areas or sectors have trumped the detailed technical experience we are so often compelled to pursue as it seems logical to do so; perhaps not anymore.

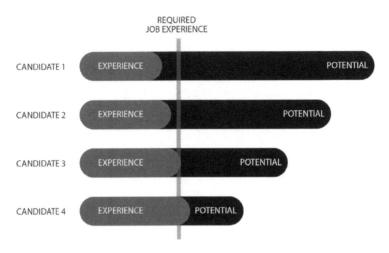

Figure 14 – Hiring For Potential

Figure 14 illustrates the conundrum we would face if we knew how much potential people had. Would we hire the person with the most experience that could do this job in their sleep, candidate 4, or do we hire the one with the least experience, but still enough to do the job, who has the most potential? Who would you hire if you knew how much potential they had? How can we even account for potential? In truth, we can't, but the clues are there.

High-performing individuals will perform highly across many domains. It does depend on many factors, of course, but if you only focus on hiring for the job and the experience, you may miss the chance to hire for potential. The closest we can get to hiring for potential is hiring those who have demonstrated time and time again the ability to outperform their relative peers. We believe we know a superstar candidate when we see one, but what about the superstar candidates that haven't yet shown their full potential? For graduate roles, that's a very tough call to make as there is little to go on.

However, once they're at the leadership level, there will be an obvious track record of progress to help you decide what their potential may be.

I believe that if more companies were focused more broadly on the evidence of performance rather than experience in certain sectors or functions, it would also be a strong catalyst for wider diversity considerations. Opening up the potential talent pool to those who have demonstrated a lifetime of delivering and performing, who have the right competencies but perhaps not the exact experience, will mean companies can think more broadly when it comes to diversity.

THE BREMNUS LEADERSHIP SUCCESS MODEL

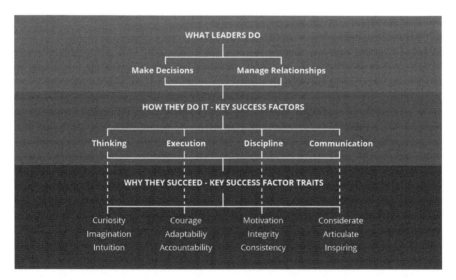

Figure 15: The Bremnus Leadership Success Model

The Bremnus leadership success model is a new framework of key success factors and traits for assessing leadership candidates. It can be traced back to the relevant and important science we explored in the first part of this book, which will be briefly revisited in this chapter for clarity. The exploration of this method then acts as the reference point to build out the question and evaluation structure covered in Chapter 9. The end goal is to show and validate a model and evaluation process that I believe should replace the out-of-date competency interviews still used by most companies today.

What is it about great leaders that makes them great? In my opinion, it boils down to two things:

1. Making decisions.
2. Managing relationships.

As illustrated in Figure 15, that is what people observe. I believe what happens behind this simplistic distillation of leadership are the key success factors and traits of the Bremnus leadership success model. The more senior a leader becomes, the more important their decisions become. For CEOs of global companies, that is the entirety of their job – to solve problems, evaluate choices, and make decisions. Their ability to solve problems and make decisions relies entirely on how they manage relationships with employees, customers, shareholders, and any other group that helps their business exist. A leader is just a single person if they have no team. It's the team that makes them the leader. Are they well positioned to attract great talent to work for them? Who they can attract to directly work for them sets the tone for who those individuals hire, and so on down the hierarchy, it goes. How will this leader inspire the business to get behind their vision for the company? How well are they going to listen to customers to really understand how their business can be improving?

There are a complex set of factors that influence their ability to solve problems, make decisions, and optimally manage a diverse set of relationships: what personality they were born with, what factors shaped their early years, how emotionally grounded they are, who they met at every stage of their lives, who they admired and studied and modeled themselves upon, how much hardship they endured and how they grew from it, and very far down the list is what work experience they've had. Every leader is unique in all of these aspects. We can't necessarily evaluate these foundational factors, but they all provide clues to help us de-risk our leadership hiring choices. We can observe the evidence of decisions they've made throughout their career and the resulting outcomes and impact of their choices. This evidence is told in the stories we carefully uncover through the very specific order of questions we ask.

BREMNUS LEADERSHIP SUCCESS FACTORS

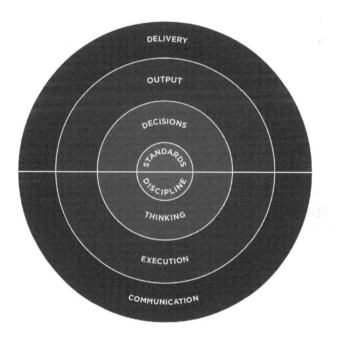

Figure 16: The Bremnus Key Success Factors

When you consider the success factors shown in Figure 15, which are repeated in the lower half of Figure 16, these are manifested in what everyone else gets to see, represented by the upper half of Figure 16. Our discipline manifests itself in the standards we keep. Our thinking manifests itself in the decisions we make. How we execute the plans and strategies we decide upon in the thinking phase manifests itself in the output and our actions. Finally, our communication is clearly evident in how we present ourselves and deliver information.

Discipline is at the center of this for a reason. It is the central foundation upon which everything is built. It's the personal discipline, the standards one holds themselves and others to, how organized they are, how they manage their mental strength to maximize their performance, and how this all translates into their drive to get it done. This is discipline.

Any leadership process starts with thinking about a challenge and how to solve it. Perhaps it's the company vision they're considering or even just how they're going to influence some key stakeholders to take action on a strategy they want to deliver. This all falls under "thinking" – the decisions.

Then it's about "execution" and holding oneself accountable for their actions and having the courage to execute in the first place. This is the extent to which they demonstrate determination and decisiveness in executing while being adaptable and ready to pivot and support others as they execute.

Then it's about "communication," how they listen to people and respond, how they understand self-awareness and how to adapt their behavior around others, and how they articulate themselves to be clearly understood and to deliver messages with conviction and integrity.

This cycle of task and idea deployment from inception to delivery is a cycle that repeats itself in every task a leader undertakes. From the board meeting to the town hall speech, to the vendor selection, to the regulatory meetings, these are the key success factors that manifest themselves in this ongoing process. Sure, one could argue that there are other success factors. However, other traits may likely fall under the category of sub-traits to those listed in Figure 15 or traits that are arguably similar enough to warrant being ignored in favor of those already listed in this model.

BREMNUS LEADERSHIP TRAITS

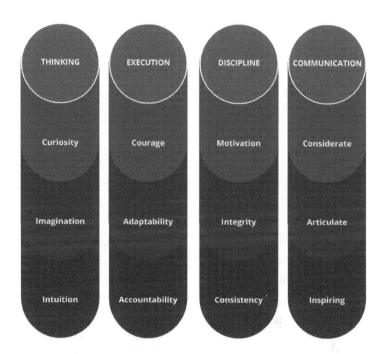

Figure 17 – The Bremnus Success Factors And Traits

Figure 17 is a condensed version of Figure 15, showing only the four success factors and each of the twelve related traits. The traits are the qualities of strong leadership that are observable in a candidate's career and life story. That is not to say they are directly observable. You will recall from the "Psychology Isn't Rocket Science" chapter it says,

"All psychological traits are constructs. We cannot necessarily see them, but we can observe behaviors that show us they exist. Constructs in psychology help us to group observable and complex sets of behaviors, emotions, and thoughts into meaningful concise language." For example, we cannot possibly hope to observe "intuition," but we can consider, in the candidate's stories, the outcomes from the decisions they made when they had little information to work with and therefore must have relied on their intuition. Similarly, with "imagination," we can't see someone's imagination, but in their stories, when recalling different options or strategies they were considering, we are observing the instances when their imagination was utilized to figure out the best way forward. Some are more obvious than others, but this is a baseline framework we can work with when evaluating leadership or management candidates. Some may apply to all leaders and managers, while others may only apply to certain types of leaders.

This whole process is about candidate selection. It is about getting as close to the perfect process as possible when evaluating candidates. For all of the reasons outlined so far as to why no process is perfect and why people can always lie, we don't have to cover every possible trait that can be measured. There is a point beyond which an interview or evaluation process can become counterproductive. For example, the answers may have little to no impact on our decision because the questions are just not fit for purpose. Maybe the questions are so open to abuse because the answers can be well-rehearsed that they're rendered meaningless. This happens when things are over-complicated, and we lose focus on what we're trying to achieve. The whole point of this model is to condense and simplify it as far as possible without losing key areas we need to recognize and focus on. I've seen models with forty to fifty competencies, which ends up being confusing and loses the impact and simplicity that comes from focusing on a condensed few. Thinking back to the science section, we saw how scientists use factor analysis to go from a large group of traits to a few. The factor analysis groups together similar traits and distills them down to common denominators. That's how they got the Big Five personality traits. Having a list of 50 traits is not only impractical, but it will undoubtedly be full of duplicate traits that sound different but have the same fundamental meaning. This is not how you design a fair and consistent selection process.

At first glance, it seems like a tough task to remember all of these traits, and how do you even measure and account for them? How can you tell if someone is considerate and inspiring? The exact method is covered in Chapter 9, but as a trained interviewer, you will learn to look for patterns and stories of these traits that you can recognize and evaluate. In thinking about these and understanding what they mean, or at least your interpretation of how I describe here what they mean, you will learn to listen to candidates' stories with these traits always at the forefront of your mind. It's like waiting in a busy coffee shop for your name to be called. At this moment, you're busy on your phone looking at pictures of your insecure friends sharing how great their Photoshopped lives are, and you hear no noise. Then your name is called, and your subconscious brain prompts you to awaken from your bubble of social media envy and go to the counter to collect your coffee. This is how your brain will start to work when spotting these traits in the stories a candidate is telling you. The trait names will pop up in your mind all over the place as you endure the monotony of yet another interview.

There are descriptions for each success factor and trait, so there can be no misinterpretation of what is meant by them. This is followed by a guide on what "weak" and "very strong" may look like in the scoring chart for these traits. You will get a better sense from the very strong descriptions of how the scales are defined. These are, of course, completely subjective. However, when the interview is conducted by more than one person on different occasions using the same framework, the average scores will be closer to a fair representation. Without such descriptions, the interpretations of what the trait names mean may be so vast that they dilute the effectiveness of the assessment. We will now explore each of the success factors and traits in greater detail.

BREMNUS SUCCESS FACTORS AND TRAITS EXPLAINED

Thinking - The Decisions

Leaders need to be able to execute, be disciplined in their execution, and communicate well, but thinking is where it all starts. From establishing a vision and strategy to imagining how various options may play out to deciding what direction to go in, this all requires the problem-solving, creative part of the brain. It may be that great leaders can excel without having all of the ideas themselves if they compensate for this by having great creatives around them, but creativity is the secret sauce that differentiates companies. Think about Apple, Nike, and Dyson. Many companies make phones, running shoes, and vacuum cleaners. What makes theirs so special? Creativity is at the heart of all of it, from creative design to creative marketing and branding. Think about any innovative company. What is innovation? It's new ideas or ways of doing things. Where do new ideas come from? Creative people. At a managerial or leadership level, it is also creative minds that are naturally curious, that envision a future state and deploy strategies to take steps forward in pursuit of the desired state.

Curiosity

Curiosity is the true definition of the Big Five personality trait, openness. The best leaders I've met always demonstrate an intense curiosity about things. They have a thirst for learning and understanding everything in order to be as objective as possible when making decisions. They don't always have the ideas; perhaps they only generate ideas from their team that may be more creative. However the ideas are generated, the leader will most certainly be the guardian of the ideas and how they are evaluated and executed. They know what's happening in their company and outside the company; the competition, the macroeconomic and sociopolitical landscape, and much more. They have a unique ability to maintain a 30,000 ft view and delegate while zooming into detail at a street level when required and know what questions to ask. They maintain an incredible capacity to hold and compartmentalize vast amounts of information on an ongoing basis and work at multiple levels with multiple styles of communication to maximize their impact at any given time.

Weak: Lacking in broad awareness you would expect from a leader of this caliber.

Very Strong: Their curiosity is evident in their understanding of things at a company and a general macro level, demonstrated through multiple stories covering a broad spectrum of role and seniority relevant knowledge.

Imagination

Imagination is not just about wild, colorful abstractions. It's the thinking and pondering of ideas and potential outcomes that, in turn, leads to strategies being formulated and then executed. If it helps to break this down into idea creation, strategic thinking, and problem-solving, these all begin life in an imagined or hypothetical state before being acted upon. Often the concept of imagination is hijacked by the creative types; you know, the ones who describe certain cheeses as having "notes of damp autumnal lambswool." That's great, but the rest of us smell mold, so that level of imagination is not required here. A vision, for example, is a hypothetical future state born from the wisdom and ideas of the person or people that imagined it. A strategy starts as an imagined path mapped out in our minds to reach a desirable future destination. Leaders don't have to be the source of imaginative ideas, but they most certainly need to be able to hypothesize about different scenarios to then decide upon what destination is most desirable and potentially attainable.

Weak: No clear evidence in their stories regarding how they process ideas and make decisions.

Very Strong: They can articulate from start to finish, on multiple occasions, what they envisioned, what they considered, how they decided, and what positive outcomes happened as a result of their decisions.

Intuition

In the chapter on intuition and biases, you will have read about the academic work done on intuition, including the views of Jeff Bezos and Steve Jobs and how intuition impacted their own success. Intuition, when harnessed correctly, is real and positive and may even be the key indicator of success as a senior leader. We cannot account for why some people have certain gifts in life, from sport to the arts to academia; some are just born to be better than others. I don't believe intuition is an exception here. Senior leaders of large corporations often work without all of the data they need to make informed choices. There isn't someone instructing them what to do next, as in the case of a manager. Sometimes they just have to make decisions using what is ultimately their intuition.

Weak: When faced with ambiguous situations, there is a pattern of sub-optimal choices being made.

Very Strong: They will have multiple stories of ambiguous situations that ended up with them having to make choices that turned out to be instrumental in their success and not just a one-off stroke of luck.

Discipline - The Standards

Motivation

Where does an individual's motivation come from? What keeps them motivated? Why are they doing what they do? How do they motivate and inspire others? The answers to these questions will most certainly be intriguing, and people can't always articulate what motivates them. It is less important that they can pinpoint exactly what motivates them. What is important is that they can communicate stories expressing how their motivation levels have impacted their life. It doesn't have to be stories about work either. For example, you can't complete a marathon without being someone who knows how to get motivated. Leaving a country to pursue your education or work goals is not a pursuit of an unmotivated individual. These stories and patterns of progression in one's life tell you a story about motivation. How do they motivate their teams? How does the way they motivate their teams resonate with the culture of your organization?

Weak: Wasn't able to share meaningful stories of how their motivation manifested itself personally or in driving performance with the team.

Very Strong: Their motivation levels will be apparent in the stories they tell about their personal journey and their approach to inspiring their team.

Integrity

Operating with integrity which can also be described as adhering to strong ethical standards and values, is a key part of discipline. Yes, we have to execute with integrity, and yes, we have to communicate with integrity, but it is grounded in our foundational ethics that require discipline to grow and maintain. Observing the standards someone keeps in different aspects of their life is a potentially greater predictor of success than many of the interview questions we ask today. Discipline manifests itself in the standards we keep, and these standards tell a story about our levels of integrity. We may never know the whole story, but there are plenty of clues about how principled people are and to what degree they value integrity.

Weak: Lacking evidence of high standards for themselves or others.

Very Strong: Everything about their perceived levels of integrity is appropriate for the role and company. They demonstrate through different stages of their life, very high standards expected of themselves and others.

Consistency

Discipline is like intelligence in that people disciplined in one domain tend to be disciplined across many domains. It is the consistency of disciplined people that tells us they are disciplined. Consistency is also about the patterns of performance and delivery that are apparent during the course of one's career. It's fair to say that the consistency of success, especially over long periods, will de-risk the chances of that person failing in a future role. That is not to say they will not fail, but rather the evidence tells us that the emerged patterns lean towards successful outcomes, or not as the case may be.

Weak: The only thing that's consistent about them is their inconsistency.

Very Strong: Everywhere you look in their career and life, there are consistent indicators about their success in relation to their peers.

Execution - The Output

Courage

The research shows us that people willing to take risks make better leaders, to a certain degree. That is not to say, the more of a risk-taker you are, the more likely you are to be an exceptional leader. Entrepreneurs are the poster people for courage from a work perspective. To give up a paying job to try to do something on your own is a risk too far for most. However, you don't have to be an entrepreneur to display courage. Having the courage to run a big company is courageous, but how does the candidate manage risk and demonstrate courage?

Weak: Demonstrated that they were more inclined to play it safe when faced with difficult decisions.

Very Strong: They can articulate more than one occasion where they took a significant risk in their work or personal life that ended up positively or that they learned a great lesson from if it was a mistake.

Adaptability

Being adaptable may appear to contrast with determination. However, not being adaptable and sticking to a strategy that turned out to be wrong, yet pressing ahead regardless because you are determined, is not the way forward. Admitting the path you're taking the company down is not working, and being able to pivot into a new direction is something that anyone in a senior enough position will inevitably be faced with on more than one occasion in their career.

Weak: In observing one or more situations when they should have changed direction, they stubbornly pursued what ended up being a lost cause and didn't change as a result.

Very Strong: Has shown, through the stories of their work history, that they have had to adapt and pivot on several occasions and can explain why this was necessary.

Accountability

A team needs to feel safe executing its objectives, knowing everyone is accountable, especially the leader. When the team knows that the leader is taking accountability and encourages them to take calculated risks and work with high degrees of autonomy, they feel empowered and safe in the knowledge that their leader has their back. Furthermore, holding oneself accountable before seeking team members to blame is a far more productive way to run and motivate any team.

Weak: When clearly they should have been holding themselves account- able, they weren't.

Very Strong: Clearly demonstrates accountability for their mistakes or targets that weren't hit while speaking about their work history.

Communication - The Delivery

Considerate

Being considerate is thinking about how to get the best out of people, share bad news, be more inclusive, show empathy, and generally listen better to others and make it known that they have been heard. Being considerate also involves self-reflecting on how you handled situations and how you can improve. Your ability to build trusting relationships, be credible, and grow professionally require you to consider your approach to situations, what you say, and how you act. Communicating doesn't begin with the words you say. It begins with your thoughts and how you regulate and process them.

Weak: Lack of self-awareness and others' well-being is very apparent.

Very Strong: Demonstrates, through their stories about interactions with team members, strong self-awareness and empathy and is clearly considerate.

Articulate

Both in terms of communicating ideas and speaking in general, being articulate is a powerful trait. It can build trust and rapport quickly, it can be used to simplify complex ideas to communicate with people, and there is an assumed level of intelligence with someone highly articulate. That shouldn't be confused with people who just use lots of big words yet speak with little substance. We've all no doubt met with these types, or perhaps you're still working with one today.

Weak: Speaks a lot but doesn't say very much.

Very Strong: Can simplify and articulate more complex concepts and stories and use engaging language that is appropriate for the audience.

Inspiring

Leaders have a team or teams of people that look up to them. A leader's job is to inspire these people. To inspire them to give their all in working there. To inspire them to get behind the purpose of the company and its vision. Inspirational communication is not about eccentric, passionate speeches. It is about connecting with people at all levels in the company and making it known that everyone has an important job to do. This is not just done through town hall meetings and newsletters, but through actions, following through on commitments made, and delivering an employee experience that inspires people to join and stay for the right reasons.

Weak: Leaves you uninspired with their stories, even as the interviewer.

Very Strong: Clearly able to communicate at all levels of the organization. Demonstrates in their stories how they inspire teams through their words and actions.

THE METHOD

It's important to understand that these four key success factors and related traits were not just plucked out of thin air. They are derived from our eight-year-long study of 1727 leadership interviews followed by analysis theoretically based on the psychometric reliability and validity measures. Just to be clear, organizational psychologists did not carry out this work. However, when you consider the failings of the Implicit Association Test (IAT) mentioned in Chapter 4, carried out by Harvard psychologists, no less, a scientific label in psychology does not carry the same weight as it does in the traditional sciences. What we have here is a real-life study of actual interviews where people qualified for leadership positions, where close attention was paid to the scientific methods of deduction, as outlined below. To better explain the method as it relates to science, let's recap on some of the reliability and validity measures we looked at when considering psychometric measurements in the science section. You will recall that psychometric tests (the measure of behaviors) had to qualify as reliable and valid, with specific definitions for each.

Reliability

1 - Reliability over time (test-retest reliability). With the Extraview interview method, because the questions are consistent and the candidates have only one story to tell, it follows that at any stage of their life, when asked the same questions, if they're telling the truth, they should be telling the same answer so the underlying construct being observed will be consistent and apparent.

2 - Reliability across items (internal consistency). With the Extraview interview method, if someone scores highly in the traits, it will indicate performance in the related success factor. For example, with the success factor, discipline, the three traits are motivation, integrity, and consistency. If someone is clearly motivated and maintains high standards consistently, as evidenced by their life and career story, then we can conclude they are disciplined, or in other words, reliability across items is demonstrated.

3 - Reliability across different researchers (inter-rater reliability). With the Extraview interview method, this is exactly why we chose to go deep into people's stories and have only one or two interviewers, with everyone else being an extra-viewer. This is outlined in full in Chapter 9. The extra-viewers are those that are rating the candidate based on the transcripts collected by the interviewers and using the same information and the same scales, which means consistent measures are applied.

Validity

1 - Evidence based on test content.

For example, when assessing for discipline, we seek to observe evidence of motivation, standards, and consistency in behaviors that are analogous to the construct, discipline. In observing evidence of these from the candidate interviews, we can infer that we are observing disciplined behaviors and, in turn, evidence of the Big Five trait, conscientiousness, which is well documented as positively impacting performance in the workplace.

2 - Evidence based on response processes.

When evaluating, for example, communication, we define communication in three traits: considerate, articulate, and inspiring. These, in turn, link to three of the Big Five personality traits: agreeableness, extraversion, and neuroticism. In asking the specific questions outlined in the Extraview interview method, we are probing for details and examples of situations that will clearly demonstrate a link between the underlying success factor, communication, the Bremnus success factor traits, and ultimately, these three Big Five personality traits.

3 - Evidence based on internal structure.

The relationship between each success factor and the related traits is evident. For example, for communication, the three traits are considerate, articulate, and inspiring. If someone is considered to be articulate and inspiring in their communication, is that likely evidence of good communication as it relates to leadership? If we're observing examples of these traits in the stories being told by the candidates, it follows that we are observing good communication skills.

4 - Evidence based on relations with other variables.

With the Extraview interview method, for example, we already know that creativity is strongly correlated with openness in the well-established Big Five personality model. We also know that "curiosity," "imagination," and "intuition" all link back to the success factor, thinking. This, in turn, relates to an already established manifestation of creativity, openness, which is also one of the Big Five.

5 - Evidence based on the consequences of testing.

With the Extraview interview method, the "test" is the interview process and the specific questions that are asked. The "intended use" is to establish patterns of behaviors and actions that demonstrate, among other things, evidence of the Big Five personality traits, with the right mix of those traits. As strong evidence links certain mixes of these traits to performance in the workplace, one can assume that with a properly conducted interview, with observable patterns adequately documented, the interviewer will be in a position to assess candidates fairly.

RECAP ON THE BIG FIVE PERSONALITY TRAITS

In the science section, we went into a lot of detail about the Big Five personality traits. There was a reason for that. Not only are they the most scientifically robust account of personality differences. The scientific method and approach used to get to the Big Five also formed the basis for our process to arrive at the four Bremnus success factors. You may recall how factor analysis distilled Cattel's Sixteen Factors into the Big Five personality traits? Figure 18, taken from the science section, may jog your memory.

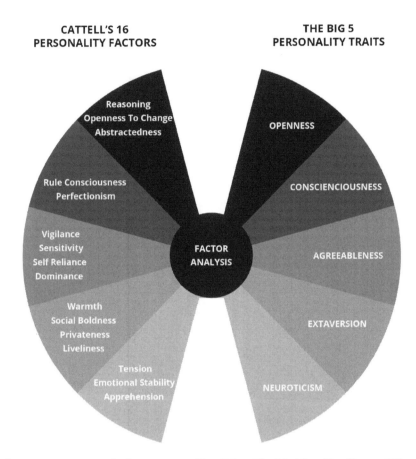

Figure 18: Factor Analysis From Cattel's 16PF to The Big Five (Duplicate of Figure 7)

With the Bremnus model, we followed a similar process. We took all of the observable traits we had gathered over 1727 interviews and condensed them down to 24 traits. Then we carried out further semantic clustering to reduce each set of words to one overarching trait, outlined in Figure 19.

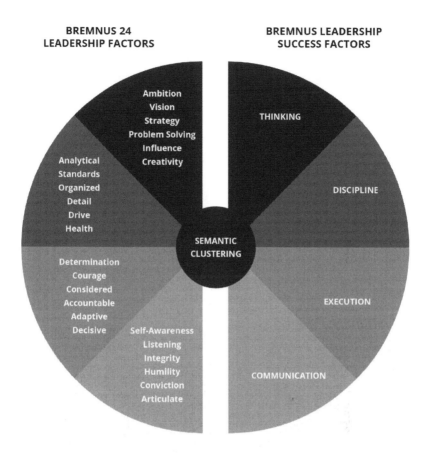

Figure 19: Semantic Clustering of Observed Leadership Success Factors

You will then recall the work done by Costa & Macrae (1995), where they developed facets of the Big Five, previously introduced in Figure 8 and now repeated in Figure 18, to better describe the breadth of what can be interpreted by these traits. Remember, they suggested, "The facets were selected to meet a series of criteria: They should represent maximally distinct aspects of the domain, be roughly equivalent in breadth, and be conceptually rooted in the existing psychological literature" (Costa & McCrae, 1995).

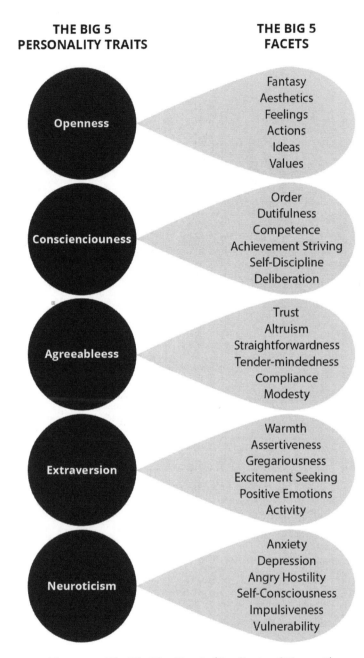

Figure 20: The Big Five Facets (Duplicate of Figure 8)

**BREMNUS LEADERSHIP
SUCCESS FACTORS**

**BREMNUS
LEADERSHIP TRAITS**

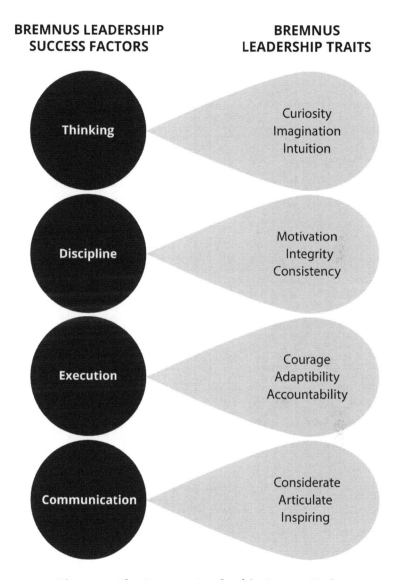

Figure 21: The Bremnus Leadership Success Traits

As you can see in Figure 21, we followed a similar process, starting with the Bremnus success factors and ending up with three traits for each of the four success factors that were maximally different but represented a broad understanding of what these success factors mean. We chose three for each, so they were understandable and easy to use in an interview where the interviewer will be measuring and commenting on these traits.

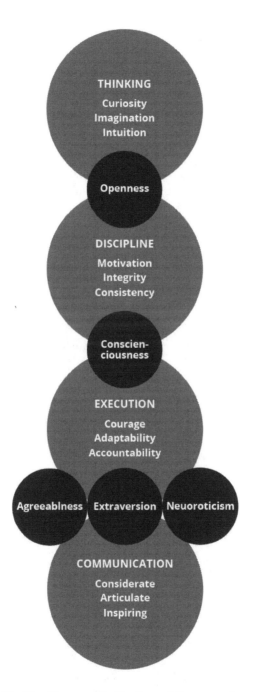

Figure 22 – The Big Five Personality Traits and Bremnus Leadership Success Model

Furthermore, as you will see in Figure 22, in relation to the Big Five personality traits, we were able to successfully overlay these onto the Bremnus leadership success factors and traits to illustrate their relationship to the Big Five personality model. You may recall that one of the validity measures outlined in the science section is evidence-based in relation to other established variables. Here we can show validity based on the relationship to the Big Five personality model as outlined below. In other words, when we observe the success factors and traits of the Bremnus Model, we also observe the Big Five personality traits.

Openness

We know from the Big Five research that creativity is strongly linked to openness. Therefore, when we are interviewing and measuring for the thinking traits, we are measuring for and commenting on the Big Five trait, openness.

Conscientiousness

We know from the Big Five research that conscientiousness is related to self-discipline. Therefore if in our interviews, we are assessing the Bremnus success factor, discipline, or its three traits, we are also assessing conscientiousness. Furthermore, when we look at leadership execution, it cannot happen without those leaders demonstrating conscientiousness, although discipline would be most closely related.

Agreeableness

We know from the Big Five research that the extent to which someone is agreeable has a large effect on their ability to communicate and execute. Therefore, especially for certain traits like considerate and adaptability, during an interview, we know we are referring to agreeableness when observing these.

Extraversion

We know from the Big Five research that extraversion is a key trait in strong leaders. That is not to say they have to be extraverts, but rather that they will often find themselves in situations where they will have to act out extraversion, like when they're speaking publicly, for example. The Bremnus traits, courage and inspiring, would most closely relate to extraversion. Therefore, we can say that we are also observing extraversion when assessing a candidate's stories and considering these two traits.

Neuroticism

We know from the Big Five research that being able to keep calm and steer the ship in troubling times is essential in leadership. In other words, coming in low on the neuroticism scale is essential. Execution and communication are where neurotic behavior will most obviously present when the interviewer listens to the candidate's stories. Therefore, in listening to a candidate's story about how they communicate and execute, we will be able to probe and observe their levels of emotional stability, or the Big Five trait, neuroticism.

CONCLUSION

What concluded in the Bremnus leadership success model started with the hypothesis that behavioral competency interviews were not fit for purpose. To establish an assessment methodology to replace this interview process, we had to start at the beginning. What has science taught us, and which parts of the science are valid and reliable? How are traits even established and defined in psychometrics? How can we best represent the most significant traits of leaders as simply as possible so we can then create a workable and effective assessment methodology?

This chapter outlined the scientific methods we followed to establish a more robust frame of reference upon which to build a more meaningful assessment methodology. With the overlapping of the Bremnus success factors and traits and the Big Five personality traits, we have established as robust a model as possible. It is robust because the Big Five personality traits are the only significant taxonomy of personality and therefore as close as we will get to being scientific. With that, we can now be confident that when we go on to build a question structure that seeks to identify where these traits manifest in people's stories, we are as close to a scientific process of evaluation as one can hope to be, given the limitations of psychometrics.

Furthermore, we have done away with the need for separate personality tests that typically measure the Big Five personality traits. In place of a competency interview and a separate self-score personality test, we have one interview. The interviewer's job is to evaluate the patterns of traits through a deep line of questioning. This is more reliable than the candidate scoring themselves for various traits based on what they think the company may want to hear, as in the case of personality tests. Ultimately, when comparing what science the behavioral interview method is based on (zero science whatsoever) to the Extraview method, it should be clear that we are taking positive steps forward in the quest to find a more robust and reliable interview method.

HOW TO FIND IT – THE EXTRAVIEW

Extraview is an interview methodology that does a lot more than your standard interview. It's like an interview, but extra. It encompasses not just the questions but also the way the information is recorded and understood. What follows is an outline of the process, the questions, the reasoning behind the questions, and how the whole process is managed.

What are we even trying to find out when we interview someone? When it's for a leadership position, we want to be as sure as we can be that this person is going to add maximum value to shareholders, employees, and customers simultaneously. For us to decide who this person will be, we first need to consider where we are as a company, how this position fits into the company, and what impact we believe a new person in this role should make. We then have to figure out exactly how we differentiate the best from the good.

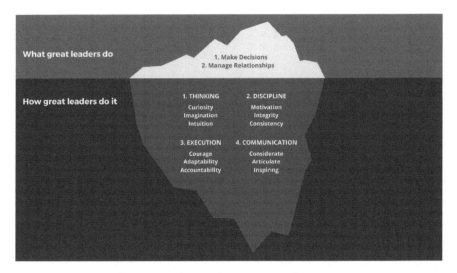

Figure 23: What Makes Great Leaders Great

The previous chapter looked at the Bremnus Leadership Success Model and outlined the four key success factors and twelve related traits. These factors and traits are once again illustrated here in Figure 23.

For leadership roles, we have to do our best to get a sense of how candidates think and operate and then map what we believe we understand about the candidate onto the role and company and figure out who has the optimal potential fit. If we can get close to understanding as many of these traits as they relate to each candidate, then we are as close as we may ever be to having an informed view on who the best candidate may be.

Existing competency interview frameworks would take the list of traits and come up with one or two questions for each of them, and then ask the candidate questions like:

"Give me an example of a problem you were faced with and how you arrived at a conclusion?"

"Give me an example of a decision you made recently and how you went about it?"

These questions only seek out the candidate's best answer from their career that most perfectly fits the question. That's not a story, and there are no patterns being identified or understood. For all the reasons laid out in previous chapters, this is not the best way to understand these factors, but how do we best understand these? We must take a step back and understand what is behind these factors. If we understand the driving forces that lead people to be differentiated across these factors, then we may have a better solution when it comes to interviewing.

	Decision Making	Managing Relationships
Thinking	x	x
Curiosity	x	x
Imagination	x	x
Intuition	x	x
Discipline	x	x
Motivation	x	x
Standards	x	x
Consistency	x	x
Execution	x	x
Courgage	x	x
Adaptability	x	x
Accountability	x	x
Communication	x	x
Considerate	x	x
Articulate	x	x
Inspiring	x	x

Table 9: A Leader's Role And The Bremnus Traits

As leadership boils down to making decisions and managing relationships, in cross-referencing these two assumptions with the success factors and traits of the Bremnus model, we can see in Table 9 how they fit together. During the interview, we would see a mixture of these traits showing up when trying to understand how the candidate makes decisions and develops relationships. These are the big picture themes we are seeking to understand when interviewing. We're not going to ask candidates, "How do you manage relationships?" because then we get a rehearsed answer about how they manage relationships. What we do instead is learn how they manage relationships by asking different questions where a set of stories will connect that informs us about patterns relating to how they actually do this.

For example, for each of their previous leadership roles, the Extraview interview method asks:

Tell me about the best and worst hires you made?

Who were you most proud of developing in your team, and why?

What percentage of your direct reports would you have wanted to take with you?

Also, from the candidate insights section, which isn't related to any particular previous role, the Bremnus interview asks:

From the three best leaders you've had, choose one trait of each that has really gotten the best out of you and explain how?

From three people that have worked for you, choose three of your leadership traits that have gotten the best out of them and explain how?

From these questions, especially when we are finding out about each of the different roles, we're observing patterns that will inform us about how this person attracts and develops people. We don't always find out from their initial direct answer, but that's why we get deeper into answers with more questions, as I'll outline shortly. If all of our interview questions seek the stories that lead us to evidence about the two big picture questions, we have a direct link to the Bremnus success factors and traits. If we've evaluated these factors and traits to the degree to which it's possible, then we have a meaningful framework upon which to base our decisions.

QUESTION VALIDITY

With existing interview methods, why do we ask the questions we're asking? We're looking to assess whether the candidate has the necessary skill set to perform a job. Fair enough. But what is the purpose of each question? How do they help us build a picture of the candidate's background and patterns of competence? Which of the criteria we are seeking to measure does the question relate to? Can their answer tell us anything about this candidate as it relates to this role? Is there a way to measure and compare the answer with other candidates' answers, or even with other candidates? Can this answer be cross-referenced to test for honesty? If these questions aren't thought through in detail, you pick your favorite questions randomly, which doesn't give you the best chance of reaching any objective conclusion regarding the candidate's suitability. Not all questions need to pass every one of the above tests. Not all questions can be measured and compared to others; in certain cases, that's okay. For example, the interviewer may be looking to build up some stories that they can then counter-question to find further specific facts.

FACTS

The facts are what we ask for initially to establish a timeline of data points in one of the candidate's previous roles. These data points then lead us to understand the beginning and end state that we can then attribute performance to. One example may be the difference between the division's revenue when a candidate joins and revenue when they leave. Of course, not all facts will be facts, as candidates can lie, but facts are the data points that relate to a candidate's role. "There were twenty people in the team when I joined, and I grew it to thirty." That is a fact, assuming they're not lying. "My performance was based on revenue growth, customer retention, and employee satisfaction." These are facts, assuming they're not lying. Fact-seeking questions can be asked by different interviewers so they can cross-reference for consistency and truth. Cross-referencing the answers to an identical question asked by different interviewers on different occasions is a great way to fact-check and get closer to the truth. More on that later.

I will get very specific about facts in an interview for three main reasons. Firstly, facts give us the data we can measure to make an informed judgment regarding performance. If I'm recruiting for a role and the company has been growing revenues by 17% year on year, and I'm speaking to a candidate that's been growing revenues by 25% at a competitor of similar revenue size, yet all other candidates are in the 10% to 15% range, then this is something I need to explore further. I don't just assume the candidate growing a business at 25% is doing better. They may have been throwing money at the business with huge cost implications compared to the other candidates. You have to do your best to qualify further any claims, which you can do in the interview by making calculations based on other metrics they share, which leads me to the second reason why I get very specific about facts.

Let's say the client I'm hiring for has been growing revenue by 17% a year with a headcount of 220 people, up from 210 the previous year (roughly 5% headcount growth). The candidate I'm interviewing tells me they grew revenues by 25% in the previous year, but they have a headcount of 200 people, up from 150 in the previous year (33% up on headcount). This puts things in a different perspective. This tells me the candidate hasn't done very well on a per headcount basis despite growing top-line numbers. If my client grew headcount by 5% and achieved 17% revenue growth, yet this candidate who looked like a superstar for growing revenues by 25% did so by adding 50 people to a smaller team, I will want to investigate further as it no longer sounds great. Furthermore, if I ask about actual revenues and their cost structure compared to other candidates, I can also make some calculations to determine what these numbers mean in real terms.

The third and final reason I get very specific about numbers is that candidates can lie. Some people believe you'll get the truth by following up on references, but the whole reference-taking process is as flawed and open to abuse as just lying on your resume is. Candidates can just as easily call up their references, which they have probably hand-selected anyway, and either get their old bosses to be vague with the truth or, as they legally can do, or just get them to say they're only willing to confirm that they worked from and to the dates written on the resume. The best way to get as close to fact-checking as possible is by getting into the detail. An interviewer has to be knowledgeable enough about business in general, or certainly the industry they're recruiting for, to be able to make calculations on the spot and push back. Crucially, the most important reason I get into the detail is so it can all be recorded. The same questions, or similar, can be asked by another interviewer later in the process, and we can cross-reference the numbers. Sure, great liars can learn that this will happen and memorize all the numbers, but good luck to anyone trying to memorize all these lies for five different roles, in the correct order, and for multiple different data points. The chances are, if they're lying, it will be found out in this follow-up interview, which is why it is so vitally important to do duplicate interviews with two different people. The other reason, of course, is so you can get two different opinions based on answers to the same questions, which also leads to minimizing bias.

STORIES

Allowing for stories to be told is the most powerful and genuine way to conduct an interview. Stories start with going back to before the candidate's career to find out how their drive and values were initially formed. The most important stories are the ones where the candidate will speak through each role, one by one. The interviewer's skill comes into play here to direct the stories in and out of key reference points so they can make observations without disrupting the flow and depth of dialogue. All of the information that an interviewer can need, from discovering competencies to learning about experiences, are contained in these stories. However, just letting a candidate tell their story of each role without it being very carefully directed by the interviewer is a wasted opportunity. This is why an interviewer needs to develop the skill of interviewing as, without it, interviewers fall into one of three camps: 1. The interviewer who already made their mind up and is just asking questions to help validate their position. 2. The interviewer who asks the right initial questions but they don't know how to challenge, push back, or fact-check the claims by asking further questions in a certain way. 3. The interviewer who spends very little time on the stories and instead focuses on a battery of competency-based behavioral questions, seeking to identify evidence of specific competencies rather than seeking to identify the competencies by skillfully navigating their way through the candidate's story. This is why I refer to it in the book title as the "art" of interviewing. It's not just about having a checklist of questions.

The easy part of developing this skill is the interview framework, which we're coming onto very soon. Part of the art of interviewing is understanding the difference between facts and stories and how both play a part in building a picture of the candidate's background and skill set. One of the tough parts to develop, and the real skill, comes with directing these stories so that the candidate maintains a degree of comfort to continue sharing information, which flows well as you're focusing on their story. However, for the interviewer, it flows in a direction where they can observe the competency/growth/success/failure patterns they're looking for. We will cover this in detail when discussing the questions to be asked and the structure and flow of these questions.

The other tough part to learn is the skill of fact-checking during the interview. This can only be done when the interviewer has a solid grasp of general business principles and understands the structure of the business to the extent that they can push back and seek further clarity on facts that don't sound right. Getting the balance right where the interviewer can direct the candidate through their story while gathering deep levels of information and building a case to cross-reference and fact-check answers is really what separates a good interviewer from an incredible one. That is, leaving the candidate feeling like they are just seamlessly taking the interviewer through their career journey when, in fact, it is a very carefully orchestrated pathway laid out by the interviewer to touch upon the various competencies and performance factors. Then on top of this, the interviewer is carefully building a catalog of data to refer back to while fact-checking differences between, for example, claimed revenue growth in relation to employee number growth or claimed revenue growth versus cost growth. Without the ability to direct these stories in a meaningful way, the interviewer is left making judgment calls based on whatever information the candidate chooses to share and taking it at face value. If all the interviewer does is ask a series of directed competency questions, where one by one, the candidate has free will to choose a time in their career where a great sounding answer can be given, the coherence of the story is completely lost. Also lost are the patterns of competencies that can be much better identified by deep diving into each role with questions asked in a way that leads the candidate to share a more natural coherent story. This, again, is the difference between paint by numbers competency interviews and the art of interviewing in a more meaningful and impactful way.

REPLACING COMPETENCY QUESTIONS

In Chapter 7 we modeled what may be going on in a competency-based interview with the highlight reel of examples masking an otherwise poor career.

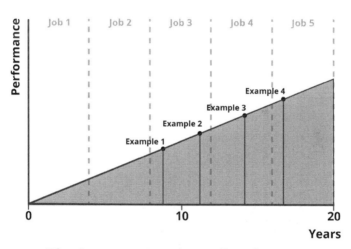

Figure 24: What Competency Interviews Believe They May Be Capturing
(Duplicate of Figure 11)

This is shown again in Figure 24, where the interviewer takes these highlights and joins the dots to conclude that this candidate has had a great career, as represented by the grey area.

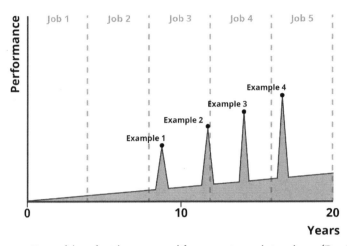

Figure 25: Everything that is wrong with competency interviews (Duplicate of Figure 12)

In the same chapter, we also illustrated that despite Figure 24 representing what the hiring manager may conclude from the competency interview, Figure 25 often represents what is actually happening. Again, represented by the grey area, we can see that these were just highlights from an otherwise not very good career. If the interviewer had been deep into the detail of the candidate's career from start to finish, they would have picked this up.

In contrast to this competency interview, the Extraview works by getting deep into the stories of the candidate's life and career without the interviewer sharing details about the competencies they're seeking to observe. This does two things: Firstly, it builds a complete story rather than a story formed by adding all the highlight reels of targeted competency questions. Secondly, the interviewer is trained to spot certain traits in the depths of these stories and observe these traits manifesting at different stages of the candidate's career, as represented by the dots in Figures 26 and 27.

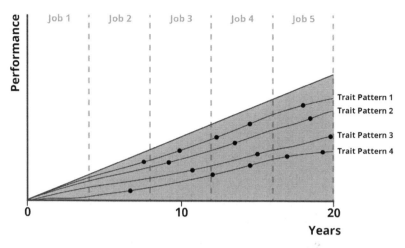

Figure 26: Extraview – High Performer

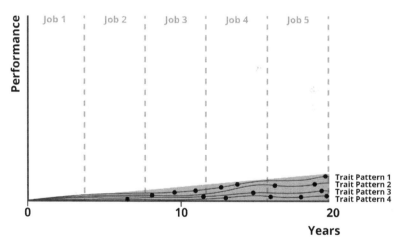

Figure 27: Extraview – Low Performer

Instead of plotting answers to competency questions and filling in the blanks, we are getting the whole story and plotting the instances of certain traits as they continue through their life and career stories. We can then observe patterns of these traits, thus reinforcing that these traits or competencies do indeed exist. When you compare Figure 25 with Figure 27, these could, in effect, be the same interview but with very different outcomes. I should add that interviewers are not actually plotting out anything on any charts. These are just visual representations to illustrate these points.

How can we observe traits and competencies without directly asking about them? To illustrate, part of the Extraview interview focuses on their earlier life before their career. Many would observe that their early life is irrelevant to a job when they're twenty years into their career. That couldn't be further from the truth. Pre-career life is incredibly important in giving clues as to how someone is wired. They don't start their career and then drastically change their motivations, intellect, or ability to get along with people. That is all shaped at a much earlier age, at least to some degree, and it's important to learn about it. For example, studies suggest that IQ is roughly 50% inherited and 50% due to the person's environment (Plomin, 2016). That's not to say that the limits of IQ are changed by the environment, but merely the extent to which someone can reach their full potential is influenced by their environment. Big Five trait dimensions have a heritability of 40% to 50% (Jang et al., 1996), so it follows that one's early life is important in building an overall picture of the candidate.

Let's say a candidate tells you a story about how twenty years ago they arrived in the US with only $800 in their pocket, and a degree in languages from a foreign-speaking university, with nothing more than a dream to work in corporate America. Twenty years later, you're interviewing them, and they are currently working in a senior role in a Fortune 500 company. In their very early career, it would be fair to suggest that they demonstrated, in abundance, three of the Bremnus leadership traits: courage, motivation, and adaptability. You don't need to be a scientist and conduct correlation analysis to conclude that this part of their story gets full marks for these traits. Then you're looking out for these traits to manifest throughout their career, taking note of when they do, in various ways, in the deep stories they're telling you as directed by the specific structure of the interview questions. If you're not witnessing similar evidence of these traits, why not? Did something change in their life at a pivotal moment, or have you just not been probing enough for answers? The interviewer's ability to maintain such an internal dialogue throughout the interview to ensure they uncover the whole story is important to get the most out of the interview.

When the interview moves from a series of competency questions to the Extraview interview process, it immediately moves from being a highlight reel of impressive anecdotes to a rich investigation into the whole story. The accountability of competency identification moves from the candidate to the interviewer. This is a significant shift in both processes and potential outcomes. The process is different because the candidate is no longer being teed up with specific competencies to comment on. Instead, the interviewer will observe competencies that are most apparent in the longer form stories of the candidate's life and career. This shift in focus also means a shift in the importance of the interviewer's experience in interviewing itself.

MACRO AND MICRO QUESTIONS

The alternative to many different competency questions is to have a much more natural flow of questions with a structure and direction that broadly follows the path of their career background. It is then down to the skill of the interviewer to navigate from macro question to macro question by also posing micro questions along the way to build a picture of these competencies without interrupting the flow of conversation. Broadly speaking, macro questions are the bigger lead questions, and the micro questions are the questions asked to probe further as the candidate talks through their answer to the macro questions.

In moving skillfully from macro to micro questions, it does several things. First, the candidate is in a more comfortable flow of conversation, so you're both likely to get more out of it. Secondly, depending on the interviewer's skill, the candidate will still be sharing evidence of competencies without necessarily being aware that these competencies are being observed. Finally, I believe this way gets more of the truth out of candidates. When you're throwing in micro questions on top of macro questions that are naturally inserted as part of the candidate's story-telling, the candidate is less able to just make something up. To illustrate, let's take two examples.

1. The candidate is being asked old-school competency questions in the same robotic way they've always been asked. Because these questions skip all over the place, the candidate can start afresh each time and tell a new story that may be completely unrelated to the previous one. So, for example, if they're asked, "Give me an example of a time when you had to influence a stakeholder's decision and what was the outcome?" they can theoretically make up a story from start to finish and even have the luxury of choosing which job this situation occurred in. If they're asked, "Give me an example of a time when you had to deliver tough news to a group of people?" again, they can, in theory, completely make up a story based on some different experiences and then choose which job that happened at, and it's unlikely to be fact-checked. So, in this scenario, you've asked two questions to gauge their level of competence in stakeholder management and communicating bad news.

2. This time we will seek to observe the same competencies but with an Extraview example.

Macro question: "What kept you awake in the first 90 days?"

"Well, I had to come up with a new strategy to move forward and present it to the board, but it meant we were going to lose some people, so it was a tough few weeks, knowing the fate that awaited a few of our guys."

Micro question: "Firing people is never easy. I understand that. So let's break that down for a moment. So you present this new strategy to the board. How radical was it?"

"Well, I can't say it was radical. I was looking to consolidate costs and knockout about five million, so it was a restructure, and there was definitely some low-hanging fruit. Had I presented what I really wanted to present, I don't think it would have gone down well, so I figured I'd give the board what they want first, which I know was a change but not a radical change. Then once I'd built their trust, I would quickly execute on my broader plan to further consolidate the cost structure."

Micro question: "So how did it go?"

"Well, the board approved my plan, and we went ahead and executed, and within about two months, we'd taken all the necessary steps to consolidate these costs."

Micro question: "And what about the team, how many people did you lay off, and how did you go about that?"

I could continue on and on, but I hope the difference between these two scenarios is clear. In scenario two, in seeking to understand more about their ability to influence stakeholders, there was a natural conversation about a specific role. It started with a very broad question, and then by asking a series of naturally flowing questions, we got a sense of this candidate's influencing skills. Because we kept this part of the conversation about one role and continued to ask more probing questions about this role, I believe we got closer to the truth. We also got to learn much more about the candidate and how they make decisions than if we just asked a standard competency question. However, this wouldn't be enough to conclude that this candidate has good influencing skills. This is merely one example where their influencing skills are demonstrated. The collection of conversations about all of the candidate's roles leads us to conclude whether or not their ability to influence is a consistently demonstrated competence.

The goal at the beginning is to identify candidates of adequate competence and most likely to excel at the job. There will often be more than one person that meets these criteria. This is subtly different from identifying "the one" from the beginning, although that is still the ultimate goal. You cannot possibly know you have "the best person for the job," as they haven't done the job yet. It is only your opinion and that of your colleagues that the person will be the best candidate for the job. If you set out at the beginning with one fixed preconceived idea about what "the one" looks like, you are at risk of missing out on certain candidate profiles that may excel but didn't get the opportunity to be in the race.

It's kind of like buying a house. Let's say you wanted to buy a townhouse in a particular area with four bedrooms. Your realtor found you three townhouses, all in the same area and all with four bedrooms. All are in the same price range but with slightly different layouts. They will all excel at serving their purpose to shelter you, make you happy, maybe, and serve as a status symbol if that is part of your intention, but how do you then choose? You don't know which house you'll like living in more, but you have to make a decision. So to expect at the beginning of the process that you're going to find the best house is realistic, yet it's sometimes hard to define what this is until you've got to the point where you have some options to weigh up. Those options can often be equally good but for different reasons, so in the end, the next best thing is to make as much of an informed decision as possible. In this house analogy, you'll likely end up going with the one that "just feels right," which is your instincts working.

Approaching it with this subtly different goal at the beginning means you have more of a realistic goal to start with, and once you get there, you can move to the next stage of selecting "the one." This way, you can focus on having a very structured interview process that can be repeated for each candidate, with different interviewers asking similar questions. I'll come on to explain why later in the chapter.

THE MACRO QUESTIONS

For each of the macro questions, there are also two alternative questions that essentially ask the same thing but in a slightly different way. This serves two purposes. Firstly an interviewer has a choice of which question to ask, depending on what they're comfortable with. Secondly, the candidate assumes they're having a different candidate experience when different people are interviewing them as they're being asked different questions, yet the information being sought is exactly the same. This can help the hiring company identify when lies may be told as the same question asked in two ways should, in theory, get the same answer. That's hard to achieve if the candidate is lying.

What you won't see here are technical questions relating to particular professions or industries. Of course, there will be different questions for different department heads and questions that are specific to certain industries. We have to start somewhere. These are questions that unite almost all leadership roles. It's as general as possible to share a meaningful framework to work with across all leadership and managerial roles. You can build on the framework and have different sets of additional questions for different types of managers or leaders. When you create additional questions, consider the logic outlined in this book and the descriptions of the questions in this chapter. Are the questions you're adding more like competency questions, or do they help build stories and evidence of patterns?

The order of questions is broken down into "previous roles" and "candidate insights." This doesn't appear to be a very exhaustive list, but most of what needs to be covered is in the "previous roles" questions. For all of the questions, the interviewer's skill is in asking pointed macro and micro questions in the right order to create an optimal flow of conversation. This is essential in gathering all the data that would otherwise typically be sourced with a behavioral competency interview. Let's start with a summary of the questions and what they mean before explaining their order in more detail, followed by the micro questions that can then be asked. The alternative macro questions are represented with the A1 or A2 prefix (alternative question 1 and alternative question 2).

Previous Roles

PREVIOUS ROLES	C-Suite Management				
	HR	FINANCE	OPERATIONS	MARKETING	TECHNOLOGY
What were you hired to do?	X	X	X	X	X
What convinced you to take this role?	X	X	X	X	X
What kept you awake in the first 90 days?	X	X	X	X	X
Talk me through the plan you made to succeed in this role and how the plan was executed?	X	X	X	X	X
What will be keeping your replacement awake in their first 90 days?	X	X	X	X	X
In terms of tangible metrics, what did you inherit?	X	X	X	X	X
Where was each of these metrics when you left?	X	X	X	X	X
What progress were you most disappointed with?	X	X	X	X	X
How was your personal performance measured?	X	X	X	X	X
On a scale of 1 to 10, how would you rate your performance and why?	X	X	X	X	X
What motivated you to stay?	X	X	X	X	X
Talk me through some of the toughest decisions you were faced with?	X	X	X	X	X
What impact did the competitive environment have on your decisions and performance?	X	X	X	X	X
Tell me about the best and worst hire you made?	X	X	X	X	X
Who were you most proud of developing in your team, and why?	X	X	X	X	X
What percentage of your direct reports would you have wanted to take with you?	X	X	X	X	X

Table 10: Leadership Role Agnostic Questions

There are sixteen main questions to ask here for each role, going back as far as you believe may be relevant to the role you're recruiting for. As you can see from Table 10, these questions can be applied across all divisions in any leadership and most managerial roles.

In opening the discussion for these, I suggest starting with an introduction explaining what you're about to ask. Something like: "For each role, I am looking to understand the start state, the end state, and the extent to which you owned, influenced, or impacted change, for good or bad. To do this, I will ask a series of questions for X of your previous roles."

What were you hired to do?

A1 – What was the broad remit of this role?

A2 – Your title was X. What exactly did this mean in terms of content and deliverables?

What convinced you to take this role?

A1 – What was so appealing about this particular role?

A2 – What were the deciding factors in you accepting the offer?

What kept you awake in the first 90 days?

A1 – In the first 90 days, what were the biggest challenges you faced?

A2 – What concerned you most about what you learned in the first 90 days?

Talk me through the plan you made to succeed in this role and how the plan was executed?

A1 – What was your strategy to deliver on your objectives, and tell me about how you executed this strategy?

A2 – How did you decide what your priorities were, and what strategy did you execute to tackle these priorities?

What do you think would be keeping your replacement awake in their first 90 days?

A1 – What do you think your successor would have been concerned about most in their first 90 days?

A2 – What challenges do you think your successor would have been most surprised to find out about in their first 90 days?

In terms of tangible metrics, what did you inherit?

A1 – When you joined, can you break down the numbers in terms of people, revenues, output, or whatever fell under your remit at the time?

A2 – When you started, how did your division look in terms of tangible numbers, be that headcount, productivity, or however it was measured?

Where was each of these metrics when you left?

A1 – At the end of your time there, how did each of these numbers change?

A2 - Before you left, how had each of these measures progressed?

What progress were you most disappointed with?

A1 - Out of these metrics, which were you least happy with?

A2 - Which of these were you expecting to be better than they were?

How was your personal performance measured?

A1 - Can you break down for me what metrics your bonus was paid against?

A2 - At your review, what metrics were observed to assess how well you personally performed?

On a scale of 1 to 10, how would you rate your performance and why?

A1 - If you were to give yourself a score for your performance out of ten, what would it be?

A2 - What number between 1 and 10 best represents how well you think you did in this role?

What motivated you to stay?

A1 - What kept you there for as long you stayed?

A2 - Why did you stay as long as you did?

Talk me through some of the toughest decisions you were faced with?

A1 - What do you remember as being the most challenging choices you were faced with?

A2 - Looking back, what big decisions were you most uncertain about making?

What impact did the competitive environment have on your decisions and performance?

A1 – How influential was your competition in driving your decisions?

A2 – How did understanding your competition change the decisions you made?

Tell me about the best and worst hire you made?

A1 - If you were to rank everyone you hired, who would be at the top and bottom?

A2 - From everyone you hired, who would you rank as the best and the worst?

Who were you most proud of developing in your team, and why?

A1- Which of your direct reports did you have the most impact on?

A2 - Who in your team do you feel responded best in terms of growing under your leadership?

What percentage of your direct reports would you have wanted to take with you?

A1 - How many of your direct team would you hire again if you could?

A2 – If you had the opportunity to hire any of your direct team again, would you?

PREVIOUS ROLES

What were you hired to do?	Fact
What convinced you to take this role?	Decision making
What kept you awake in the first 90 days?	Decision making
Talk me through the plan you made to succeed in this role and how the plan was executed?	Decision making
What will be keeping your replacement awake in their first 90 days?	Decision making
In terms of tangible metrics, what did you inherit?	Fact
Where was each of these metrics when you left?	Fact
What progress were you most disappointed with?	Decision making
How was your personal performance measured?	Fact
On a scale of 1 to 10, how would you rate your performance and why?	Decision making
What motivated you to stay?	Decision making
Talk me through some of the toughest decisions you were faced with?	Decision making
What impact did the competitive environment have on your decisions and performance?	Decision making
Tell me about the best and worst hire you made?	Relationships
Who were you most proud of developing in your team, and why?	Relationships
What percentage of your direct reports would you have wanted to take with you?	Relationships

Table 11: Asking Questions With Purpose

I wrote at the beginning of the chapter that leadership boils down to two things:

1. Making decisions.
2. Managing relationships.

Table 11 shows how we can categorize each question into making decisions and managing relationships. For some, it will be both, but only the predominant ones are shown here. Also in here is a third category, which is the facts. These are asked to build factual points into the story from which we can extract timeline-related progress indicators. All the questions have a purpose – either to build out the story or understand how people manage fundamental leadership skills.

Candidate Insights

Going as far back as you can remember, what drove you to get this far in life?

A1 - How did your drive to succeed manifest itself in your childhood?

A2 - Thinking about your early years, where did your drive to succeed come from?

How did your potential for success manifest itself in your high school and further education years?

A1 - What significant events from your high school and further education years exemplify your potential to succeed in your career?

A2 - What memories from your high school and further education were significant in shaping your later success?

What are you not currently getting that you think you'll find in this role?

A1 - What's missing in your career that you believe you may find in this opportunity?

A2 - Why do you believe this role may bring you the satisfaction and inspiration you may not currently be getting?

What's going to keep you in this role beyond the first year?

A1 - What's going to drive you to stay beyond the initial challenges posed in the first year?

A2 - After year one, how will you maintain the focus and standards you demonstrated in achieving your year one objectives?

Where has your previous role failed you that led you to be here today?

A1 - What frustrated you most about working at your previous employer?

A2 - What has been the biggest letdown for you working at your previous employer?

How do you maintain the mental strength and balance required to lead people?

A1 - How do you minimize the impact of stress that comes with leading people?

A2 - What do you do to optimize your capacity to deal with the stresses of leadership, mentally or otherwise?

From the three best leaders you've had, choose one trait of each that has really gotten the best out of you and explain how?

A1 - Choose three traits of previous bosses that were really effective in developing you, and explain how?

A2 - Thinking of your previous bosses, what three traits would you say were instrumental in developing you as a leader?

From three people that have worked for you, choose three of your leadership traits that have gotten the best out of them and explain how?

A1 - In your toolkit of leadership skills, which three traits do you feel are most effective when managing people, and explain how?

A2 - When you're developing people, what would you say are your three most effective traits, and explain why?

How do you manage your team to maintain the standards you expect of yourself?

A1 - How would you summarize your approach to management that maximizes your collective team's performance?

A2 - How do you inspire others to lift themselves to the standards you expect of yourself?

What is it about your management style that is so impactful?

A1 - Referencing how you manage people, why are you such an effective leader?

A2 - What is it about how you lead that gets the most out of people?

If you were the perfect leader, what would you be doing better?

A1 - How big is the gap between your leadership style and that of the perfect leader, and how will you fill this gap?

A2 - What do you have to work on the most to improve as a leader?

QUESTIONS EXPLAINED

Previous Roles

1. What were you hired to do?

This question is deliberately open to see how they define what they were asked to achieve in this role. The objective is to get a simple overview of what their role was, which can then be referred back to in some of the other more complex questions.

2. What convinced you to take this role?

How did the candidate decide at the time? Was it a jump in salary, a new challenge, a change in career focus, or some personal reason? There could be useful information here that helps you land this candidate and understand the decision-making patterns that lead them to make a career move.

3. What kept you awake in the first 90 days?

The answer to this question provides a foundation to understand how they prioritize, how they deal with stress, how they influence, how they problem-solve, how they think strategically, and so much more. It is also an unusual question that elicits a deeper response than typical questions. Therefore, the candidate must stop and think about how they will construct an answer. To do so, they have to think deeply and recall what they found tough in the beginning.

4. Talk me through the plan you made to succeed in this role and how the plan was executed?

Because you've just asked what kept them awake in the first 90 days, it is impossible for the candidate to now speak about anything that didn't involve how they resolved the items that initially kept them awake at night. That sounds obvious, but had you not asked that question first, they would have been freer to talk about anything they wished rather than referring back to these initial burning issues.

5. What will be keeping your replacement awake in their first 90 days?

When candidates are talking about what they inherited, it can sound like a horror show in such bad shape that it was barely savable, but a hero came to the rescue and saved the day. It is always interesting with this line of questioning and how those types of candidates describe what their replacement will be inheriting. It's never quite the same.

6. In terms of tangible metrics, what did you inherit?

Their answer could involve anything from team size to direct report titles, structure, revenue, profit, offices, cities, countries, or anything else under their managerial remit. You may need to prompt the candidate with some of these metrics so you can get maximum information and value from their answer. Given the previous questions, they may already have answered this one in a roundabout way. If they have, just ask them to repeat any metrics they've already shared. If they've been lying, you may catch some of it here. Either way, it's important to get as many data points as possible as they can all be useful when referring back to at a later date or comparing these answers with the answers shared with other interviewers.

7. Where was each of these metrics when you left?

You may have already found out some of this information, but it's important to get it reframed by them. Then you have to ask yourself, do these metrics all make sense? Is it possible that team size could have grown, yet costs have come down? Is there a net revenue increase that factors in the increased cost structure?

As an interviewer, you have to know the basics of how a business works to ask the right questions to call out where things appear to have fallen short. Also, remember, you've already asked about what kept them awake at the beginning and the end. Only now are you finding out about what was achieved in terms of the metrics. How do these tally up with what concerned the candidate initially and in the end? Does everything make sense, or are there areas you now want to probe further?

8. What progress were you most disappointed with?

This is one of those questions that require a story to be told. They can't just say, "Everything I did was incredibly impressive, and I have no comment." Even a list of the most impressive achievements contains a least impressive one, so they will have to speak about something here. How do they address it? How do they tell the story? How accountable are they? What did they learn from this?

9. How was your personal performance measured?

Only after you've asked all the above questions do you then ask how their performance was measured. Between questions about start and end metrics, what kept them awake at the beginning and the end, and how they delivered on goals they set out, you'll have a good understanding of what they claim to have achieved. How does the way they were measured and rewarded tie in with this? Look back and reconsider the actions they took and how these relate to how their performance was measured. Does everything seem to tally up and make sense? If not, probe further.

10. On a scale of 1 to 10, how would you rate your performance and why?

Now you know how their performance was measured, and you've learned most of the start and end-state metrics, you will have an informed view of how their perception of their performance relates to reality. Does it all add up?

11. What motivated you to stay?

This is an important question to ask at this stage because you now have a full picture of what happened, at least according to them. Depending on what you've been told, what challenges they faced, and how they were treated, it will be most telling to understand now what motivated them to stay. What does that tell you about how they will stay the course in a new company?

12. Talk me through some of the toughest decisions you were faced with?

From all the previous questions, you will have a good idea of what tough decisions they had to make, but how do they define which were the toughest decisions? How do they reflect and learn from their misjudgments or mistakes? Do they now mention something not previously discussed?

13. What impact did the competitive environment have on your decisions and performance?

It doesn't matter if a candidate is a CEO, an HR Director, a COO, a Head of Technology, or any other leader; if they don't understand how their employer makes money, who they compete with, and on what basis they are competitive, how can they add optimal value? They need to understand how to contribute and win, and to do that, they need to know what race they're in and what, if any, competitive advantage they can utilize.

14. Tell me about the best and worst hire you made?

This is a very specific question. Even if the candidate doesn't end up being honest, they will have to process all the data in their mind before constructing an answer. They should know instantly who did and didn't work out under their watch, but how do they share that news with you? Are they learning from their mistakes? Are they even holding themselves accountable?

15. Who were you most proud of developing in your team, and why?

Special leaders don't just attract good talent; they grow and nurture talent. Again, this is a very specific question. They will have to think of someone. If they can't, did they not develop anyone? Did they just inherit a team of rockstars that would have done a great job anyway? How do they speak about what they did to develop the employee? Was it really someone they developed, or was it someone who was a star anyway that came into a role and grew with little input from them? How does this story compare to their stories from other roles?

16. What percentage of your direct reports would you have wanted to take with you?

You can get a lot from this question. How did they view their team? If they wanted to take everyone with them, did anyone join them when they moved? If they weren't that excited about most of their team, how did they tolerate them in the company? Weren't they able to develop any of them to the point where they'd want to bring them along to their next company? This is always an interesting discussion.

Those are the sixteen questions about previous roles. You don't have to go back through their whole career and do this for every single role, but it should go far enough back that patterns can emerge, for good or bad. This line of questioning doesn't allow the candidate to jump to some rehearsed answer from any randomly selected part of their career where they will have the best example. Of course, they can lie, but when you're into this level of detail, asking questions in this way, it's much more difficult for them to lie over and over, job after job, especially when different interviewers are going to be asking the same or similar questions.

It is very important to understand that these are not technically difficult questions. They're being asked to retrieve quite a basic set of information that they should remember from each role, depending on how far back you go. There are no trick questions or questions that set them up for failure. You're asking them to think deeply and reflect on their time there. These questions, collectively, seek to get a full picture of the candidate and their performance in each role. Once repeated over several roles, you will see the emergent patterns related to the Bremnus success factors and traits.

With competency questions, the interviewer simply asks a long checklist of questions that go along the lines of, "Give me an example of a time when....?" candidates can easily lie and make up a story. When a second or third person conducts an interview that aims to cross-reference information, more than one person asking the same competency question can get different answers, and the candidate may have different examples. Instead, with these sixteen questions that ask specifically about particular roles and metrics, it will be very easy for them to get it wrong more than once if they're telling lies. Given the nature of interviewing in general, where candidates are susceptible to embellishing the truth, we are limited in our ability to fact-check, so we have to work with what we have. Therefore, the order of these questions is designed to make it less easy for people to lie.

Candidate Insights

Candidate insights are not role-specific. This is one set of questions asked about the candidate to try and get a snapshot of who they are, generally speaking, and how they grew to be where they are today. It's a bit like a balance sheet of them as a person. How did their early years shape them? What motivates them? How do they self-reflect and understand their skill set, and what is unique about it? Why do they believe they're a good leader? After running through the role-specific questions, the interviewer should have formed some opinions, and now we can cross-reference what they're telling us compared to the stories we've heard about their jobs and career progress. Does it all fit together and make sense?

Going as far back as you can remember, what drove you to get this far in life?

Here you're starting with a compliment. They have come far in life. What were the drivers that led them to get here? There will always be clues regarding what makes them so driven in their earlier life. Can you pinpoint them? What do you even do with the answer? This is all part of building the story, starting at the very beginning.

How did your potential for success manifest itself in your high school and further education years?

The aim here is to touch upon some of the highlights during their latter years of education immediately before entering the workplace. The candidate should share stories about achievements during these times that help you formulate a view of the early patterns of success.

What are you not currently getting that you think you'll find in this role?

This question forces the candidate to process their answer through a series of filters to construct an answer. They will think about what was wrong in their previous role, then process how much of that they can share. Then they'll assess how much of what they can share sounds like what may be on offer in the new role as they won't want to second guess the wrong thing or admit to looking for something that isn't on offer. When you ask this question, take your time to observe their problem-solving face, as that's exactly what they'll be doing here.

What's going to keep you in this role beyond the first year?

Their answer to this question may give you further insight into what they're looking for in the longer term and perhaps how realistic their ambition and vision are with the reality of a role in this company.

Where has your previous role failed you that led you to be here today?

At first glance, this seems like another way of asking the first question.

However, there is a subtle difference between what someone wants (the first question) and how they feel they have been let down (this question). In exploring how they feel they've been let down, you have the opportunity to gather more honest information about what it will take to land the star candidate.

How do you maintain the mental strength and balance required to lead people?

This question is about more than just motivation. It's about the standards the candidate keeps and how these standards are manifested in different aspects of their lives. From goal setting to discipline and actively working on oneself, what clues do you see that this individual works to maintain the optimal capacity to lead and make decisions?

From the three best leaders you've had, choose one trait of each that has really gotten the best out of you, and explain how?

Here's another question where the candidate has to process their answer through a series of filters before you hear their answer. This filtering process is them thinking deeply and hard about their answer, which is a good thing. They're not just being asked how they like to be managed. You're calling upon them to recall exact traits about specific individuals, so they're forced to tell you stories rather than just give you answers. In hindsight, you can learn a lot from their answer to this question, and often more than the candidate may have wanted to share.

From three people that have worked for you, choose three of your leadership traits that have gotten the best out of them, and explain how?

Fresh off the back of the previous question, the candidate now has to share what it is about their approach to managing that's effective, in their opinion. This question is much more robust than "How would you describe your management style?" You're getting them to tell you stories about actual people that have worked for them and making it specific to these individuals. Furthermore, compared to the previous question, you can see which traits of their boss are similar to the traits they claim to have.

How do you manage your team to maintain the standards you expect of yourself?

Again, this is a little more exploratory than asking, "What is your management style?" They may have had a rehearsed answer to the management style question. With this new question, the candidate has to think about the standards they maintain for themselves and how they tie in with how they manage their team to aspire to the same standards. Remember, many macro questions are designed to start the story, which you can then follow up with micro questions to get deep into details and build it out further.

What is it about your management style that is so impactful?

You've already referenced their management style in the previous two questions without directly speaking about it. Now you know how they describe their approach to managing. If you hadn't asked the two previous questions, they could speak about anything they want here. Because you have asked the two previous questions, the candidate will have to reference which of the previously mentioned approaches stand out as their most impactful style and approach.

If you were the perfect leader, what would you be doing better?

No, this isn't another way of asking, "What are your weaknesses?" Weaknesses refer to areas where the candidate believes they are least strong. This new question doesn't assume the candidate has weaknesses per se; it could refer to what is already great but could be even better. In this case, how do they believe they can go from good to great?

PREVIOUS ROLES ORDER EXPLAINED

1. **What were you hired to do?**
2. **What convinced you to take this role?**
3. **What kept you awake in the first 90 days?**
4. **Talk me through the plan you made to succeed in this role and how you executed the plan?**
5. **What will be keeping your replacement awake in their first 90 days?**
6. **In terms of tangible metrics, what did you inherit?**
7. **Where was each of these metrics when you left?**
8. **What progress were you most disappointed with?**

By asking questions 3 and 4, you're seeking to understand what they inherited and how they went about fixing or changing things. Then with question 5, you're asking them to stop and think about what their successor will be inheriting, and with their answer to that question, they're really saying what they would do if they inherited that role at that stage. Here you may get further insight into how they perceive their performance. By asking questions 6 and 7 after exploring what kept them awake at night and how they executed their plan, you can see what impact their priorities had on their results.

For example, they may have said one of the things that were keeping them awake at night was the fact that their costs were too high. Let's say they told you they needed to reduce costs by $5m, which included making over 100 redundancies. Then, after questions 6 and 7, you learned that they started with 1000 employees and ended up with 1100 employees, and the revenues had gone up 20%, but their costs had also gone up by 20%. There's a disconnect somewhere there. They fired 100 people to reduce costs, but they hired 200 more (1000-100+200=1100). Also, the costs and revenues grew in line with each other. So there was no net cost reduction, and any half-decent company can increase revenue by increasing resources, so you have to call them out on this.

This is part of what the interview is for – to go beyond the face value of the questions being asked and the answers you're getting. This is why you can't just leave the interviewing process up to HR or recruiters if they are not also trained in understanding the business, as they simply won't know what to ask as follow-up questions. Traditional behavioral competency questions are a "paint by numbers" approach. You ask a question, and you get an answer; therefore, anyone can conduct the interview. This isn't the case with a proper interview where we're trying to understand the candidate's performance and decision-making processes.

9. How was your personal performance measured?

Asking this question only now means that you can spot any disconnect between how they were measured and what they prioritized in answer to question 4. If they were being measured and rewarded on new customer acquisition and new product releases, why were these not part of the priorities outlined in answer to question 4? That's not a question you necessarily have to ask them, but the disconnect can certainly be observed as you score them for problem-solving and strategy in the creative, discipline, and execution sections.

10. On a scale of 1 to 10, how would you rate your performance and why?

Asking this question after gathering all the information about how they prioritize (question 4), how they performed (the difference between metrics in questions 6 and 7) and how their performance was measured (question 9) may seem odd. However, you now know exactly how they performed, or certainly, you have as many indicators as one can hope to gather. So how do they view their performance? If they're giving themselves a 9 after showing such poor results, why is that? Is their self-awareness a red flag? If they're scoring themselves a 7 when they knocked it out of the park on all measures, why is that? Are they just super tough on themselves? There are a lot of rich observations that can come from this one answer asked this late on in the process.

11. What motivated you to stay?

If you'd asked this at the beginning, before understanding everything they've been through and what they've achieved, you'd have no information to push back, depending on their answer. This is also a follow-on from question 2 (what convinced you to take this role?) to further clarify their motivation, why they join companies, and why they stay. Why is this important to understand? You may observe some clues about the kind of company they like to work for. You may be a startup firm where people have to come in and roll their sleeves up and not wait to be told what to do. It may be an environment where people have to make decisions with little information. If the candidate is telling you they joined the previous company because they had a huge support team in place, allowing them to focus on customers, then this will be something to dig deeper into because "that's not what it's like here."

12. Talk me through some of the toughest decisions you were faced with?

It may seem a little counterintuitive to ask this question towards the end.

It's typically asked as an opening question rather than a closing question. However, after going so deep on many of these questions, you will have learned a lot of stories of what went well and what went not so well. By this stage, you should be well aware of the main challenges they were faced with and the choices they made. Therefore, seeking only now to understand what they feel were the toughest decisions means you can get a better idea of how they think and how they have categorized which of the decisions they made were "tough." Now you have some context, and the question is about a role you now know a lot about. Furthermore, unlike with competency questions, the candidate doesn't have the luxury of choosing just any role; their answer has to be in response to this particular role.

13. What impact did the competitive environment have on your decisions and performance?

By now, you have a good understanding of the decisions they made in their role. Asking them only now about the competitive environment allows you to understand how closely they paid attention to the competitive landscape when shaping and delivering upon their strategy. Do all the stories tie together?

14. Tell me about the best and worst hire you made?

15. Who were you most proud of developing in your team, and why?

16. What percentage of your direct reports would you have wanted to take with you?

As you will now have the full picture of how they executed their strategy, how did their approach to their team contribute to their success? How do they treat their team? How does their team view them, and how will this reflect on this person if they join your company? Is everything they're now saying about their team interactions consistent with how they performed in their role? This is another way to fact-check and see if everything adds up.

MICRO QUESTIONS

What we have to do with these macro questions is interject with micro questions to get much deeper into the detail, identify patterns, and build stories that we can record and come back to when we're fact-checking. What follows are some examples of questions you can ask, but it depends on the flow of the conversation and your objectives with the information you're trying to gather. This is down to the interviewer's skill to direct the conversation naturally through a series of questions encompassing the competencies and facts we're looking to discover. Below you'll see, in order, the macro questions previously discussed, with examples of micro questions and descriptions directly below.

Previous Roles

1. What were you hired to do in this current role?

Tell me more? How did that develop? What else? Can you be more specific?

How do these extra questions add value?

Be careful not to go too deep here; otherwise, there will be a lot of duplication during the rest of the interview. It should be clear how these questions can add value, and you will be able to use other questions that will roughly be similar to, "Please elaborate."

2. What convinced you to join the company?

Can you be more specific? What else got you across the line? Did they deliver on their promises?

How do these extra questions add value?

You're looking for as many clues as possible about how they made this choice. This can help with understanding their motivations for joining, which may give some clues as to how you're going to land this candidate should they turn out to be a candidate you really want to hire.

3. What kept you awake in the first 90 days?

How did that develop? What else? Can you be more specific? How did you react when you found out?

How do these extra questions add value?

With most of these extra questions, you're seeking clarity, so their answers are crystal clear, and they cannot backtrack when you're fact-checking later in the process.

4. Talk me through the plan you made to succeed in this role and how the plan was executed?

1. What autonomy did you have in the decision-making process? 2. Who did you lean on for help, and why? 3. Talk to me about some of the resistance you faced and with who? 4. How much of what you wanted to do was roadblocked or scaled back? 5. Tell me about three different sets of people and how you got their buy-in? 6. What was the toughest part to execute? 7. Did you lose or fire anyone as a result? Tell me more?

How do these extra questions add value?

These are just some of the many questions you can be asking here. If they're in a leadership position, talking about their plan and how they executed it may be the one area where you should spend most time digging deeper, as this is central to what they were doing. For question 1, you're trying to find out how involved they actually were. Often people will have these grand statements on their resumes about what they've been doing; then, when you drill down, you find out they really didn't play that big a part in it at all.

Question 2 is a gateway question to them speaking about how they engaged other people, delegated, and worked with their peers and other stakeholders.

Question 3 assumes they must have faced some resistance, and this is one of those questions where, unlike traditional competency questions, you are finding out "about a time when they were faced with conflict and how they dealt with it," but in this specific role. It's not just any random role they can select from their ten, twenty, or thirty-plus-year career. Because we are asking about this particular role and we are already deep in the detail of if, good luck to them trying to lie, at least to the extent they can do when they can pick any role when answering traditional competency questions.

Question 4 could be asked in addition to question 3, to come at it from a different angle, or just instead of question 3, depending on how the conversation is going. Remember, this is not a prescriptive set of micro questions you always ask in these scenarios. Instead, they are optional questions to call upon if and when the moment is right.

Question 5 seeks more detail on the different types of people they had to interact with. This may be their bosses, peers, the direct team that reports to them, or their direct report's teams. This question is looking for clues about how they manage relationships in the business. Does it sound like their approach is the kind of approach that would work in your company?

Question 6 is similar to one of the macro questions, but if the previous questions have helped the candidate remember some of the fine detail, it's good to ask again.

Question 7 brings context to the broader questions about how big their team was at the beginning and the end of that role. This is where you will again be using your skill as an interviewer, not only to ask the question but to gauge if it all makes sense. For example, if they fired a whole bunch of people, does that fit with the story they've spent the last few micro questions telling you about?

5. What will be keeping your replacement awake in their first 90 days?

What would be a different yet effective leadership approach to yours that could still get the job done? Which of those items do you wish you'd had a chance to tackle the most? How will they benefit most from what you've been able to achieve?

How do these extra questions add value?

The first question is tough for the candidate to answer as it assumes there may be a better approach. Perhaps you, as the interviewer, don't yet know how they define their current style. Perhaps you've already worked it out based on how they've answered their other questions so far. Either way, the structure of this question really pushes them to do two things: 1. Define what leadership style may have been more effective than what they currently have, and as a consequence, 2. Define in their own words what their current leadership style is. Is that a leadership style that will be effective in your business?

6. In terms of tangible metrics, what did you inherit?

How did you go about identifying what the priorities were? After under-

THE CEO'S GREATEST ASSET

standing everything fully, which of these metrics did you think you could move the needle on the furthest in the least amount of time?

How do these extra questions add value?

There's a lot of rich potential data in here. There's actually a lot in the initial question itself, and this is definitely one to spend a lot of time on as these are the facts, or as close to being facts as potential half-truths can be. From here, you, as a skilled interviewer, can make some calculations to identify outlier data that should be further explored and quantified.

7. Where was each of these metrics when you left?

In hindsight, which metric do you think you could have improved more than you did? If you were inheriting that role as you left it, what would be your top three metrics to focus on, and what would you do?

How do these extra questions add value?

You're really putting the candidate on the spot with these extra questions to reflect and self-analyze about where they may have gone wrong, or at least what they could have done better. If they draw a blank for this question over a series of past jobs, what does that tell you about the candidate? It seems like it may be quite strong evidence that they find it difficult to hold themselves accountable for mistakes.

8. What progress were you most disappointed with?

What makes you say that? With the benefit of hindsight, what would you go back and do differently?

How do these extra questions add value?

As this question asks for self-critique and reflection, their initial answers can often be vague. You will likely have to probe further here to get a fuller story. How does their answer about what could have been done differently inform you about their accountability, thought processes, and strategy skills?

9. How was your personal performance measured?

How did you score on each of the measures? What do you think were the right performance measurements to use? Let's talk about two people on your team. How did you manage their performance? Do you feel these measures were fair, and were the goals achievable?

How do these extra questions add value?

Is the candidate really deep into the details, or can they not even remember how their performance was measured? This may be forgiven if it was years ago, but otherwise, it's quite telling about some of the different leadership traits and the candidate's shortcomings. In the interview process, when we're entirely reliant on what the candidate tells us, we have to get creative about identifying areas where the answer may be disingenuous. In spotting these patterns over many different questions and different roles, the interviewer can better gauge how much of it may or may not be true.

10. On a scale of 1 to 10, how would you rate your performance and why?

You gave yourself a ___. What would have made it a 10? Is that even achievable? How?

How do these extra questions add value?

Do they speak about how they could have improved or how the company, opportunity, or bosses could have been better? What does this tell you about their accountability? What does it tell you about their confidence? How justified is their confidence, for good or bad?

11. What motivated you to stay?

What was it about ___that kept you there? How have those motivations changed now you're thinking about a new role?

How do these extra questions add value?

Before the micro questions, you've already ascertained why they chose to stay. This may have given you some clues about the sort of things that motivate the candidate, in general, to work at a company. By asking these further questions, you're not assuming that these motivations change; you're seeking clarification on what will help get them across the line if you decide you want to hire them.

12. Talk me through some of the toughest decisions you were faced with?

Tell me more? How did that develop? What else? Can you be more specific?

How do these extra questions add value?

You may have already covered this in answers to previous questions, and that's okay. This is not a prescriptive model where every question has to be asked. For the micro questions relating to the formative years, motivation, and leadership sections, you should already have a feel for what you should be asking. Your job is to build out the deepest story possible that is optimally useful for you to observe potential patterns of competencies. Once they have nothing more to share and no more answers to "What else?" you can re-orient your line of questions with the macro list.

13. What impact did the competitive environment have on your decisions and performance?

Who would you say your competitors are? Where were you winning against them? What were they fundamentally doing better? How much did they influence what you were doing?

How do these extra questions add value?

These questions really seek to understand how well the candidate knows the competitive environment. Regardless of their position, they should be able to articulate how their competitors win and lose market share. Knowing what influence the competitors had on their strategy will also tell you more about where they saw themselves in the market in comparison to their competitors. Are they really leading, or are they followers?

14. Tell me about the best and worst hire you made?

Did any of these experiences change your mind about how you hire? If so, in what way? What are they doing now?

How do these extra questions add value?

Here you're really seeking to understand what they learned from these hires, what they can try to replicate, and what they will no longer do as a result. Also, in asking what they're doing now, you're really asking if they kept in touch with their best hire. If not, why not? There may be a perfectly valid reason for it, but this is definitely an area to probe further.

15. Who were you most proud of developing in your team, and why?

Can you tell me a little more? How did that develop? How have they progressed since? What specifically was it that made this one stand out?

How do these extra questions add value?

These questions seek to further clarify the story as much as possible. These stories can be rich in content that helps you understand how they may manage their people.

16. What percentage of your direct reports would you have wanted to

take with you?

How many did you take in the end? Out of those that stayed, who would you have wanted the most and why?

How do these extra questions add value?

Firstly you may get a different perspective on how well they got on with their team? Did they manage to bring anyone with them? There are many reasons why that may not have been possible. For example, they may have left the industry or gone somewhere to work to turn around a business that was high risk and messy and therefore wouldn't have wanted to bring people with them. However, you may get some further insight here. At the very least, you'll get to see how they really rated their team. If they wouldn't have wanted to take them all with them, why is that? Did they have people on their old team that they didn't want to manage? Why keep a team that they didn't feel was up to scratch? This question alone can lead to quite a deep and telling discussion.

Candidate Insights

1. Going as far back as you can remember, what drove you to get this far in life?

What else can you remember that may have had a significant impact? Have you ever considered a link between that and your success today? How different do you believe you would have been had it not been for these moments in your life?

How do these extra questions add value?

The whole point of this approach to interviewing is to get deep into their stories and do so in a way that helps them uncover all depths of their stories. Ultimately, with these questions, you're seeking to better understand their drive and motivation, but secondary to that, you're discovering more about their levels of self-awareness.

2. How did your potential for success manifest itself in your high school and further education years?

What else can you remember? How different do you believe you would have been had it not been for these moments in your life?

How do these extra questions add value? How does the candidate self-reflect on their earlier years? When they're talking about what could have been different, are they positive or negative? Are they reflecting on what could have been rather than being grateful for what actually did become of them?

3. What are you not currently getting that you think you'll find in this role?

What else?

What's the most important factor for you?

How do these extra questions add value? Getting to the bottom of all potential factors is important here. It's also important for them to rank order their importance, or at least share the most important one. Their answer will tell you a lot about what their expectations are and how you may potentially be able to hire them.

4. What's going to keep you in this role beyond the first year?

What else?

What's the most important factor for you?

What are the deal breakers for you?

How do these extra questions add value? The value here is mostly explained in the previous question. Asking the third question after the second one sounds like you'll get the same answer, but it is different enough to help them reframe their thoughts on what is important and see if you get the same answer.

5. Where has your previous role failed you that led you to be here today?

What else? How different would things have been if this hadn't happened?

How do these extra questions add value? This second micro question is difficult to avoid answering, so you should witness some introspection here. How are they processing and communicating this answer?

6. How do you maintain the mental strength and balance required to lead people?

What else?

Where does this come from?

What triggers your breaking point when leading people?

How do these extra questions add value? Great leaders have to be extremely resilient to high-pressure situations. In considering the Big Five trait, neuroticism, being low in this trait and calm under pressure is essential in strong leadership. Some candidates will talk about fitness, reading, holidays, and generally taking time out to focus on things other than work. Some will just describe an aspect of their character that they believe makes them resilient. In asking the third question, you're deliberately assuming they have a breaking point, so it is linguistically difficult for them to answer this question without directly addressing their breaking points. It's always interesting to hear what they have to say here.

7. From the three best leaders you've had, choose one trait of each that has really gotten the best out of you and explain how?

Which of these three do you feel has impacted you the most?

Which of these leaders did you admire the most and why?

What else was unique about that person and how they led?

How do these extra questions add value? You're building out their story, getting deeper and deeper, to tease out as many clues as possible that can help you formulate an opinion concerning the traits or at least the scoring metrics you're using. The first question is really seeking to understand what they value the most regarding how they're led. This is likely to be a trait or value they have adopted in their leadership style. The second question, again, is getting them to rank order their preferences, and in doing so, you will learn more about what type of leader they admire, which is often not too far away from what type of leader they are or aspire to be. The final question seeks to get even deeper into the story, but also, you're asking them what was unique about that person. What does the candidate describe as being unique? Is it actually a unique trait, or is it just something the candidate admires? Either way, it will help you build out the story of how this candidate thinks and leads.

8. From three people that have worked for you, choose three of your leadership traits that have gotten the best out of them and explain how?

Tell me more about how you developed these people?

Where or who do you believe you inherited these traits from?

Which of these do you believe makes you most effective?

What did you learn from managing these specific individuals?

How do these extra questions add value? The first question is helping you build a full story of their leadership style through real stories with real people. The second question seeks to understand their self-awareness about how they have been shaped as a leader. Their answer to this question also tells you more about what values and traits they consciously decided to identify with. That in itself will be very telling. The third question is asking them to rank order which of the traits are most impactful in their opinion. What does this tell you about their values system? The final question is a very open question designed to get further information about how they manage people. This is achievable because they are invited to tell stories about actual people, which should be easier to remember. This will make it more comfortable for them to share their stories.

9. How do you manage your team to maintain the standards you expect of yourself?

What is your no negotiating standard that your team simply has to abide by?

Are you as tough on your team as you are on yourself?

How do you identify those in your team that you can push further?

Tell me more?

Talk me through your typical approach to managing those who fail to meet your standards?

How do these extra questions add value? The first question is seeking for them to rank order their most valuable standards. What do they stand for as a leader, and what do they simply not tolerate? If they say something obvious or virtuous, just ask, "What else?" The second question seeks to get deeper into the stories about their values, standards, and ultimately their levels of integrity. Most will say they're tougher on themselves, but why do they say this? Have them explain it to you with stories. The third question seeks to find out how they approach leadership at an individual level. How do they evaluate people, whether explicitly or subconsciously?

Without identifying the right people to push in the right way, they can't possibly hope to maximize their team's performance. The final question seeks to understand how they manage underperformers. We're looking for more stories about actual situations they have encountered in their career.

10. What is it about your management style that is so impactful?

Where did you learn to lead like that?

How has this approach changed over the years, if at all?

Tell me more?

How do these extra questions add value? You will already have a good idea of what shaped them as a leader and what turning points in their life and career led to their current approach. The first question seeks to reframe similar previous questions to see if their answer is consistent with what they've already told you. The second question seeks to understand how they believe they have grown as a leader and what has changed. This question has the potential to get deeper into their story.

11. If you were the perfect leader, what would you be doing better?

What else?

Who have you seen or read about that does this very well?

What are you already perfect at?

How do these extra questions add value? The second question will help you to understand who they admire or recognize in business and, therefore, who they potentially model part of their approach on. The third question is another way of asking what they're really good at. What is it about their leadership that they believe to be exceptional? How consistent is their answer with everything else they've already been telling you?

FACT-CHECKING

As previously mentioned, one of the biggest issues in interviewing is the inability to fact-check. Interviewers that base their whole interview strategy, or a big part of it, on competency-based interview questions are just leaving themselves wide open to being told lies. That's not to say that all candidates will always tell lies. However, how can the interviewer know when they're just hovering around the shallows of the detail bouncing from one competency question to the next, with the candidate having a whole career to choose each answer from? It is mind-blowing to me that this has been going on forever in nearly all companies, including nearly all Fortune 500s. Why has nobody stopped and questioned this? The question is: "If I ask this person this question about their ability to deal with conflict, and they have given me an example of a time that occurred one, three, five, or twenty years ago, what does that tell me about this persons ability to deal with conflict?" The correct answer is, "Not much," or certainly "not enough to conclude that if they were to be in a similar situation, this is exactly how they'd do it again."

We have already established that evidence of competencies exists within candidate stories about previous roles. It's up to us as skilled interviewers to identify evidence of these competencies as we go through the questioning of each candidate. Aside from the poor utility of competency-based questions, or at least the ones that pick a competence and ask a candidate to recall one situation out of their whole career, there is also the fact that people can just make up their responses. I understand why some people may choose to make up a response, as some people may not remember a situation so specific yet so unmemorable that their hard drive has long since erased the memory in favor of other more important ones. To try and combat this breach in the system, we have to ask questions in a certain order that builds a story with deep information that can then be fact-checked in three different ways:

Firstly, by identifying separate timelines in a role and asking about facts in each of these timelines, then comparing all listed facts to see if they add up. An example of this may be that the candidate shares a story about how their team size grew by 20%, and their revenues grew by 10%. Without exploring here and understanding the revenue and cost numbers at the beginning and end of the period, you have no idea whether these percentage increases represent a good or bad performance.

For example, if revenues grew by $5m (from $50m to $55m), but the team size grew from 300 to 360 (up 20%), that's not necessarily good performance. Or is it? It looks like it is if you just ask about revenue growth, but there has to be some relevant context to the revenue growth. Growing at 100% a year in the first three years of business isn't necessarily as impressive as growing at 30% per year in the 20th year of business. But even then, you have to consider the context. Did that business grow organically at 30% in its 20th year, or did they just acquire a company? If they acquired a company, there's another new story to explore while having all of the Bremnus success factors and traits in the back of your mind.

Without further questioning, you don't know what's behind the numbers, and there may be a good reason for it. In the above example, the cost structure has increased (to hire so many people), and although revenues grew, profitability will inevitably be down. That may not be bad if the company's goal is to grow, but this information is something to explore further. For example, you could go on to ask another micro question like, "You obviously invested in growing the team, which clearly impacted the revenue, but no doubt also negatively impacted your profitability. Tell me more about how you projected this would play out in the year following this investment in growth?" That's kind of a vague question, but deliberately so. What the candidate goes on to say will be dripping in evidence of competencies, or lack thereof.

The second way to fact-check is by asking micro questions during the review of each of the previous roles to build such deep information that you can then further compare previously answered questions and see if it all adds up. Thirdly, one of the most important ways to fact check is by having different people interview and ask questions that may sound different but are seeking the same information. This could be only two people on two separate occasions, but it could be more. Think of these two examples:

1. When you started, how did your division look in terms of tangible numbers, be that headcount, productivity, or however it was measured?

2. When you joined, can you break down the numbers in terms of people, revenues, output, or whatever fell under your remit at the time?

Both of these questions seek the same information but are asked in a slightly different way. If interviewer A and interviewer B conduct their interviews one week apart, with slightly different questions but seeking the same information, any misrepresentation of facts should be obvious. Candidates can lie here and there, but getting into such detail about each role is a far more impactful way to manage this than asking competency questions where the candidate gets to pick any of their previous roles to respond with. With the Extraview interview method, when two interviews with the same candidate are conducted, they are automatically transcribed, and question by question, the answers are then shown side by side. The answers to two seemingly different questions seeking the same information can be played back or read, and a score is given by anyone reviewing the answers. This also means everyone is assessing the same answers from the candidate's one and only life story, thus minimizing bias and speeding up the process.

It's difficult to consider every scenario when this may play out. Interviewing is a very developed skill unless all you do is ask competency questions. In that case, anyone can perform the role of an interviewer. They just need to have a long list of competency questions and ask away. However, getting into detail and balancing between macro and micro questions asked in a particular order is an approach that must be practiced. As we can't cover all potential scenarios, let's consider an example to give you a sense of what I mean by fact-checking.

SCENARIO

A candidate is interviewing for a job as a leader at a business services company, and the interviewer is about to ask the candidate about the three years he spent as the leader at another similar firm:

Interviewer (I): "So you were there for nearly three years. Let's go back to the beginning of your time there. In the first 90 days, what was it that kept you awake at night?"

Candidate (C): "Honestly, I sleep well at night. I tend to leave my work at the office and not worry about things."

I: "Okay, well, that's great to hear. Let me ask that in another way, then. What were the burning platform priorities in those first 90 days?"

C: "Well, we had a lot of attrition in the company. There were 200 people in total, and they were losing about 30% of their staff per year. Our website and branding were terrible. They were looking to move overseas into the UK market. We didn't really have a strategy for growth, and generally, the company was just in bad shape."

The whole point of this interview process is to give the candidate an experience that flows and where you don't give anything away. For it to flow, you have to listen very well, keep the broad line of questioning on a tight path, but never miss the opportunity to pick up on a point they've just made and explore it further. Remember, with this interview structure, when asking about previous roles, you have these macro questions to help re-orient the line of questioning if you digress off into micro questions, so you can never get totally lost.

In the above example, the question and answer flow is typical of the early stage questions. The candidate claims that nothing keeps them awake at night. Perhaps they're trying to be smart, or perhaps they just sleep well at night and take the question too literally. That's okay because we were ready with a slightly different question asking the same thing, and this time appealing more to their ego, which was so clearly present. In asking what were "the burning platform priorities," it appeals to their ego as you're now saying, "What was wrong with the business that you came along and saved?" No surprise, the candidate goes in hard talking about the disasters that he came and saved. This is typical of this particular type of candidate during these early stages. Often they calm down in their critique once they learn that they also have to comment on what they left behind for someone else to fix once they left.

From his response, I want to understand what he meant by "just in bad shape." The candidate's response to this query could set up many reference points that we can come back to further on in the interview. The following question isn't on the list of micro questions. This is why it's so important to realize that as an interviewer, you have to work hard to learn how to interview, as you can't just be reading through your questions and while they're answering, just making sure you're ready for the next question. You have to be in the moment and listen out for these cues to ask more micro questions, some of which won't be written down on your list. You have to improvise with micro questions to get to where you need to be. Let's get back to the scenario and see how it continues.

I: "When you say the company was in bad shape, what do you mean by that?"

C: "Well, their revenue was terrible on a per-person basis, and their cost structure was ridiculous."

I: "At the time you joined then, what were the revenues for the previous year?"

C: "Around $16m."

I: "Okay, well, help me to understand how bad that was. What was it by the time you left?"

C "$24m."

I: "Okay, so you grew the revenues by 50% over three years. That's fantastic."

We still have two more rounds of these questions for this one role. With this particular answer, I'm just going to write it down, and I'm going to come back to test it when asking about what kept them awake in their final 90 days. It's important here to just pay the candidate a compliment for such great work and move on like you're done with this piece of data. At this point, as the interviewer, I'm looking at my notes and see in the beginning, the candidate had a team of 200 people, with 30% attrition, and revenues had gone from $16m to $24m under his tenure as the leader — time to test.

I: "So here we are. You've been there for three years, and it sounds like it's time for a change for you. Talk me through the number of where you got the business to? Let's start with revenue?"

C: "Uh, $26m."

I: "Okay, and team size?"

C: "300."

I: "Okay, and how many people did you lose in the last year?"

C: "10%."

A great interviewer will gather all of that information before the test begins because clearly in there, there are some lies, but there are also some performance issues that have come to light. Can you spot them? Well, the first lie is obvious. In the beginning, he said $24m in revenue, but now he's saying $26m. With that, I would call him out:

I: "So, $26m, yes?"

C: "Yes."

I: "I wrote down here $24m from when I asked you a couple of questions ago. Where does the $2m difference come from?"

C: "Sorry, yes, it's $24m."

At this moment, the candidate had an answer that will pass off as one you can't really further contest, as arguably, they could have just made a genuine mistake. That's not important. What is important is that they know you're on the ball, and for the other roles, the answers better be more honest, or they'll be caught out.

"I: Now you also mentioned that the company was in bad shape in the beginning. You had 200 people and were doing $16m, correct?"

C: "Yes, correct."

I: "And on a scale of 1 to 10, 10 being incredible, how would you rate your performance as

CEO in the three years you were there?"

C: "Probably a 7."

I: "What would it have taken for that to be a 10?"

C: "Increasing revenue by 100% instead of 50%."

I: "Anything else?"

C: "Probably hiring more people."

I: "Anything else?"

C: "No, that's it."

Always keep asking "anything else" until they tell you there's nothing else. Here the interviewer asks the potential CEO to rate his performance at what appears to be the end of the questioning, but it's not over.

I: "When you took on this role, you told me the business was in bad shape. You increased the revenues by 50%, but you also increased staff by 50% and reduced attrition to 10% from 30%. So, according to these numbers, you haven't increased the output of your people at all. It's flat. Did I miss something?"

C: "No, that's correct. You're right."

I: "Okay, I just wanted to check. So you decreased attrition, yet you seem to have kept a lot of underperformers as the per-person revenue number is flat. How do you account for this, and did you factor this into your performance score of 7?"

The chances of candidates thinking they will be able to lie through the rest of the interview is quite slim. It's important not to be confrontational when calling them out on these facts. Your tone and body language should represent curiosity and intrigue rather than suspicion and critique. Ultimately you want the candidate to be as relaxed as possible, so they have the best chance of doing well, but if they're blatantly lying, you have to call them on it. Using the technique where another interviewer repeats the question at a different time helps you to not only build a story and a profile of their successes and failures, but more importantly, it helps you to be able to cross-reference their answers. Remember, we don't have a scientific test to qualify the truthfulness of answers. All we can do is take nothing at face value and find ways to cross-reference what we're being told.

This is the way you can revolutionize interviews and turn them from being a prescriptive competency-based checklist into a deep review of the stories where the competencies are evidently abundant or not, as the case may be. It leads to an interview that flows better, goes deeper, and keeps the candidate focused while you, as the interviewer, are writing down information you can cross-reference. Furthermore, when memories are recalled, they, in turn, uncover other memories simply by association. Therefore, keeping questions deep and long on each role should bring out more information than simply asking random competency questions where the candidate is free to choose which role to reference.

CAPTURING TRAITS

What we currently have in large companies are different people asking different questions and reaching their own bias-laden conclusions. We also have a very inefficient process where candidates may have to attend numerous interviews to tell different people the same story. For this to change and to minimize bias as best we can, we have to do two things. Firstly we have to have an interview framework that doesn't just seek out a highlight reel of a candidate's best moments. It has to be purposeful, complete, and robust. Secondly, once we've gathered the candidate's full story, everyone needs to be assessing the same story with the same measures and with the same understanding of what those measures are.

Do you remember getting interviewer training that was anything more than a description of which questions to ask? Have you ever had interviewer training, or did you learn based on how you were interviewed in the past? We're not going to solve diversity issues, for example, by having software cover up for people's biases. We need humans to make better-informed decisions who understand more of the literature about performance in the workplace and assessing humans. We need to train people to know how to extract maximum information from a candidate so we can lean on our experiences and knowledge to make confident decisions about who to hire. We must improve our own intelligence rather than just trying to replace it with artificial intelligence.

If all we have is software making decisions for us, what use is the years of experience we gain? If our biases are based on our lived experiences, we don't stop having lived experiences, and our biases can and do evolve. The process in our brains of creating biases may be hardwired, but the biases themselves are not. If they were, we'd never change our minds about anything or evolve as human beings. Nobody would ever convert from one religion to another or change political preferences. We don't need to replace our brains' hard drive; we just need to update our software. Updating our brain software is not just being told which questions to ask; it's understanding why we're asking them and how to interpret the answers.

With the Extraview interview software, everyone involved in the hiring process goes through seven hours of on-demand online training which focuses on the research presented in this book. The training aims to help people be better informed and make better choices. Better humans making better choices will lead to better outcomes. Then once the training is complete, the platform enables users to perform consistent and detailed interviews with this new method.

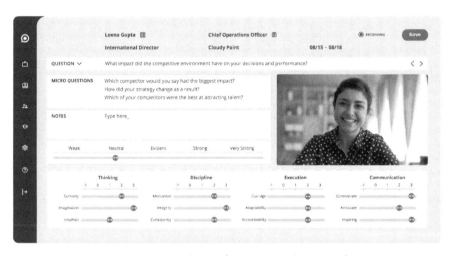

Figure 28 - Extraview Software Interview Interface

With Extraview, the interviewer can focus on the candidate more as the conversation is recorded and transcribed (in-person), or it can be deployed remotely using the software via one or two-way video. The questions and structure are all laid out for the interviewer, as you can see in Figure 28. Furthermore, with flowing questions that focus on the candidate's one and only story, the candidate is likely to perform better.

Then, all other assessors who, in the past, may also have interviewed the candidate are what we now call extra-viewers, where the name of the software, Extraview, originated. They are called extra-viewers because the candidate has told their whole life story in great detail already. They have no more things to tell. Now, all other assessors simply view the interview and use the same scoring metrics to evaluate the candidate. Our leadership consulting firm, Bremnus, can also conduct these interviews on behalf of our clients. This further minimizes any bias as the interview that Bremnus conducts is entirely impartial and focuses on the questions and the candidate's story.

Figure 29: Extraview Assessment Interface

Weak	Neutral	Evident	Strong	Very Strong
-1	0	1	2	3
Fell short of levels expected for this role.	No observation of this trait so cannot comment.	Observed evidence of this trait but not to an outstanding degree.	Observed strong evidence of this trait. Clearly identified.	Observed multiple strong instances of this. Very strong evidence.

Table 12: Interview Scorecard Description

The interviewer and extra-viewers would then score the candidate using the interface shown in Figure 29, using the scoring method shown in Table 12. Alternatively, the company can customize its scoring and questions using the same software, which may be necessary for different types of leadership roles or less senior roles. They don't have to use this software to conduct the interviews, but the software was specifically designed to make this process much easier, based on this book.

This Extraview interview process is not intended to replace all interviewers for all hires, all of the time. For very senior roles, for example, it may be perfectly justified to have several executives meet with the candidate. At a bare minimum, this interview process could replace the out-of-date 'HR interview,' which still, to this day, uses the behavioral competency interview framework and STAR method created in the 1970s. We are all familiar, I believe, with the saying, "The definition of insanity is doing the same thing over and expecting a different result." We are now in a different century with a different expectation of how our workforce should look, yet the HR interview is still made up of a series of questions established fifty years ago. This has to change.

Figure 30: Interactive Extraview Candidate Report

Once each interviewer and extra-viewer has completed their scoring and notes, we have a full report to reference to start making some choices. Figure 30 shows what the beginning of a report looks like. Anyone viewing this report could also click on any extra-viewers to see their assessment of the candidate. All assessors' names can be anonymous, depending on who sees the report. The result is a report automatically compiled with all the scores aggregated to get a true "top candidate" for the job, as shown in Figure 30.

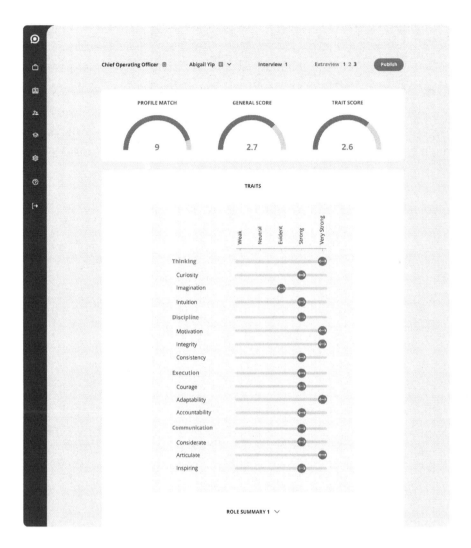

Figure 31: Extraview Candidate Traits Report

Those viewing the interactive report can also see the recorded interviews just as they appear for the extra-viewers in Figure 29. Viewers will also have access to the scoring of the different candidates by each assessor. An example of the deeper insights is shown here in Figure 31. Despite how complex this all appears it takes less time to create than a normal interview as the software does most of the work in pulling all the data together.

The scoring of traits is not the only measure we use to assess candidates. Multiple potential candidates will likely score well on these traits. Ultimately these are only contributing indicators, and someone has to decide based on all the available data. You may recall the quote from Daniel Kahneman in Chapter 4:

"You're better off if you collect information first and systematically collect all the information and only then allow yourself to take a global view and to have an intuition about the global view" (Our Crowd, 2019).

It ultimately comes down to this post-data-gathering intuition when weighing up two great candidates. With this in mind, all interviewers and extra-viewers are asked to provide an overall profile score after completing their review of the candidate interview. This score from one to ten represents how closely the assessor believes the candidate matches the success profile. You may recall the success profile from Chapter 6, which is the document created to align everyone involved in the hiring process concerning the ideal candidate profile and potential external candidate sources. There is also room in the reporting function to make written notes on exactly why the reviewer believes the candidate is a match for each of the points listed in the success profile.

The decision-maker has to consider, in great detail, the content of the stories, the success profile, and the trait scores, and then triangulate all of these before making an informed call on who they will choose. Of course, you don't need to use the software to be able to conduct this kind of interview. All you need is the questions and to learn the process, much like you will have learned about competency interviews. However, for deploying company-wide, consistent, bias-minimized interviews, the software does all the hard work for you, including training your hiring managers and HR teams.

When addressing some of the issues identified in Chapter 7, this method, compared with the current interview frameworks used in companies, needs no further dissection. This new method does not eradicate biases altogether, which cannot be done but can minimize them significantly. At the very least, you have a group of people contributing their opinions based on the same information. With competency interviewing, the information is incomplete, so having people assess the same incomplete data is not sufficient. Furthermore, the speed at which such a process can occur dramatically reduced the hours spent getting candidates back in and coordinating diaries, reducing the risk of candidates going elsewhere. With this process, the candidate interviews can happen over a day or a week, maximum. Then all extra-viewers can be notified and given as little as 24 hours to complete their assessment. This reduces an inefficient and incomplete interview process from weeks and months to an efficient and complete interview process completed in a matter of days, with any biases being drastically minimized.

CONCLUSION

We are recruiting someone into a role where the future is not certain, as predictable as it may be. The external competitive environment is not certain. The macroeconomic environment is not certain. The team dynamic is not certain. Even our ability to predict who the best candidate will be is not certain. So our goal is not to do the impossible and predict, with certainty, who the best candidate will be in a future role; that's not technically possible. Therefore, our goal is to make as accurate a prediction as we can with the available information we have. We need to be getting better information than that which is available through the lottery of competency behavioral interview questions.

Furthermore, our goal is also to get as close as possible to understanding if what the candidate is telling us is indeed true. This cannot be done when we don't cross-reference information at that moment, and when we don't ask questions in a certain order, that leaves the candidate with fewer trap doors to escape from. Also, the truth can be further checked by asking the same questions on two or more separate occasions with different people conducting the interview. With the detail we get into using the Extraview method and how freely candidates will speak due to our depth of focus on each role, it's harder for them to lie about all the facts and then tell the same perfect lies on another occasion in the correct order.

There is no perfect way to interview. We are human beings with all of our errors of judgment, interviewing other human beings who make mistakes as they learn to be better employees, leaders, and people in society. Who are we to judge? Well, "we" are anyone tasked with making a hiring decision, and we have to find a way that is fair and fit for purpose. With the Extraview method, the candidate has to withstand the deep scrutiny of an interview that is structured to make it easier for them to tell more of their story but more difficult for them to lie. For a candidate to triumph under such scrutiny, they have to prove that they are not only smart, creative, disciplined, great at execution, and strong communicators; they also have to demonstrate that they have integrity, that they know their numbers, and that they take accountability for their mistakes. If the same depth of accountability and rigorous candor cannot be achieved by your existing approaches to interviewing, then perhaps Extraview can take you one step closer.

HOW TO CHANGE - THE PEOPLE AGENDA

Everyone in the company agrees; "We're great at recruiting, but a lot of that is down to our brand, so we must get better at the process of recruiting itself." We owe it to the candidates coming through the process, we owe it to our colleagues, and we owe it to our shareholders and customers, who will all benefit from better value hiring practices. So all the main executive board has to do now is pass this off to HR and see what they come up with, right? Wrong. This is everyone's responsibility, but if the CEO doesn't know what to expect and how to hold HR accountable, then HR will be forgiven for doing what they've always done, given the budget they have to work with.

For companies who truly want to take their senior talent acquisition seriously, and by seriously, I don't mean they get an RPO (Recruitment Process Outsourcing) solution and a set of LinkedIn Recruiter subscriptions, things have to change. That should already be evident if you've had the opportunity to read through the rest of the book. It is also important to reemphasize that I'm writing about experienced senior hires, not the higher volume entry-to-mid level or contract/temp roles. So how does the CEO take charge of the people agenda, and what should they expect from HR? First, it is not just what the CEO should expect, but rather what the whole business should expect from a truly strategic recruiting function, and not just one that performs an internal placement service. The difference between a truly strategic recruiting function and an internal placement service is quite vast. Unfortunately, most companies are closer to the placement service model than they are a strategic partner, despite their claims and best intentions, and there are very few exceptions.

In the last ten to fifteen years, at least, internal talent acquisition teams have been growing at an incredible pace, with some Fortune 500 companies now having hundreds of internal recruiters. While this may seem like great progress, a sizable vacuum exists between the C-suite narrative about people being the greatest asset and the cost-saving focus on the internal recruiting function. Of course, cost-saving should be a focus, but like anything that ends up getting too cheap, at some point along the axis of cheapness, things really get cheap, as does the quality. There are several reasons this vacuum still exists, and of course, not all companies are the same. For example, I know of a very small number of Fortune 500 companies that have done a great job of setting up real in-house executive search teams for their senior hiring. I'm not referring to those that call themselves executive search, yet just manage a group of external search firm suppliers, but rather, companies who have almost entirely brought the function in-house and done extremely well with it.

Fundamentally, either the senior TA leaders aren't telling the business what they can be getting out of their leadership TA function, or the business doesn't care to know, or the business is dictating how much the TA function can spend and year on year having to cut corners and deliver greater cost savings. I write this because if there were a proper dialogue between senior TA and the business, the case would be very clearly made; to have a full-service senior-level in-house search function. The sheer lack of such functions in the TA organizations of Fortune 500s leads me to believe these conversations just aren't happening.

If you're a CEO reading this or someone else in the business who isn't part of HR or TA, there's a big difference between recruiting high volume low-level hires in terms of the process and hiring senior people. For example, if you're a global bank hiring a junior technology project manager, there will be thousands of potential candidates, so it makes sense to post a job advert. On the other hand, if you're looking to hire a global head of equities technology, your potential talent pool will be more like twenty to fifty people. That requires a senior person to do a very thorough job of identifying every potential candidate, calling them all, and converting enough of those individuals into potential candidates so you have a shortlist to choose from. Again, this requires a very different approach and skill set to writing a job ad and sifting through hundreds of applicants. However, this difference is rarely reflected in what is expected of the recruiters and the cost allocation to deliver a set number of hires. If the cost of hire is applied equally or even on average across all hiring, these numbers will be wrongly skewed.

Let's say you are that senior person in the business, and your company doesn't have a senior TA function set up, where they work on a search-only basis. If that is you, then you're likely doing one of two things:

1. For very senior hires, you use external search firms. This will get you what you need in terms of getting the role filled, but you are missing out, as I will come on to explain.

2. TA has agreed to keep costs low, so they are trying to recruit everyone at all levels using cheap recruiting techniques that are only fit for high volume lower level recruiting. You and your colleagues may be disappointed with the results and revert to hiring search firms.

If you are doing any of the above, what follows is what you may be missing out on.

MARKET INTELLIGENCE

Interviewing candidates from other firms is one of the company's greatest assets when gathering information about the market. So much important information can be captured and put to good use. Of course, people have signed away their ability to share secrets, and understandably so, but we're not seeking to steal the source code here. Rather, piece by piece, interview by interview, over months and years, we should be subtly growing a set of data points that, when brought together, form a powerful dataset of valuable information. This data is not only valuable when looking at pipeline planning, but when discussed regularly with the right senior leaders in the business, it can also be an invaluable asset to the strategic direction of the company. Unfortunately, that theory, for almost all Fortune 500 companies, gets thrown out of the window when costs are brought into the equation.

Think about when this process is outsourced to an external search firm. Sure, you get to interview the shortlist of four candidates, during which time you can extract quite a lot of information, but what about the other twenty to forty candidates that the search firm spoke with as part of the process of this search? Very little of that data will make its way to you, but your search firm partner, who are providing outstanding value in their task to find your new hire, are enriching themselves with vast sums of data at your expense. You probably don't ask for it, and that's not necessarily what they're being hired to do, so there's no issue here, but what if you took that process in-house? In the current in-house recruiting landscape, there's little room for time-consuming data gathering through lengthy discussions with long lists of candidates, but the value of such an approach is incredible. Whether it's an external search firm or someone internally in a senior in-house search role, afforded the time to do this correctly, the information they can get during the interviewing process is immense. Done subtly and progressively throughout a call or interview and done 30-50 times throughout a search, multiple times a year, you will build incredible market intelligence worth far more than the $100k fee you spent on paying an external search firm to find one person.

The purpose of this chapter is not to act as a training guide on how to gather information in a headhunt call or interview, but consider the following path of questioning and think about what information you're building as part of the broader process. The following four questions don't feature in the Extraview interview method. The Extraview interview method is a basic framework to build upon depending on the situation and role. Some of the following questions may be appropriate for a screening call or perhaps adding to the Extraview interview questions where part of the objective is to build market intelligence. Either way, there are many more you could be asking; these are just some examples to illustrate how to build market intelligence.

1. Tell me about the relationship you have with your boss?

The primary information you're getting here is building a profile of clues about how this individual interacts with their colleagues. That's the purpose of the interview. However, the headhunt perspective is also taking this information to map out the organization. Also, it may be to find out if their boss is a superstar who may be worthy of a call at a future date for another search.

The flow of conversation from here can lead you to understand, for example, that their boss has six direct reports, one of whom you are interviewing. You may also learn there are 400 people in the broader team. That's data the headhunter uses to build out profiles of that company. Over time and searches, the headhunter identifies all six of these direct reports, finds out how the 400 people are categorized, where they're all based, who is doing well, what is working for the teams, and who are most likely to be fired, and so on it goes. That all comes from the seed of one question that then leads into a discussion. If you're using an external headhunter, they gather all that information, which builds value in their service because they become increasingly knowledgeable about the market. However, that knowledge doesn't reside in your company because all your recruiters are too busy hitting cost of hire and unrealistic volume metrics to have a moment to do anything that can add such long-term value.

2. Let's talk about how you manage people. Let's take your direct reports. For each of the six direct reports, talk me through how you adapt your style to manage each of them to get the most out of them? What do you personally do to ensure you keep your best people?

Again, here's another line of questioning with some primary goals to understand how this person manages good and bad people in their team. A good headhunter will also be steering this conversation in a way that dives deeper into the context of the answers to pick up other information, like the names of some of these people, for example. By the way, for senior people, you won't even always need to ask for names. Sometimes if they're talking about titles, like "Head of Design" or similar, you can do research afterward, and over time you will piece together the jigsaw that is their org structure. Why is that important? Well, don't you want to know how your competition organizes themselves and who the key talent is in their company? There's so much other information that can be acquired from this line of questioning with subtle diversions along the way to serve two purposes: 1. To assess whether they're a good candidate, and 2. To build market knowledge that can be fed back into your company.

3. In what ways do you contribute to the company's cultural fabric that makes people want to stay? Why do people stay at X company? Give me some examples?

This line of questioning has a genuine primary purpose. The first one won't be for everyone; it will specifically be for someone in a senior leadership role. You're asking what it is about them that contributes to the bigger picture culture of the company. Perhaps they'll tell you some stories to articulate their contribution. The secondary purpose of this line of questioning is to find out about their culture. This is likely to be the culture of your competitor, and whatever they're doing that leads them to have market share and people that you don't have, is information you should be keen to understand further.

4. Why did you join, and have those reasons changed over the years? If so, in what ways have they changed?

The primary purpose of this question is to open a dialogue about what has changed over the years. The follow-up questions focus on what they've done to contribute to this change and what they would have done differently. This serves to understand more about what they've really done to contribute. The secondary purpose as a headhunter is, again, to build up stories about what is happening in that company, to understand how it's changing, and for better or worse, to find out what decisions were made that led to that change.

I could continue with many questions, but hopefully, you see the picture that's building. In trying to form an internal narrative on culture, success, on doing things right to keep the best people, there are plenty of clues in the outside world that can be harnessed if captured correctly. This data can be easily captured in interviews and as part of the onboarding process. However, it is lost in a high volume, low-cost recruiting game where in-house recruiters just aren't afforded the time to undertake such value-add work. Furthermore, if it is all outsourced to an external search firm, which is a perfectly good way to find the best candidate, you are essentially paying

THE CEO'S GREATEST ASSET

for them to understand the market better than your company ever will by not taking this in-house.

BUT WE'RE NOT ALLOWED TO DIRECTLY HEADHUNT

Oh, yes, you can. In fact, in the US, if you openly admit to preventing proactive candidate sourcing from your competitors, you may find your company in court, like Google, Apple, Intel, Adobe, Intuit, and Pixar did in 2010. In September 2010, the U.S. Justice Department settled with each of these companies over claims they colluded to not "poach" from each other (cold call each other's staff) (U.S. Department of Justice. 2010). Yes, the U.S. Justice Department pursued these companies for agreeing not to cold call each other on the grounds that it was anti-competitive for the labor market.

In a statement released by the U.S. Justice Department on September 24, 2010, Molly S. Boast, Deputy Assistant Attorney General in the Department of Justice's Antitrust Division, said, "The agreements challenged here restrained competition for affected employees without any pro-competitive justification and distorted the competitive process." "The proposed settlement resolves the department's antitrust concerns with regard to these no solicitation agreements" (U.S. Department of Justice. 2010).

In a blog post, Google Associate General Counsel, Amy Lambert, said: "While there's no evidence that our policy hindered hiring or affected wages, we abandoned our 'no cold calling' policy in late 2009 once the Justice Department raised concerns, and are happy to continue with this approach as part of this settlement."

People outside of the recruitment industry, and even some inside the industry who don't understand headhunting, use the word "poaching," which to me conjures up images of fishermen under cover of darkness stealing fish from a private lake. If this word correctly described both practices, you would have headhunters doing all of their recruiting in the winter months when it was dark by 5 p.m., so they could hunt the unsuspecting competitor employees under cover of darkness as they were innocently leaving their place of work. Headhunting is not poaching.

Poaching implies that the target prey or, in this case, employee, is taken against their will or is illegal.

No senior executive leaves a firm because they were bullied and pestered by a headhunter to move. Good professional headhunters approach potential senior candidates, call them, and in that first conversation, establish if they are open to a discussion about a potential career move at the moment. If they say they're not, the headhunter may ask permission to tell them a bit about the role to establish who else may be in that person's network to call, at which point the target may reconsider his or her response based on the information they just heard. That's it. Consent to enter the discussion is sought, and if not given, the conversation ends there. Whether that's done by a direct competitor or a third party, it's all the same.

If it is so unethical for corporate firms to go and directly headhunt their competitors, and the U.S. Justice Department disagrees with you, why is it, therefore, ethical for almost every Fortune 500 company to still engage senior-level headhunters to find their executives? Is it more ethical because a third party is doing the calls your firm has instructed them to make? In the criminal world, you're still considered as bad as the person who pulled the trigger if you hired the hitman to do it. The person who hires the hitman can't just stand there in court and say, "Well, I didn't do it, your honor. I paid this man to do it, so it's all his fault." Isn't the hirer just as guilty as the hitman himself because he ultimately instructed the hit in the first place? Of course, they are. So why, after eighty-plus years of professional headhunting, when we do look to take the initiative in-house, are we all of a sudden dealing out the ethics card?

The healthy way to deal with the threat of headhunters coming to "poach" your staff is simply by creating the best possible work environment for your employees. That responsibility falls on every single employee in the company, starting at the top, inspiring people to want not just to join the firm but to stay there. Good people are always going to be pursued by other companies. Smart headhunters, either in-house or external, will know their market very well and know where the best people are, and will come knocking if your company has the star employee(s).

The in-house recruiting teams can play a huge part in creating that work environment, starting with the candidate experience. This is not a book about employer branding or candidate experience, but in summary, your company can start to address this by:

· Training the actual hiring managers on how to interview and how to best represent your brand. Not just training, but sitting in on interviews and giving constructive feedback.

· Having a structured end-to-end interview process where candidates aren't faced with countless repeat interviews where too many people can't reach a consensus on a hiring decision.

· Having a clear and well-defined feedback policy for all candidates who come to interview with a service level agreement that hiring managers must adhere to in terms of providing feedback.

· Having a first-class onboarding process with adequate feedback channels to track, in real-time, the effectiveness of the process and the satisfaction of the newly on-boarded candidates.

· Working with your internal recruiters and suppliers to maintain accurate and up-to-date competitor salary and benefits information and leaning on the business to take action to maintain a competitive environment.

It takes a lot more than the in-house recruiting team doing a good job to keep your employees, but ultimately good people should be able to decide their career fate, not their captor employers. Your company will no doubt have benefited in the past few years from a star candidate being approached at another firm to come and work for yours, so it works both ways.

HOW COST OF HIRE ERODES THE VALUE OF SENIOR IN-HOUSE RECRUITING

Earlier I wrote about the contrast between the C-suite narrative, claiming that people are the greatest asset and the cost focus of in-house recruiting teams. One of the biggest reasons that this contrast still exists is that cost was the single biggest driver taking recruiting in-house in the first place. There were other factors, but the cost was the key one.

Whether we work in external recruiting or not, we all know that recruiting is expensive. Many of us working in the external market can kid ourselves that "It's not expensive; it's valuable." Well, to me, it's both, and at times, only expensive, especially in this day and age with the advancements in technology for lower-level hiring, yet external recruiting fees have barely moved. Sure, fees have gone down for high-volume recruiting, but back in the days, predating LinkedIn, a recruiting firm's database and its network was their unique proposition. Now, despite all of the claims that "We are different" and "we have a unique approach," the only real differentiators any recruiting firm has are its people, and that's not always a good thing. Sometimes it is, sometimes it isn't, and it's not defined by the company. Great people exist in terrible recruiting companies, and terrible people exist in wonderful recruiting companies. The same can be said of most industries. That's all that's unique: a different collection of individuals that can't be replicated but can easily be replaced.

For the most part, recruitment has become commoditized, and rightly so, given the advancements in technology. The same can't be said for very senior hiring, and again, rightly so, because the process of hiring the right senior people takes a lot more time and focus. Nowadays, for the most part, there's nothing valuable about a "proprietary database of candidates" when most people are visible on LinkedIn anyway. I know there are exceptions, but proportionately not many. In the executive search world, where ads are not used and instead its pure market mapping and headhunting, relationships can still mean something, and fees are comparatively more justifiable compared to contingency recruiting. In the contingency world, where firms are still getting paid $20k for posting a $100 advert for a $100k role (20% fees), it's mind-blowing that fees haven't dramatically dropped over the years.

In the in-house TA world, when the cost becomes the defining focus, measures like "cost of hire" are put in place to keep track of costs and compared each year. If cheaper recruiting is to remain the focus, then for sure it's going to get cheap; it will be all kinds of cheap. Here, the value and the potential of what in-house recruiting can do are largely lost in the cost race to the very bottom. At some point, value starts being compromised, which isn't as much of an issue for lower-level roles, but for senior hires, compromising on quality will always be at the cost of the business in the long run. To clarify, for lower-level recruiting, the quality of candidates is not compromised by cheap recruiting as the talent pool is far greater with less specialized skill sets in far greater abundance. Therefore, the process itself doesn't have to be as thorough and time-consuming, hence why it can be done cheaply, relatively speaking.

In my opinion, a big part of the issue stems from the lack of two-way dialogue between the business and HR/TA, where different recruiting levels are much better defined. Perhaps in many cases, it's the internal lack of dialogue between HR and TA, depending on the organization's size. If HR is acting as the intermediary between the business and the TA team, which is a mistake in my opinion, then better communication needs to exist between HR and the business about the vast differences in cost and time required to hire at different levels.

If HR or TA cannot articulate to the business why the blanket cost of hire metrics across all levels of recruiting is a terrible idea, then they are doing a disservice to their employer. I don't believe enough pushback is happening. To be fair to the HR and TA executives, though, after decades of being defined as a cost function and not much more than a decade of being told to make things even cheaper by building in-house recruiting teams, they can be forgiven for thinking their main purpose is to cheapen the recruiting process. This belief contrasts drastically with the business leadership narrative about their people being their greatest asset. Somewhere in the middle of these conflicting views, the books are not balancing. If people are the biggest asset, why is it still a cost function with a one size fits all cost approach?

Herein lies the problem. The blanket recruitment banner often gets placed across a wide range of roles, from junior to senior. It's just not practical. The average cost to hire is a corrosive data point eating away at the value of senior hiring in any company unless it is categorized and broken down: junior temp recruiting, contract recruiting, graduate recruiting, experienced hires, experienced senior hires, and so on. An equally simple and somewhat fair categorization could also be salary-based. The more these are broken down, the better. How these can all be bundled together when considering cost is beyond me. How "experienced hires" are bundled together, which, for argument's sake, could be any role from say $80k to well over $1m, is beyond me. This is evident in any significant company that has teams of recruiters and also has a big RPO focus. RPO is clearly effective for volume hiring, but the higher up the corporate structure you go, the less effective a high volume approach is; somewhere in the middle of that journey, it starts to break down. With the key driver for hiring an RPO being cost, in addition to some other reasons, cheap hiring doesn't create as much value at a senior level of recruiting.

To give it some context and perspective for anyone that doesn't work in the recruitment world, in the external recruiting market, in a senior executive search firm, a consultant may be responsible for placing 10-20 people a year, often with the support of a researcher or two. Those don't seem like big numbers, but these are super senior hires and often six-figure fees. An internal recruiter working in a global company, working on mid-level roles in the $100k salary range, may be responsible for placing 120+ people per year; sometimes, it's way more, sometimes way less. If you're placing 120 people a year, you simply don't have the time to do value add activities; you are at best able to perform an administrative function of getting people through the door. This is not interesting for the recruiter, and it's not maximizing the recruitment function sufficiently enough to have any confidence that great hires are being made. The bottom line is, that using the cost of hire for senior hiring and trying to compare it to the cost of hire for less senior roles may save money on hiring, but it is arguably going to have the opposite effect on the value to the company.

Here's an abstract illustration to make the point. This isn't a scientifically robust hypothesis, but if you're hiring an individual to run a $100m division of your company, what is the value of that person? Let's say you've got two candidates, and one is 5% better than the other. There's no way of proving this unless you hired two people to do the same job and waited to see how they got on. However, if one was, in theory, 5% more effective than the other, that's $5m in revenue you're potentially speaking about.

Compare that to hiring a $25k a year security guard. That security guard cannot positively affect the company's value in the same way. Of course, their service is valuable to the organization and necessary, but from a cost-of-hire perspective, if you have a recruiter hiring 120 of these junior roles per year and that recruiter is earning $60k per year with $20k of costs attributed to their sourcing efforts, that's arguably a $667 cost per hire. Is the senior in-house executive search person supposed to do 120 hires per year? That's not possible if they're doing a proper job. If they're doing a proper job and working alone, it will be more like 15-25 hires per year. They're more likely to be on at least $150k per year at the lower end of the spectrum; many are on a lot more than that. Even with similar costs attributed to their sourcing efforts, $20k, the cost per hire of this senior search person may be as much as $12k, or 18 times the cost per hire of the entry-level recruiter. That's the kind of number being observed and frowned upon because "the cost of hire must be lower."

When done properly, where the internal search executive is truly a trusted adviser to the C-suite and their direct reports, placing candidates is no longer the sole purpose of the role. There are many purposes, not least, to act as a direct feedback loop of market information. Also, with the right level of seniority, that person can act as a trusted adviser with an expert view of the external market and the competitive landscape. I've experienced this firsthand while working in-house for a global investment bank in that capacity. All of that said, in the short history of the evolution of in-house recruitment, the number of companies that have adopted these practices is still staggeringly low. Even for those that have fully embraced internal search, many still fall short in terms of process, productivity, and consistently demonstrating the true value of what they can do. Why? Well, for one thing, proper market mapping headhunting is very time-consuming and tough. It's not difficult; it's tough. It takes time, but it is time well spent.

Consider the scenario where someone headed up in-house executive search for one of the big global banks. If the right budget and time were allocated to them ten years ago, and the individual spent their time meticulously mapping out the market and understanding how many of the key players were at the competitors, how valuable would that person and function be in the company? Being able to sit down with the Group CIO at any moment and discuss a particular business line, how X bank is approaching infrastructure, cloud, AI, or, for example, who the top people are in, say, blockchain technology is extremely useful. This is a powerful asset, and yet only a small number of the world's biggest companies have such a function.

If senior-level hiring is to evolve in in-house TA functions, there needs to be a seismic shift in focus away from the current cost-of-hire blanket approach to all hiring. The most senior part of the TA function needs to sit much closer to the business, working on long-term pipeline planning, key competitor and target company market mapping, and data gathering, and delivering the kind of value that can only be achieved when it's not appraised in the same way as the higher volume, lower level recruiting function. People in this role have to come from the search world, with a proven track record of delivering on such senior assignments and already acting as a trusted adviser to the C-suite and their direct reports. This is not just a case of promoting an internal recruiter into the role because they managed to place 150 candidates the year before against a target of 120. It's a vastly different skill set, as previously mentioned. Until this happens, companies will continue to do one of three things:

1. Overspend on external search firms because they're the ones that can deliver the right value of service. In doing so, they're getting the right hires but are not building long-term market intelligence in the same way it could be done internally with the right people in place.

2. Try to do it themselves with the same recruiters that are placing lower-level roles. Sure, it can be done, but over time and several hires, it cannot possibly be done consistently to the same standard as someone working with a proven track record in a low volume search capacity.

3. Avoid having the conversation with the business that this new function needs to be created because it will cost a lot more money per recruiter, and they're unsure how to articulate its value compared to lower-level recruiting.

These less desirable outcomes can be avoided with the correct effort and focus. What kind of TA function is your company going to have moving forward? If you don't have the right one, you can be sure at least one of your competitors will, and with that, they'll have the upper hand when it comes to competitor knowledge. With that, they'll know where the best people are, and with the gathered information, they'll also know how to attract them.

CONCLUSION

This book resulted from my curiosity to understand how the seemingly useless interview process we've all used for our whole working lives still appears to be somewhat effective at hiring good candidates. It never sat well with me when interviewing people that the prescriptive process I followed was inherently flawed in many ways. There are the questions that are bad enough, but also the process of having different interviewers asking different sets of questions and conducting the whole process over weeks and sometimes months. Competency and behavioral interviews have been masquerading as a real process for years when in actual fact, they just served as a decoy to the underlying biases that have really been driving our candidate choices all this time.

What else could have been driving the process? It wasn't the coherent structure and flow of the competency questions. If only it was coherent. It wasn't the comparability of answers of different candidates because nobody was asking the same questions in the first place. I just felt that while so much progress had been made with diversity and technology, these interview processes were stuck in the dark ages, or at least in the 1970s when they were created, and just not fit for purpose anymore.

I started with a deep dive into academic research to understand what we at least know from an empirical evidence-based perspective. In joining the dots between IQ and learning ability, it was clear that nearly half of the population were trainable for most professional jobs, which goes some way to explaining why poor interview processes still have positive outcomes. It's not the interview processes that are robust and effective; it's the people that are highly trainable, adaptable, and motivated to succeed.

In learning about IQ and the Big Five personality traits, I established the four Bremnus success factors and twelve traits, which formed the basis for candidate evaluation metrics. If we are evaluating these, we are, to the extent that it is possible, evaluating leadership in general and the Big Five personality traits.

The interview methodology made it clear that both the questions and the process needed to change. Candidates only have one story, so it made sense to get as deep into their stories as possible. Instead of asking for a highlight reel of great rehearsed responses that would paint an amazing picture of one's career, the focus was on getting very deep into each role to understand how the candidates think and develop relationships.

Instead of having multiple people asking different questions, we have one or two trained interviewers who ask very specific questions in a very specific order. Then all other assessors are called extra-viewers; hence the interview process is called Extraview. The extra-viewers log in to see or hear the interview, review it question by question, and use the same evaluation system to grade the candidates. Then all grades are collected, and the natural best candidate emerges.

Given the wide spectrum of roles at many different levels an organization will typically recruit for, this framework has to have some built-in flexibility. For example, there has been no reference to any technical questions in this book. If there were, we would have to include every profession from finance to aerospace and everything in between. This was more about finding a common denominator model upon which any other questions, technical or otherwise, can be built.

As a leader in the business, I encourage you to reflect on your own experiences and look at how you can incorporate anything you've learned in this book with what you already know. Consider implementing a universal process for leadership interviewing where bias is minimized through much more structured interviews. Don't think your current hiring methods are working well just because your company is doing well. It could be doing better. A good company can be built by hiring good people, which isn't hard. Good people are easy to spot, and most recruiting processes are sufficient to identify good people. However, this is about hiring the best, not just the good ones. The Extraview is about going deep into the stories of a candidate's history to spot patterns of competence and to weed out shortcomings not typically evident in other interview approaches. It is in this detail that you have more chance of spotting greatness than you can by taking a candidate through a series of competency interview questions.

Given the current frameworks, it is fair to say that the decisions you make about who you hire could be better informed. The process and candidate experience could be vastly improved by delivering a much more structured and thorough interview process. In reflecting on what you've read, I hope it is clear that a lot more can be done to empower your people and ultimately make your company more profitable, more efficient, better for customers, and better for its employees, as, after all, people are the CEO's greatest asset — all of them.

References

Agor, W. H. (1986). The logic of intuition: How top executives make important decisions. Organizational Dynamics, 14(3): 5–18.

Agor, W. H. (Ed.). (1989). Intuition in organizations: Leading and managing productively. Sage Publications, Inc.

Allport, G. (1937). Personality: A psychological interpretation. New York: Henry Holt & Co.

American Educational Research Association (AERA), American Psychological Association (APA), & National Council on Measurement in Education (NCME). (2014). Standards for educational and psychological testing. Washington, DC.

Antonakis, J., House, J.R., Simonton, D. (2017). Can Super Smart Leaders Suffer From too Much of a Good Thing? The Curvilinear Effect of Intelligence on Perceived Leadership Behavior. Psychology, Medicine. Journal of Applied Psychology.

Banaji, M. (2013). Blindspot: hidden biases of good people. New York :Delacorte Press.

Bar-On, R. (2007). The Bar-On Model of Emotional-Social Intelligence (ESI). Consortium for Research on Emotional Intelligence.

Barrick, M., Mount, M. (1991). The Big Five personality dimensions and job performance: A meta-analysis. Personnel Psychology, 44, 1–26.

Becker, K. A. (2003). History of the Stanford-Binet intelligence scales: Content and psychometrics.

Berry, C. M., Sackett, P. R., & Landers, R. N. (2007). Revisiting interview-cognitive ability relationships: Attending to specific range restriction mechanisms in meta-analysis.

Boyatzis, R. (2018). The Behavioral Level of Emotional Intelligence and Its

Measurement. Frontiers in Psychology.

Buckingham, M., Goodall, A. (2019). The Feedback Fallacy. Harvard Business Review.

Campion, M. A., Palmer, D. K., & Campion, J. E. (1997). A review of structure in the selection interview. *Personnel Psychology, 50*(3), 655–702.

Carson, S., Peterson, J., Higgins, D. (2005). Reliability, Validity, and Factor Structure of the Creative Achievement Questionnaire. Creativity Research Journal. 17(1):37-50.

Cattell, R., Eber, H., & Tatsuoka, M. (1970). Handbook for the Sixteen Personality Factor Questionnaire. Champaign, IL: Institute for Personality and Ability Testing.

Cattell, R. (1987). Intelligence: Its structure, growth, and action. Amsterdam: Elsevier Science.

Clarke G.M., Cooke, D. (1978). A basic course in Statistics. 3rd ed.

Costa, P., & McCrae, R. (1992). Revised NEO Personality Inventory (NEO PR-I) and NEO Five-Factor Inventory (NEO-FFI): Professional manual. Odessa, FL: Psychological Assessment Resources.

Costa, P., & McCrae, R. (1995). Domains and Facets: Hierarchical Personality Assessment Using the Revised NEO Personality Inventory. Journal of Personality Assessment.

Costa, P., McCrae, R. (1997). Longitudinal stability of adult personality. In R. Hogan, J. A. Johnson, & S. Briggs (Eds.), Handbook of personality psychology (pp. 269–290). San Diego, CA: Academic Press.

Cronbach, L., and Meehl, P. (1955). Construct validity in psychological tests. Psychological Bulletin, 52, 281-302.

Dane, E., Pratt, M. (2007). Exploring Intuition And Its Role In Managerial Decision Making. Academy of Management Review, Vol. 32, No. 1, 33–54.

Deary, I. (1996). A(latent) Big Five Personality Model in 1915? Are analysis of Webb's data. Journal of Personality and Social Psychology, 71, 992–1005.

Deary, I. (2000). Looking down on human intelligence: From psychometrics to the brain. Oxford, England: Oxford University Press.

DeYoung, C., Quilty, L., & Peterson, J. (2007). Between facets and domains: 10 aspects of the Big Five. Journal of Personality and Social Psychology. 93.

880-96.

DeYoung, C., Peterson, J., Higgins, J. (2005). Sources of openness/intellect: Cognitive and neuropsychological correlates of the fifth factor of personality. Journal of Personality. Volume 73. Issue 4.

Duckworth, A., Seligman, M. (2005). Psychol Sci. Self-discipline outdoes IQ in predicting academic performance of adolescents.

Evans, J., Stanovich, K. (2013). Dual-Process Theories of Higher Cognition: Advancing the Debate. Perspectives on Psychological Science. 2013;8(3):223-241.

Gawronski, B., Morrison, M., Phills, C., Galdi, S. (2017). Temporal stability of implicit and explicit measures: A longitudinal analysis. Personality and Social Psychology Bulletin, 43(3), 300-312.

Gladwell, M. Blink: The Power Of Thinking Without Thinking. New York : Little, Brown And Co., 2005.

Gigerenzer, G., & Goldstein, D. G. (1996). Reasoning the fast and frugal way: Models of bounded rationality. Psychological Review, 103(4), 650−669.

Goleman, D. (1995). Emotional intelligence. Bantam Books, Inc.

Goleman, D. (2001). Emotional intelligence: Issues in paradigm building. In C. Cherniss 60 and D. Goleman (Ed's.), The Emotionally Intelligence Workplace. San Francisco: Jossey-Bass.

Gottfredson, L. S. (1997). Mainstream science on intelligence: An editorial with 52 signatories, history, and bibliography. Intelligence, 24(1), 13−23.

Gottfredson, L. S. (1997). Why g matters: The complexity of everyday life. Intelligence, 24(1), 79−132.

Gough, H. (1990). Testing for leadership with the California Psychological Inventory. West Orange, NJ: Leadership Library of America.

Greenwald, A. G., & Banaji, M. R. (1995). Implicit social cognition: Attitudes, self-esteem, and stereotypes. Psychological Review, 102(1), 4−27.

Greenwald, A. G., Banaji, M. R., & Nosek, B. A. (2015). Statistically, small effects of the Implicit Association Test can have societally large effects. Journal of Personality and Social Psychology, 108(4), 553−561.

Greenwald, A., McGhee, D. & Schwartz, J. (1998). Measuring individual differences in implicit cognition: The Implicit Association Test. Journal of

Personality and Social Psychology, 74 (6): 1464–1480.

Hayashi, A. M. (2001). When to trust your gut. Harvard Business Review, 79(2): 59 – 65.

Higgins, D., Peterson, J., Phil, R., Lee, A. (2007). Journal of Personality and Social Psychology Vol. 93, No. 2, 298–319.

Hinkle, D.E., Wiersma. W., Jurs, S.G. (2003). Applied statistics for the behavioral sciences. 5th ed. Boston: Houghton Mifflin.

Hirsh, J., Peterson, J. (2008). Predicting creativity and academic success with a "fake-proof" measure of the Big Five. Journal of Research in Personality. Vol, 42, Issue 5.

Hodgkinson, G., Langan-Fox, J., Sadler-Smith, E. (2008). Intuition: A fundamental bridging construct in the behavioral sciences. British Journal of Psychology (2008), 99, 1–27.

Humphrey, R., Pollack, J., Hawver, T., Story, P. (2011). The relation between emotional intelligence and job performance: A meta-analysis.

Hunter, J. E. (1980). Validity generalization for 12,000 jobs: An application of synthetic validity and validity generalization to the General Aptitude Test Battery (GATE). Washington, DC: U.S. Department of Labor, Employment Service.

Hunter, J., Hunter, R. (1984) Validity and utility of alternative predictions of job performance. Psychological Bulletin.

Hurtado, P. (August 17th, 2020). Why the U.S. Is Threatening Yale Over Race and Admissions. The Washington Post.

Jang, K. J., Livesley, W. J., Vernon, P. (1996). Heritability of the big five personality dimensions and their facets: a twin study. Journal of Personality.

Jensen, A. R. (1994). Spearman, Charles Edward. In R. J. Sternberg (Ed.), Encyclopedia of intelligence (Vol. 1, pp. 1007-1014). New York: Macmillan.

Judge, T., Heller, D., Mount, M. (2002). Five-Factor Model of Personality and Job Satisfaction: A Meta-Analysis. Journal of Applied Psychology.

Judge, T., Piccolo, R., Kosalka, T. (2009). The bright and dark sides of leader traits: A review and theoretical extension of the leader trait paradigm. The Leadership Quarterly. Elsevier.

Judge, T.A., Bono, J.E. (2000). Five-Factor Model of Personality and

Transformational Leadership. Journal of Applied Psychology. Vol. 85, No. 5, 751-765.

Judge, T. A. Bono, J.E. R. Gerhardt, M. (2002) Personality and Leadership: A Qualitative and Quantitative Review. Journal of Applied Psychology. Vol. 87, No. 4, 765–780.

Jung, C. G. (1933). Psychological Types. New York: Harcourt, Brace, and Company.

Kahneman, D. (2011). Thinking, Fast and Slow. New York: Farrar, Straus and Giroux.

Kahneman, D., and Tversky, A. (1979). Prospect Theory: An Analysis of Decision under Risk. Econometrica, Vol. 47, No. 2.

Khatri, N., & Ng, H. (2000). The role of intuition in strategic decision-making. Human Relations, 53: 57– 86.

Kell, H., Robbins, S., Su, R.,Brenneman, M. (2018). A Psychological Approach to Human Capital.

Klein, G.A., (1998). Sources of Power: How People Make Decisions. MIT Press, Cambridge, Mass, pp. 1–30.

Koch, C. (2015). Intuition May Reveal Where Expertise Resides In The Brain. Scientific American Mind.

Kyllonen, P. C., Christal, R. E. (1990). Reasoning ability is (little more than) working-memory capacity?! Intelligence, 14, 389–433.

Lane, K., Banji, M. Nosek, B. Greenwald, A. (2007). Understanding and Using the Implicit Association Test: IV. Implicit Measures of Attitudes. The Guilford Press.

Levashina, J., Hartwell, C. J., Morgeson, F. P., Campion, M. A. (2014). The structured employment interview: Narrative and quantitative review of the research literature. Personnel Psychology, 67, 241-293.

Levashina, J., Hartwell, C., Morgeson, F., Campion, M. (2014). The structured employment interview: narrative and quantitative review of the research literature. Personnel Psychology.

Lieberman, M. (2000). Intuition: A social cognitive neuroscience approach. Psychological Bulletin, 126: 109 –137.

Lord, R., De Vader, C., Alliger, G. (1986). A Meta-Analysis of the Relation between Personality Traits and Leadership Perceptions Procedures. Journal of Applied Psychology, 71, 402-410.

Ma, D. (2011). Introductory Statistics. Retrieved August 8th, 2020 from: https://introductorystats.wordpress.com/2011/09/.

Mayer, J., Roberts, R., Barsade, S. (2008). Human Abilities: Emotional Intelligence. Annual Review of Psychology.

Messick, S. (1989). Validity. In R. L. Linn (ed.). Educational Measurement (3rd ed.). New York: American Council on Education/Macmillan. pp. 13–103.

McCrae, R., Costa, P. (1997) Personality Trait Structure as a Human Universal.

McDaniel, D. Whetzel, F. Schmidt, S. Maurer. (1994) The Validity of Employment Interviews: A Comprehensive Review and Meta-Analysis. (1994). Journal of Applied Psychology .Vol. 79, No. 4, 599-616.

Microsoft. (2022). Understanding Unconscious Bias. https://mslearningc ontent.microsoft.com/UnderstandingUnconsciousBias/story.html, 2022.

Murray, C. (2009). Intelligence and College. National Affairs, Inc. and the American Enterprise Institute.

Nafukho, F., Muyia, M., Farnia, F., Kacirek, K., Lynham, S. (2016). Developing Emotional Intelligence Skills among Practicing Leaders: Reality or Myth? Performance Improvement Quarterly.

Norman, W. T. (1963). Toward an adequate taxonomy of personality attributes: Replicated factor structure in peer nomination personality ratings. Journal of abnormal and social psychology, 66. 574-583.

Norman, W. (1967). 2800 Personality trait descriptors: Normative operation characteristics for a university population. Ann Arbor, MI: Department of Psychology, University of Michigan.

NPR (2016). How the Concept of Implicit Bias Came Into Being. https://w ww.npr.org/2016/10/17/498219482/how-the-concept-of-implicit-bias-c ame-into-being.

Ohio State University. (2017, June 19). Why the 'peculiar' stands out in our memory. ScienceDaily. Retrieved June 20, 2020 from www.sci-encedaily.com/releases/2017/06/170619092713.html.

OurCrowd, (2019). Prof. Daniel Kahneman: Art & Science of Decision

Making #OCSummit19. [Video]. YouTube. https://www.youtube.com/watch ?v=WKSts1lNZhc.

Peterson, Jordan. (2018). 12 Rules for Life: An Antidote to Chaos. Toronto: Random House Canada.

Pittenger, D. (1993). Journal of Career Planning and Employment. v54 n1.

Plomin, R. Is intelligence hereditary. (May, 2016). Scientific American.

Polya, G. (1945). How to solve it; a new aspect of mathematical method. Princeton University Press.

Poropat, A. E. (2009). A meta-analysis of the five-factor model of personality and academic performance. Psychological Bulletin, 135, 322–338.

Pretz, J. E., Naples, A. J., & Sternberg, R. J. (2003). Recognizing, defining, and representing problems. In J. E. Davidson & R. J. Sternberg (Eds.), The psychology of problem solving (pp. 3–30). New York: Cambridge University Press.

Project Implicit. (2022). https://implicit.harvard.edu/implicit/takeatest.h tml/.

PWC. (2019). 22nd Annual Global CEO Survey.

Quillian, M. R. (1967). Word Concepts: A Theory and Simulation of Some Basic Semantic Capabilities. Behavioral Science 12: 410-430.

Reber, A. (1989). Implicit learning and tacit knowledge. Journal of Experimental Psychology: General, 118: 219 –235.

Roulin N., Krings F., Binggeli S. (2016). A dynamic model of applicant faking. Org. Psychol. Rev. 6, 145–170.

Rynes, .S., Colbert, A., and Brown, K. (2002). Human Resource Management, Summer 2002, Vol. 41.

Sackett, P. R., Burris, L. R., & Callahan, C. (1988).Integrity testing for personnel selection: An update.

Salgado, J. F. (1997). The five factor model of personality and job performance in the European community. Journal of Applied Psychology, 82.

Salovey, P., Mayer, J. (1990). Emotional intelligence. Imagination, Cognition, and Personality, 9, 185-211.

Schmidt, F. L., & Hunter, J. E. (1998). The validity and utility of selection methods in personnel psychology: Practical and theoretical implications of

85 years of research findings. Psychological Bulletin, 124, 262–274.

Schmidt. F., Hunter, F., J. (1998). The Validity and Utility of Selection Methods in Personnel Psychology: Practical and Theoretical Implications of 85 Years of Research Findings. Psychological Bulletin 1998, Vol. 124, No. 2, 262-274.

Schulte, M., Ree, M., Carretta, T. (2004). Emotional intelligence: Not much more than g and personality. Personality and Individual Differences, 37, 1059–1068.

Seger, C. (1994). Implicit learning. Psychological Bulletin, 115: 163–196.

Shannon, C. (1950). Programming a Computer for Playing Chess. Philosophical Magazine. 41 (314).

Simon, H. 1947 [1997]. Administrative Behavior, 4th Ed. New York: Free Press.

Simon, H. (1957) Heuristic Problem Solving: The Next Advance in Operations Research. Reprinted from Operations Research Vol. 6, No. 1, Jan-Feb, 1958.

Simon, H., & Newell, A. (1958). Heuristic Problem Solving: The Next Advance in Operations Research. Operations Research 6(1): 1–10.

Spearman, C. (1904)."General Intelligence," Objectively Determined and Measured. American Journal of Psychology 15, 201-293.

Thoresen, C. J., Kaplan, S. A., Barsky, A. P., Warren, C. R., & De Chermont, K. (2003). The Affective Underpinnings of Job Perceptions and Attitudes: A Meta-Analytic Review and Integration.

Thorndike, E. (1920). A constant error in psychological ratings. Journal of Applied Psychology, 4(1), 25–29.

Thurstone, L. (1935).The vectors of mind. Psychological Review, 41, 1–32.

Tupes, E., and Christal, R. (1992). Recurrent personality factors based on trait ratings. Journal of Personality, 60, 225–251.

Tversky, A., and Kahneman, D. (1974). Judgment under uncertainty: heuristics and biases. Science 185, 1124–1131.

U.S. Department of Justice. 2010. Justice Department Requires Six High Tech Companies to Stop Entering into Anticompetitive Employee Solicitation Agreements. Retrieved from: https://www.justice.gov/opa/pr/justice-depar

tment-requires-six-high-tech-companies-stop-entering-anticompetitive
-employee.

Viswesvaran, C., Ones, D.S. (1990). Meta-Analyses of Fakability Estimates: Implications for Personality Measurement. Volume: 59 issue: 2.

Waterhouse, L. (2006). Multiple Intelligences, the Mozart Effect, and Emotional Intelligence: A Critical Review, Educational Psychologist, 41:4, 207–225.

White, R. W. (1959). Motivation reconsidered: The concept of competence. Psychological Review, 66(5), 297–333. https://doi.org/10.1037/h0040934.

Wickelgren, W. A. (1981). Human learning and memory. Annual Review of Psychology, 32, 21–52.

Wiesner, W., Cronshaw. S. (1988). A meta-analytic investigation of the impact of interview format and degree of structure on the validity of the employment interview. Journal of Occupational Psychology.

Xiaohong Wan et al. (2012). Developing Intuition: Neural Correlates of Cognitive-Skill Learning in Caudate Nucleus. Journal of Neuroscience, Vol. 32, pages 17,492–17,501.

Y Combinator. (2020). Mark Zuckerberg: How To Build The Future. [Video]. YouTube. https://www.youtube.com/watch?v=Lb4IcGF5iTQ&feature=emb_title.

Notes

Visit extraview.io, where we have brought this book to life with over seven hours of training for all hiring managers, not just those in HR. Also, we have a customizable platform for you to conduct interviews using this methodology, both for enterprise clients and startups. Here you can conduct face-to-face interviews using our technology or even interview candidates online using our portal. All answers and data are automatically recorded, transcribed, and organized for your review. Alternatively, you can also outsource your company's interview/selection to Bremnus where we will conduct full interviews on your behalf, with the results accessible via the same portal.

For in-person leadership consulting or speaking engagements with the author, Fraser Hill, go to www.bremnus.com or contact Fraser directly at fraser.hill@bremnus.com.

About the Author

Fraser grew up in Scotland and, after graduating from university in 1999, moved to London to start his career in recruiting and executive search. In the early 2000's he moved to Hong Kong to work in technology executive search before moving back to the UK, where he worked in-house for one of Europe's fastest-growing billion-dollar companies at the time. Following this, he moved to Poland, where he headed up a team of recruitment professionals in six Eastern European countries. Then he moved to Canada, where he set up and later sold his first headhunting firm before coming back to the UK and joining J.P. Morgan in an in-house leadership executive search role. In 2012 Fraser left J.P. Morgan and set up Bremnus in London, UK, an executive search and leadership advisory firm. In 2016 he moved the business to California, where he now lives and works, advising Fortune 500 and high-growth tech companies on leadership hiring and strategy. Additionally, in 2022, Fraser created and launched Extraview.io, an HR technology platform for all companies to manage experienced hire interviewing as well as training all hiring managers in the art and science of landing leaders.

You can contact Fraser directly at fraser.hill@bremnus.com, fraser.hill@extraview.io, or via LinkedIn at https://www.linkedin.com/in/fraser-hill-270 4a134.